My Body Politic

My Body Politic

A Memoir

SIMI LINTON

THE UNIVERSITY OF MICHIGAN PRESS   *Ann Arbor*

2009   2008   2007   2006   4   3   2   1

A CIP catalog record for this book is available from the British Library.

Library of Congress Cataloging-in-Publication Data

Linton, Simi, 1947–
   My body politic : a memoir / Simi Linton.
      p.   cm.
   ISBN-13: 978-0-472-11539-6 (cloth : alk. paper)
   ISBN-10: 0-472-11539-1 (cloth : alk. paper)   1. Linton, Simi,
1947–   2. Women with disabilities—United States—Biography.
3. Paraplegics—United States—Biography.   4. Traffic accident victims—
United States—Biography.   I. Title.
HV3013.L56A3 2005
362.4'3'092—dc22   2005017907

Acknowledgments

It is for the pleasure of their company that I dedicate this book to the disabled people I know: the ribald, the kind, the uncompromising, the surly, the burly, the invincible . . . the mothers of invention.

And then, with thanks, to:

Bob Lescher, my wise and steadfast agent, my very good friend, for all he has done, for the muffins and for his wonderful stories.

The expert Barbara Craig and Carolyn Larson at Lescher and Lescher, Ltd.

Sara Bixler, for unleashing her smarts on this book and strengthening it immeasurably.

The executive editor of all time, the gracious LeAnn Fields, a friend to books everywhere and, to my great benefit, a friend to mine.

The staff at University of Michigan Press, in particular Mary Bisbee-Beek, Marcia LaBrenz, Rebecca Mostov, and Pete Sickman-Garner.

Alvaro Gomez, for the words, and for being, with grace and good humor, my right and, on alternate days, my left brain.

Myrtilda Cissy Tomlinson, for her great care.

Everyone who read large and small quantities of these words: Gene Chelberg, Anne Finger, Rosemarie Garland-Thomson, Cathy Kudlick, Paul Longmore, Corbett O'Toole, Harilyn Rousso, Barbara Waxman-Fiduccia, Florence Weiner, and others.

My darling David, who, despite being confined to a pair of roller skates lo these many years, has managed to triumph over his affliction and lead a serious life. Skate-bound, as it were, he is a credit to his kind and an inspiration to us all.

Contents

1. Conscripts to the Cavalry   1

2. Brave New World   18

3. Coming Out in the West   38

4. A Special Education   56

5. Going Away   70

6. Pleasures and Freedoms   77

7. The Design of My Life   89

8. I Sing My Body Electric   102

9. What I Learned   108

10. Weddings and Marriages   121

11. Citizens in Good Standing   134

12. Lessons from Children   156

13. Rufus   172

14. Odyssey of a Sure-footed Man   194

15. The Cripple Girl & the Blind Boy
    Go to the Museum   213

16. Our Body Politics   223

17. Epilogue   246

1 *Conscripts to the Cavalry*

On a spring day in 1971, my husband, my best friend, and I set off from Boston, Massachusetts, bound for Washington, D.C. We walked down the street together, we stood together near the entrance to the Mass Pike, and in unison we thrust our thumbs out, looking for the ride that would take us far on this first leg of our journey. We got the ride, and then another, and then another. And with each ride we got closer to Washington. But we never got there, and by the end of the day, my friend Carol was dead and my husband John, the ferociously smart man I'd married much too young, was in a coma he would never wake up from. I lay down the hall from him, tethered to tubes and machines, breathing hard to keep myself alive.

We had been on our way to Washington to protest the war in Vietnam. We had no doubts on that day we set out. This was the demonstration that would end the war, and we would—we must—voice our outrage. While it hurt us to know about the horrors, we lived at a safe distance from danger. Just two years before, John and I had been planning to go to Canada so that he could escape the draft, but then, just weeks before we were to leave, he fell and damaged his knee and his draft status was changed to 4-F, an immediate exemption from service. Carol and I had been training at a local center to be draft counselors, to assist young men who were trying to avoid the draft. We wanted to do something meaningful—something to show that we were not just tie-dye hippies, flashing peace signs to passersby.

We all knew of men who had been killed, and of those who were wounded and wouldn't ever walk again, or hear again, or breathe properly. But we were safe from that. We could only speak out against the injustice, and so we set off.

Suddenly, this became my story alone to tell. I lost my husband John, a wry wit who rebuked all that was hypocritical and phony. He led a frantic life, and was heard to say openly and with assurance that he knew he wouldn't live long. He had a nervous energy and a long lean body that caught my eye the first time I saw him. John dropped out of college shortly after I did, and we both had a defiance about us. Neither of us wore it comfortably. Mine was tinged with self-doubt, and his with a brashness and a lust for beer that often muddied his righteousness. We were living together and apart. He had loved me and been my friend, but he had hurt me too. He pulled and pushed, wanting too much, or nothing. I loved him too, and pulled and pushed back, and neither of us was wise enough to make it better.

And I lost Carol, an upright oak tree. A woman who made art of everything she did. Her long fingers were constantly weaving, twirling, braiding—threads, rope, string; wherever she was, she would pull from her pocket a small crochet hook and some yarn, and hook and loop, hook and loop, catch and knot, cutting the thread with her teeth, tucking in the ends, sliding it back into her pocket when her turn came up on the supermarket check-out line. On her face, she wore a red birthmark that slipped across her cheek, and gave her a soft glow. I told her many times how beautiful it was, as were her almond-shaped eyes and the long brown hair that flowed to her waist. She lived with a man named Rick, and they were a lively, playful pair. The four of us spent most of our weekends together. Carol and I had met at one of the temp secretarial jobs I took to make ends meet, and we insisted that we all get together. We would tease the guys later on because neither trusted our judgment, and had put off getting together for months. Once we did, we stuck. Rick didn't go with us to Washington, as he was the only one among us who had a steady job, and he had to work. He would hear when he got home that night how his life had been shattered too.

So Carol and John were lost to us. And John and Carol lost life. I breathed, and breathed, and breathed, and in beds down the corridor from me in a Baltimore hospital they each stopped breathing. Carol that same day, and John, they told me, a few days later. I never saw them. Or, if I did, I don't remember. I've blotted it all out. The crash, the ambulance, the airlift in the helicopter, and the emergency room are locked up somewhere, I hope never to be found. But now, many years later, what I do remember, and want to reconstruct here, is the life I grew into. The new shape and formation of my body were set on that April day; the meaning this new body would have for me took years to know.

For it wasn't until some time after I sustained the injury to my spine that immobilized my legs, after I learned to use a wheelchair, and after I had reckoned with myself and the world for a while in this new state—it wasn't until then that I gained the vantage point of the atypical, the out-of-step, the underfooted. It took being turned away from restaurants because they would not provide a table for me and discovering that my local polling place, library, post office, and movie theater were now off-limits to me. I first had to endure strangers coming up to me in public to offer a pat on the head and tell me how brave I was and obstinate college professors who thought it was my responsibility to get to classes scheduled in buildings that had no ramps or elevators. Crucially, though, it was banding together with other disabled people for good purpose that taught me what I needed to know for this new life.

The injury was a sudden cataclysmic event, and the paralysis in my legs was instant. Becoming disabled took much longer. I learned along the way how a young woman of privilege, although living at the time as a college dropout and self-fashioned hippie in rented rooms on the outskirts of Boston, could, by the collision of a tinny Volkswagen bus into a cement embankment on Interstate 95, become a marginal citizen, her rights and liberties compromised, and her economic advantage, white skin, and private school education weakened currency in this new world she inhabited. It was, of course, the same world I had always lived in, but when I was a nondisabled person I hadn't recognized the ways that world had favored me. I had always taken it for granted that if I could go places or get jobs that disabled people couldn't, it was because *I* was strong and healthy and *they* had their deficits and incapacities. While I probably (my memory is fuzzy here) felt sorry for those who "couldn't," I saw no agency on the part of those of us who "could." Certainly not those of us who were concerned about the plight of the unfortunates. We would at least want them to be cared for, housed, and fed.

Once I was pushed over to the other side, shelter and nourishment seemed meager fare for a body and mind that wanted a full life. I had ideas, I yearned to go to college, take a trip, get a job, and live on my own. I was a twenty-three-year-old robust and excitable young woman—ready for more life, not less.

After the accident, I spent almost a year in two different hospitals and a rehabilitation institute. I don't remember much of the first few weeks. I was in an ICU and heavily sedated. Someone, I think it was a nurse, did tell me that John and Carol had died, but she must have had to tell me several times, because I kept asking for them.

It wasn't until the third or fourth week that a doctor came to tell me that my legs were paralyzed. It seems strange now that I didn't realize it. I seem to have been able throughout this ordeal to shut out many things. I must have known it on some level, but kept the thought at bay. I was lying in bed on my back unable to move anything but my left arm, since my right was fractured and in a cast, and I must have thought (if I let the thought in at all) that I was just too weak to move.

The doctor stood over me and delivered his news, not hurriedly, not insensitively, but briefly. It seemed he might leave then, but he turned back to me lying there in my bed.

"You know," he said, "there are many young men coming back from Vietnam in the same situation as you, and I know you'll find someone really nice to settle down with."

That woke me up. How absurd this man was. Did he not know my husband had just died; did he not remember why I was there? Did he think this limp woman had lost her convictions? Did he think that I could now simply be matched up with a Vietnam vet, two people with nothing in common but our wounds?

I spoke. "Don't assume you know what will happen to me, what I might do."

Would I be able to decide what I would do? I didn't know; I didn't know a thing. I didn't know what "paralyzed" meant. Not for me.

After a month in the Baltimore hospital I was moved by ambulance to New York. There were surgeries to repair broken bones and damaged organs. A shoulder, a thumb, and some ribs had to be set right. The bones that house my spinal cord were pinned in place with metal plugs you can still see on x-rays. In the hospital I lay in bed being fed, ministered to, coddled, and soothed by my mother and my sister, and by a stream of nurses, slipping in and out of my room. My mother made me chicken soup and brought flowered pillowcases to rest my head on. She was with me all the time. In between the quiet moments were the surgeries, the painkillers, the nightmares. Snarling tigers and rabid beasts attacked me in my dreams, and I was their captive, penned in by the metal bars of my narrow hospital bed.

My doctor promised me that once I got to the rehab center I could get out of bed. We both knew that meant into a wheelchair. He'd said it before, I knew it, but he didn't repeat it each time, and I didn't think too much about it. Everything was very immediate—whether I hurt or not, who was in the room, how scared I was at night, and also my family and friends who surrounded me, feeding and distracting me. It must have been hard for them not to talk about the past, about John or Carol, nor talk at all about the future, a future none of us could quite imagine.

They did everything *for* me, and doctors and nurses did everything *to* me. I was exempt from my responsibilities as friend and sister, daughter and cousin. I didn't call people; they called me, and someone held the phone to my ear so I could talk with them. I didn't visit them; they visited me. I didn't bring them birthday presents or run errands for them; they did that and more for me. They were generous and steadfast. My sister, Chick, went to John's funeral in Lexington, Massachusetts, and absorbed for me the shock and the sorrow of our Boston friends and family.

Months passed, and I was transferred to a rehab center in New York City. The first day there, in a room not much different from the one in the hospital, in another bed with metal side bars, I was visited by a group of other patients. They came into my room, five or six young women and men, all in wheelchairs, waving and smiling, introducing themselves, offering to show me around. "When will you get your chair?" someone asked, like it was something I should want.

They soon left, talking loud, kidding around. Two guys tried to push their chairs out the door at the same time so they crashed into each other. "Fuck you," said one. "No, fuck you," said the other. I understood it as performance for my benefit, and I was flattered. I was left alone, wanting to be part of the group, wanting to move. Wanting to be like them.

I lay there in bed, on my side where the nurse had positioned me, with pillows tucked behind my back to keep me in place. I felt so helpless. The call button to summon the nurse was there, just a few inches from my hand, but I could think of nothing to ask for. I scanned the vacant room. I had three roommates, but they were all out of bed, down the hall somewhere, doing their scheduled activities. A clear plastic cup with urine sat on my nightstand, taken from the long tube inserted in my bladder. I jiggled the cup and watched the little white bits float up and down in the yellow liquid. Had it been just weeks before that I had been splayed out on my living room floor in Cambridge, tripping on LSD, entranced by the oily purple globules rising and falling in my lava lamp?

And had it been just a couple of years before that when I stood tall on the roof of my apartment building in the East Village, with the New York City skyline rising up behind me? Dressed in John's black V-neck sweater and a pair of tattered jeans, I was having my picture taken for an underground newspaper, the *East Village Other*. I would be the centerfold for the next issue, with a bold caption over my head: SLUM GODDESS.

Now, I was a slight, horizontal body draped in a loose white hospital gown. It opened in the back so if a doctor or nurse approached my bed, I would be available for their examinations and ministrations. I was more at home on the sooty roof than on my antiseptic hospital pallet. I was clothed then, costumed as an ethereal symbol of the counterculture. I stood in profile, with my face tilted upward, and my long wavy hair blowing out behind me.

My hair had been chopped off by a nurse in the emergency room and was slowly growing back. It was just long enough to comb behind my ears and fold into a little wave on top. The harsh fluorescent lights in my room sapped all tone and nuance from the atmosphere. There was nothing ethereal about me now. I had become an assemblage of body parts, notable only if they worked or not.

I got the wheelchair, but it took me a while to catch up to the others. Even sitting up in it made me dizzy. I had not been out of bed since the accident and weighed under ninety pounds. I hadn't used my arms for anything more strenuous than scratching. Slowly I began to gain strength, move around a bit, and eat. Thick milkshakes, bread and butter, mashed potatoes. I had the wild cravings of a pregnant woman. I'd wake up thinking about jelly donuts, and couldn't rest till I had one. Sitting up at a table to eat was an amazingly pleasing activity. Whatever I hungered for, my sister appeared with shopping bags filled with it: rich, smelly cheeses, olives, peanut butter sandwiches, apricot nectar, or a packet of vegetables and brown rice she had cooked on her stove, wrapped up in tin foil, and transported to the hospital at breakneck speed so it arrived still warm. And she acted as if this were a natural act, not heroic, not to be fussed over.

Treats were shared with my roommates. We ordered Chinese food at odd hours. Greasy egg rolls for everyone. We made each event as festive as possible. We were in a sorry place. Gray and alien. And there was nowhere to hide. We were thrown in together and exposed in all that was messy about our lives at that time. Our piss and our shit, our tears and our awkward visits with people who didn't know how to talk to us. The flimsy curtains that surrounded our beds hid little, but nurses and aides would appear at any time, day or night, and fling them open or snap them shut in order to do things to us: adjust our position, take blood from our arms, ask out loud to all around—including the aunts and uncles, boyfriends, and such clustered around each bed—if we'd had a bowel movement that day. Most of the nurses and aides were champions. They were sensitive and caring, and knew just what we needed. But there were others who were peculiar, self-involved, or sometimes downright hostile, and they had us in their grip.

I went to physical therapy every day. I lifted, stretched, pulled. I hurt. My legs were stock-still, and my feet in red sneakers perched on the footrests of my wheelchair, but the rest of my body kept moving, working hard to get us around. I'd never had very strong arms, but now these were becoming the most robust parts of my skinny little body.

The most difficult task was to learn how to move my whole body as a unit. The top half acted automatically, performing as it had for twenty-three years, but I had to consciously take charge of the lower half. Not only did it not move of its own volition, but the sensations below my waist were radically different from those I'd felt before. At the very beginning, when I was first injured, my legs felt numb, like when you get Novocain at the dentist. I couldn't feel if anyone touched me, nor could I sense where my legs or feet were unless I looked down and made an assessment of their position. But, over time, that changed. Feeling returned in my pelvis and genitals, and in other spots like my knees, my thighs, and the bottoms of my feet. The sensations that I feel in the lower half of my body, and there are many, are familiar to me now. The precise and specific sensations above the level of my injury meld into the more diffuse and varying feelings below, but they are all part of me. There is no longer a clear line of demarcation between these zones. There is a gradual change along the length of my body. Although my toes can't always tell the difference between hard and soft, rough and smooth, they alert me when they have encountered an object, and they tingle inside and tell me where they are. While initially I had to find my legs with my eyes, I can now reach down with my arm, hook it under my knees, and reposition my legs with as little conscious thought as it takes to reach out my hand and pick up a pencil on my desk.

Learning all of this and gaining strength took a long time. In the current managed-care climate, people with similar injuries are shut-tled out of the hospital, into rehab, and then out the door as soon as they are medically stable, sometimes just three weeks post-trauma. In 1971, people stayed in the hospital and then in rehab for months, gradually getting stronger, learning to do the familiar in a strange new way. I was in the hospital for four months and then six months in rehab. Day after day, the physical therapists and the aides worked us hard. They were relentless; little fazed them. Their job was to get us strong and keep us moving forward. If someone got tired, or angry, or depressed, the solution was more exercise. But if you were really hurting, they would circle around you and help you out.

Much of the day was filled with stupid activities that I had little patience for, like learning to make a cake from a packaged mix in the occupational therapy room, or the meetings they scheduled for me with a staff psychologist. Most of the time, I wouldn't talk to him. I didn't show up for the appointments, or I would stop by and give him a report of my activities with few embellishments. He was a soft, mild-mannered man, and did seem concerned. Yet his tailored slacks and sports jacket and slicked-back hair showed him to be "straight," and certainly over thirty. I feared he might talk me out of myself.

I had only vestiges of my life with me in that place: a big brown suede pocketbook with floor-length fringe I had on the trip to Washington, emptied now and folded into a drawer in my nightstand, and a beaded headband I put on every day. The clothes I wore were loose pants and t-shirts my mother bought in a hurry at Macy's. They were not what I would have chosen, but I could not go to Macy's to choose them. So what I was left with were the few decisions I could make in a day: whom to talk to, what flavor ice cream to eat, whom to trust. Small as I was in that hospital-issue clunky metal wheelchair and my baggy clothes, I said yes and no to things.

I remember one day the psychologist sought me out to report the results of an IQ test he'd administered the week before. He seemed excited with his news that I was quite smart. I had scored even higher on the test than he thought I would, he told me, and I quickly discovered that the more casual I acted and the more disinterested I seemed, the more insistent he became that I take this seriously.

The man earned his pay that day by patiently listening to me rant about his simplistic, meaningless, rote tests, which did nothing but affix a number to people, taking all that they are and shrinking it down to bits and pieces. Indeed, he may have been very talented and allowed me the adolescent thrill of getting a rise out of an adult, and the opportunity to vent my anger at him for making me think about my future. Maybe, somewhere in my response, he could see my first try at the kind of opinion-rendering I would one day get paid for.

I didn't puff myself up like that often. Mostly, I think I was nice to people. It was a humbling experience being there. All these people in pain and needing so much, and most of the staff were decent people doing a hard job.

I often brushed off people's kindness to me, showing an upbeat face, saying I was fine today, no need to worry. But not always. My friend Kevin found me once huddled in a vestibule outside the urologist's office, crying. A few weeks before, they had taken out my indwelling catheter, and I was trying so hard to keep from peeing all over myself, but I couldn't hold back and there I was again, wet and sad. "Kevin," I sobbed, "he told me that maybe it would get better, but if not I could wear a pad when I went out. He said that it wasn't so bad, people did that. But it is bad," I said, "it's terrible. I can't do that."

Kevin said, "Yeah," and pointed to the bulge in his pants leg where, as we both knew, there was a tube coming out of his penis, running down his leg, into a bag strapped to his ankle. But it was Kevin's turn to comfort me, and he did, and before long we were laughing at how much beer he'd drunk the night before to make his bag so fat.

Another day I hung around the nurses' station waiting to talk to one of the nurses I liked. I didn't want to approach her, or make a big deal of it, like there was really something the matter, so I just waited till she was alone there and I could casually pull my chair up to hers. I asked how her day was going.

Then I said, "You know that salesman who you order equipment from? Yeah, well, he came to my room last night and said he had to measure me for a back brace. It was late," I said, "so it was weird. The room was pretty dark, there was no one around, and he sat on my bed, and every time he reached down to measure my waist, or the length of my back, he rubbed my breast."

She said that it was hard to do that measurement without touching me, maybe it just seemed like he was rubbing my breast.

"No," I said, my voice getting louder, "it was wrong. What he did was wrong. When I tried to stop him, he got annoyed and told me to hold my hands over my head."

I found the courage to name him. "He's a creep," I said. "Please don't let him near me." I began to cry.

She took my hand. "Don't worry," she said. "I'll make sure that won't happen again."

He never came into my room again, but I saw him move easily about, visiting other patients on the floor.

I stopped going to the sessions with the psychologist, but physical therapy made sense, and I did everything they told me to do. As I got stronger and learned how to use my chair, I wanted to get out of my room, to go somewhere—anywhere. I teamed up with the group that had visited me that first day, and we would barrel down the hall, get on the elevator, go to the snack bar, sit out in front of the hospital, do anything for privacy, fresh air, space, and just to move. Our favorite spot was the roof, which in the summer and fall months when I was there was often hot and dirty, but it got us out of the stifling rooms and corridors where you smelled medicine, heard groans, and saw nothing that wasn't starkly white or hospital green.

We snuck bottles of scotch up to the roof, and some of us smoked reefer. We had a couple of portable radios and were always fighting over which stations to listen to. Here was a group of women and men who were anywhere from seventeen to around thirty-five. We had landed in this place with little in common—a college student who smacked up his sports car on spring break, a country boy thrown from his horse, a construction worker who toppled off a high rigging, a young woman who fell off the back of a motorcycle, and me, a college dropout, a young widow, kind of drifting, kind of working, kind of OK, sideswiped on her way to an anti-war demonstration.

The scotch drinkers and the pot smokers tolerated each other's habits. In the days before the hospital I remembered that these groups had been divided along party lines, but here we had to mingle, there was only one party for us.

The songs "American Pie" and "Bridge Over Troubled Water" were big hits that summer. Whenever the first came on the radio we'd sing along, driving our Chevy to the levee. Screeching at the top of our lungs, we were a group of caterwauling bruised creatures, eager to cut loose with our voices, our bodies tied down by our impairments, and held captive in this institution. Yet when we heard the first plaintive strains of "Bridge Over Troubled Water," we'd get quiet and sad. Even late at night, with everyone in bed, if the song came on, someone would turn the volume way up and each of us in our rooms up and down the hall would hear Simon and Garfunkel reassure us.

> If you need a friend
> I'm sailing right behind.
> Like a bridge over troubled water
> I will ease your mind.

Up on the roof, after visiting hours, when all our friends and families, girlfriends and boyfriends had gone home, when our loneliness and isolation were at a peak, we huddled together and talked about sex. Most of us had sustained spinal cord injuries to our necks or backs, others had brain injuries. All of us were radically altered in the way we moved, felt our bodies, responded to sexual stimulation. How did we know this? This group of relative strangers, women and men, adolescents, married people, probably both gay and straight people (though no one said that they were gay), we shared our stories—our attempts at masturbation, our furtive fondling with girlfriends and boyfriends up here on this same roof, our few private moments at home when we had the precious weekend passes that got us out of the institution. Our bodies had changed, our lives had changed. Some had partners who wanted them to be the "way they were before," some didn't know how their partners felt and were afraid to ask, and some of us, like me, were alone, not knowing how we would meet anyone now. What was clear and uniform across the group was that we had strong desire. We felt lust in our hearts, and our bodies tingled and stretched out toward sex, toward pleasure.

Like the young adolescents we had only recently been, we didn't know what to do with all the pent-up feelings. Here we were, swept into this dormitory, living four in a room, trying to stretch our curfews, surrounded by worried, hovering parents—parents whose clutches we'd just escaped from. Now they were back in charge, and we needed them. It was very hard for both sides.

So when questions about sex came up, we turned to each other. "What did you hear?" "Can we get any books?" "What happened when you went home last weekend?" We could start putting the pieces together. The doctors were a mixed group on this score. Some were well-meaning, but awkward. Others didn't offer much help. There were no women physicians there, and the only male doctor I would have liked to talk to was handsome and appealing, and I dreamed about him at night. I couldn't ask him. So I picked out one of the other doctors who seemed nice enough. Although he looked like my Uncle Harry, I plucked up my courage and asked him if he could explain a couple of things about sex to me.

"You know," he said, "most of the research and most of our experience is with men. It's not as complicated for you women, you can do everything just like before. And don't worry, your period will come back soon." I hadn't had my period since the accident, and no one had said why or that it would return.

"But," I asked, "does that mean I could get pregnant?" It hadn't occurred to me.

"Well, yes, sure, if you want, and there are a couple of doctors around the country who have experience delivering babies of women with spinal cord injuries." I had not wanted to have children; my concern had always been not getting pregnant. I didn't even know what else to ask him. It was all too much for me, and too abstract. "Well, thanks," I said. He leaned in across the desk and said, "We don't have much information yet on women, but you go out and give it a try and come back and tell us all about it." Come back and tell him? Why would I do that? Why was the information only about men? I knew I would never tell him anything personal.

Another time, I approached one of the physical therapists, a young woman about my age, kind of a cheerleader type. When I asked her if, maybe, we could talk about sex and stuff, she looked down at the floor, rang the button to call the elevator, and said maybe I should speak with my doctor.

Finally, a group of us found a physical therapist and a nurse who were great allies. They kept saying we were going to be fine, we could have a pleasurable sexual life. Many people before us were doing well, had lives, jobs, and relationships. "You make the adjustments," they told us. "It's not always easy, give it time, don't give up." The nurse said to a friend of mine: "Try to relax and just see what comes, see what feels good."

We weren't completely convinced, but their optimism was helpful, particularly because they seemed to really know the people they were talking about. We had heard that one of the therapists was married to a former patient.

One of the people I particularly remember was an aide named Charles, a tall lanky man, wiry body, dark black skin, a warm, funny guy who used to help me with the exercise equipment in the physical therapy room. After I'd been there about three months I got my first pass to leave the rehab center, and spent the weekend at my mother's house. I came into the PT room on Monday morning still a bit dazed from a weekend spent trying to figure out how to live and function in a world more complex than the simplified routine of institutional life I'd gotten used to. My major accomplishment for the weekend was that I had bought cookies for everyone. I actually went into a store, opened a wallet, and purchased cookies. Sure, my mother had given me the money and the wallet, sure, my sister had gone with me and helped get my wheelchair up and down the curb on the corner, so I could get to the bakery, just a block away, but I'd done it. I was in good spirits and had a big grin on my face as I passed the cookies out. Charles came up to me, leaned way down, and, with a sly chuckle in his voice, whispered to me: "Been doin' them horizontal exercises?" That is the sweetest memory I have of that place. Here was my big brother telling me: "You're OK. You're attractive. You're going to make it. Go ahead, enjoy your life."

Such moments made me strong. A few members of the rooftop gang petitioned the doctors to bring in an educational film that we'd heard about on sexuality and disabled people. I was to be one of the spokespersons in our meetings with the doctors. Before our meeting, our allies from the staff came to help us prepare. They had just returned from a conference on sexuality held at a rehabilitation center in the Midwest and spoke with excitement about the development of a new area of research in sexuality, and about the presentations made at the conference. They mentioned something in passing that caught my attention—many of the people speaking at the conference were disabled people who were actively involved in the work.

That thought was in my mind when we went to speak with the doctor. When he dodged our questions, and when he let it be known that this was his decision to make, I persisted, saying it was about *our* lives, we had a right to know. It was not many weeks after that, while still an inpatient at the rehab center, still not knowing where my life was going, that I decided to go back to college to get a degree in psychology. I would come back to this place with the authority to implement a sexuality program. I would listen to what patients wanted and needed, and I wouldn't be high-handed or patronizing. I wouldn't tell them I knew what was best for them. I would listen.

I had no idea what it meant to "get a degree in psychology." Graduate school? It had never even occurred to me. I had been a lousy student in high school, had gone to the only college that accepted me, and lasted two months. I had met John there, and he lasted just a few months more than I did. We both read books, and paid attention to things, but we nurtured the belief that anything worth knowing could be learned outside of the college classroom. At the time the accident occurred I was faltering in that conviction, and tired of flopping from job to job, unable to find anything that met my criteria of "meaningful" and "creative." The only thing that had held my interest was volunteer work for the anti-war movement, and the training I went through to be a draft counselor.

While this idea about going back to college was brewing, my friend

Barbara had been coming to visit me at the rehab center. She speaks French and offered to give me lessons twice a week. She brought grammar books and notebooks, and threw herself into the job. I hadn't even read a book or watched television in all those months. Nothing had held my attention until this. During the day, when I snuck out of the cake-making sessions or wanted to get away from the shrink, I went to the library in the basement of the hospital next door and did my French homework. I was surrounded by medical students poring over their thick anatomy textbooks. They didn't look at me. Even the young intern who had been in my hospital room many times on rounds, when I said hello to him, glanced quickly at me and, just as quickly, looked away. I turned back to my books; I would have to get stronger.

Something serious had happened to me, and I was starting to feel like a more substantial person. A woman now, although no longer a married woman and no longer a walking woman, I was, mercifully, no longer a girl. Even in this forest of overseers, where every move I made was scheduled and every quantity of liquid I drank and eliminated was measured, I had opinions. I was cowed by the outside world, the walking world, but here inside I had a role and a point of view. I was on leave from the anti-war movement, and left the skewering of the big guys at the Pentagon to others, they were beyond my reach, but doctors were all around me, and I saw the mischief in their brand of power-wielding and the hierarchies they imposed on others. They had saved me, and saved all my new friends, but I was outraged when they spoke for me or spoke down to a nurse I liked. I thought they shouldn't be entitled to say "yes," or, more significantly, "no," to me with such finality. As a participant in the workings of an institution, I had something before me each day that I could think critically about.

During my fifth month in the rehab center, my doctor told me that I would be discharged in another month. On my weekend passes I went with my sister to look for an apartment. John and I had moved in together soon after I dropped out of college. I was eighteen and he was twenty-one. We married a year later, in 1967, and I took his name. We set up house and I learned to cook and do laundry and clean. I was an experienced, if not enthusiastic, housekeeper, but this would be my first apartment on my own. Now the bed would be my bed. The possessions that had been *ours* would be *mine* to share, as I saw fit, with others.

I was starting to take back some control over my life. Where I would live, when I would move there, what colors to paint the rooms in my new apartment, who would come and go in those rooms. The organization of my life had been under the control of others for so long that the simplest choices seemed monumental. Was this what I really wanted, or was I doing it because someone else wanted me to; was I doing it because I was now disabled and had to do things a certain way, was I doing it because I was scared not to, was I really in charge, was this really mine to choose? Would everything be a compromise now? A half, or even less, of what might have been?

Over the last months, I had had no choice who visited me. All the people who had come to see me since the accident had been told about it by someone else, and they showed up during visiting hour unannounced, offering flowers or books. I imagine that my mother or my sister had called them, or Rick, Carol's boyfriend, had. The only people I had told about the accident were the group on the roof, but that was just some of the details, everyone knew why we were there.

There was one friend I hadn't seen in a couple of years. She was living in a small town in upstate New York. I knew she didn't know what had happened to me; none of my other friends knew her. A couple of weeks before I left the hospital, late at night after everyone was in bed, I took a bunch of change down to the phone booth at the end of the hall and called Delia. I just plunged in and told her about the accident, about John and Carol, the outcome, the plan to leave the hospital soon, stay on in New York and go back to college.

I then said, "I'm OK, you know."

"What?" she said, letting out a gasp. "Oh yeah, sure, you're fine. John is dead. You're fucking paralyzed, you're in a fucking wheelchair, what do you mean, you're OK?"

"But I am," I said.

I woke from the nightmares, lived on the edge for a while, frail and hurting, dopey from rounds of painkillers and the numbing bleakness of hospital life. The accident had taken some material worth from me. There were lumps and bumps and scars. A couple of my ribs were missing, and they had even taken my appendix just for good measure while they were in there rooting around for broken bones. But now, a few months later, I liked the same things, got outraged just the same, laughed at my sister's jokes, and still hated Nixon. I was scared of going back out into the world, a world I knew would not treat me well, but I was hungry for it.

I laughed when Delia said, "You're fucking paralyzed!" Everyone had been so nice, so tentative, like maybe I didn't know what had happened to me.

If Delia could talk rough to me, I must be OK.

2 *Brave New World*

One by one the rooftop gang disbanded as we were discharged to go back out to the world. Sex wasn't all we had talked about. We talked a lot about reentry and how we would manage. None of us knew anyone else like us out there. We had gotten used to a place where disability was commonplace, at least for the patients, but it wasn't like that elsewhere. Even at the hospital only a handful of the people we saw working there had disabilities: a couple of the secretaries used wheelchairs, a psychologist with foreshortened arms, a lab technician who used crutches. Were we now like them? Were we "handicapped"? What was that? What would it mean for us? What should we call ourselves?

Some of us would go back to the homes where we'd been living before, but most couldn't. There may have been stairs, or other unnegotiable terrain. Some wound up going to their parents' homes, at least for a while. Some of us needed help with the daily routines of life, and parents seemed the only option, and most of us no longer had the resources to live on our own. There were some so young they hadn't left home in the first place.

Few of the places that people would go were fully accessible, and most of us used wheelchairs or walked with crutches or canes. Ramps had to be built, doorways widened, kitchen counters lowered. My friend Bob was going to wind up sleeping in the living room of his parents' suburban home, the only space on the ground floor for him. He said he felt guilty about disrupting everyone's life, and knew too that he would have no privacy there. Kevin would go back upstate, but didn't know what he would do there. He and his girlfriend would move to the first floor of the house, once the ramp had been built and the bathroom renovated, but he wondered how he would get his wheelchair around the farm and into the barn. Sara went to stay with her father. She was walking now with a cane, and thought she'd be able to manage the few steps at the entrance to his building.

I spent two weeks at my mother's house and then moved into an apartment in Manhattan that I had found while on one of my weekend passes from the rehab center. My mother would pay my rent and help me out with expenses, and the social worker at the hospital worked with me to secure funding from the state for college tuition, and for transportation to go back and forth to class. I won a small court settlement from the accident, and that helped ease the way.

Life was bound to be more expensive now. I didn't think I could work the temp secretarial jobs I had relied on in Boston to earn money. Would they hire me? How would I get there or fit in those crowded offices? Into the bathroom? I certainly wouldn't be hitchhiking anymore, and the bus and subway were inaccessible. I'd have to take taxis or buy a car. I could no longer live in a third-floor walkup. Even the apartment I'd found, in a building that had a flat entrance, an elevator, and wide doorways, would need some work for me to be able to live there. I had to buy kitchen cabinets that could sit on the floor, and have a carpenter remove the existing counter and build a lower one that was open underneath so I could pull up to it, like sitting at a table. At that height, I could chop and stir, sift and blend. I had gone to enough of those cake-mix classes to know some of the tricks. The shower door in the bathroom had to be removed, and I purchased a sturdy plastic chair that sits inside the stall. When I take a shower, I pull my wheelchair alongside the opening, like parallel parking, do a push-up with my arms on the seat of my wheelchair, which lifts my bottom up, then shift my body over to the plastic chair, hook my arm under my knees, and pull my legs in with me. This is the same way I get into bed, onto the sofa, and into a car.

The building faced Riverside Park and the Hudson River, and I could see them and smell them, and feel the breezes off the river. I chose a bright pumpkin orange paint for the bedroom and various shades of violet for the living room walls and ceilings, with a touch of magenta on the mantle. The view, the smell, the breeze, and these manic colors would ward off my fear of being cooped up, of living a compromised life, of people seeing sadness in this place.

My mother was in the moving and warehouse business, and I made an excursion to her office way uptown to pick out some furniture from the storage area where they kept the goods people left behind. This was a business my mother and father had started in the 1940s, before I was born. My father died when I was eight, and my mother remained in charge of the company. Growing up, it seemed perfectly natural to me that women work, that they can be the boss and know what they're doing.

I spent a lot of time at the warehouse when I was a kid, and then in high school I worked in the office during summer breaks. That day when I arrived to pick out my furniture, all the men and women who worked there, some who had known me since I was a baby, came out to see me. Each said hello to me, calling me Cookie, the childhood nickname that had stuck with me through adolescence, and here, apparently, even longer. People looked awkward and uncertain, like they didn't know what to say to this disabled young widow. For my own sake probably more than theirs, as each person approached me, I smiled and extended my hand or reached up to hug the women who worked in the office with my mother. I said, "How ya doin'?" "Good to see you," "What's new?" This would be casual and upbeat, I signaled to them. I was here to pick out furniture for my new apartment. I was getting out of rehab next week. This was a good thing. You mustn't feel sad.

I don't think I convinced everyone. Particularly Mitch, a broad-shouldered, lumbering man, with doleful eyes and long ears, who drove one of the moving vans for the company. When I was little he used to take me for rides around the neighborhood in the red truck. One time when I was about five, I rode with him all the way up to the cottage my family rented for the summer. When we were almost there, he got lost, but I remembered all the roads, and showed him the way. Every single time he saw me after that he would laugh at how little Cookie had showed up the big truck driver. But that day, when he saw me seated in my wheelchair, his sad eyes held tears. When it was coming up to his turn to greet me, he took his cap off and held it in his big, rough hands. He came forward and patted my shoulder, murmuring something I couldn't hear, but which I thought had the word "sorry" in it, and then he quickly moved away.

I went upstairs in the huge freight elevator with my mother and

Pete, the warehouse man. We found a couch, a couple of bookcases, a dining room table that sat eight, a queen-size bed, and a desk. Pete pointed to the room where my stuff from Boston was stored. I was not prepared to think about that material yet. John was gone from my life, and in the last months there had been hardly anything around that proved that I had a previous existence, let alone that he ever existed. What was left of him was contained in that storage bin.

"How did the things get here?" I asked my mother, trying to sound casual.

"Pat and Susan packed up everything, and we sent a truck up there," she said.

John's mother and sister, then, had been to our house. Whatever dirty underwear was on the floor, whatever moldy food was in the refrigerator, they had to handle. Were there secrets they may have unfolded?

Were all of John's things here, left for me to sort through, or had they given them away already? People do this all the time when someone dies, I thought, but the job seemed cruelly hard.

How had they gotten into the apartment? Did our nasty landlady let them in? Did she soften at the news of her tenant-victims?

I felt beholden to Pat and Susan, and guilty, as I often did in those days, for bringing so much pain on people. I was embarrassed that I had taken the risk of hitchhiking and they had to pick up after me.

Mitch and one of the young drivers showed up at my new apartment on moving day. They drove the red truck which carried the old and the new fixings for my house. One by one, my sister and I unpacked the boxes, and each one scared me. I wanted to look forward, not back. What would I see that would make me compare my life before to my life now, my body then to the one I now owned? I quickly put back in their boxes: the high heels I didn't think I could wear anymore, the suede vest with the long fringe that had swung around my legs as I walked through Harvard Square, and the photos of me, and John, and Carol, and Rick, and one snapshot of all four of us, nonchalant, unfettered, standing on a beach on Cape Cod, our faces turned up toward the sun, assuming we could always be there, could always do that.

Over the next days, weeks, and years I would take all of these out of their boxes and the drawers I had tucked them into and revisit them, try them on, feel it all, but today I would look for the things that could bring me pleasure in my new life—my red flannel shirt, the hairbrush that made my scalp tingle, my camera, and the flowered dishes I'd bought at a yard sale.

John's clothes were not there, but our collection of books and records and such was. His Howard Zinn and my Par Lagerkvist; his Frank Zappa and my Joan Baez.

I had Mitch's young partner help me set up the stereo in the living room. We took two empty cartons and draped a tablecloth over them, to hold the turntable, and placed the small walnut KLH speakers on either side. In those days, that was a sound system. I picked out my favorite album, Otis Redding's *Live in Europe,* and slowly turned the volume up until I made Mitch smile.

My mother had given me a portable typewriter for my recent birthday, my twenty-fourth. It had sat in its case in my locker at the rehab center. Maybe she thought that I would be able to write down all that happened as a way to help me through it. When the men brought my new desk upstairs and we positioned it in the living room, facing the river, I ceremoniously took the typewriter out of its case and placed it on my desk, along with a dictionary and other signs of serious endeavors. I was going to college, I had work to do. My sister and I made plans to go to a stationery store the next day and buy the paper, pens, stapler, paper clips—the list was long—that would set me in motion.

As night came, everybody went home except the woman who would be living with me and helping me out for a while. I wanted her to go too. Francine had been my mother's housekeeper, and her new position in my household was my mother's idea. A large woman, she took up a lot of space. She had a hearty laugh that I could hear when she was on the phone, even when her door was closed and mine. I hated that I needed her there, handling me, fixing things, and protecting me, or at least so my mother thought, from danger. My mother paid her salary and my rent, and Francine's big presence reminded me of that.

As Francine settled in for her first round of phone calls, I went to my closet and picked out an old shirt, a pair of underpants, and my favorite jeans, and placed them on a chair. I would put them on tomorrow and look like me again. But then I saw one of the long macrame belts that Carol had made for me. She had woven and tied it with her beautiful long fingers, and sprinkled it with shiny blue beads. Here I was in this strange apartment, but Carol wasn't. I lost her. I misplaced her. I misled her. Was it me that had urged her to go with us to Washington? I couldn't remember. And where was my John? *I want you to be alive, to breathe like I'm breathing, to feel.*

I came out of the closet into my orange bedroom. With the night and soft lighting it had a warm glow, not like the garish Day-Glo of afternoon. I practiced. "This is my room." "This is my apartment." "I live here." It would take years until I felt it was so, felt that I was in charge there. I brushed my teeth, put on a t-shirt, and called Francine to help me take my back brace off and lift my legs so I could get into bed. I had to wear the brace to support my back when I was sitting up, I couldn't get in or out of the damn thing myself, and I had been told not to move too vigorously until my back was stable.

Francine and I were to cohabit for several months, until I no longer needed the back brace and could move more easily. I soon learned, though, that we had a common goal. She wanted to go out at night, and I wanted her to go out too. Friends could come over or they could pick me up and we could go somewhere, and I didn't have to tell Francine, who, I was sure, told my mother everything I did, and what my mood and my appetite were. At twenty-four I was again playing the adolescent games with my mother that I had left home six years before to get away from. Then, I had packed some things in a shopping bag and walked out in a huff, dropping out of college to live in the East Village. Now I needed her and I felt so much for her, and so guilty for all she'd been through because of me. I knew that she worried about me, and was even more uncertain how to keep me from harm. Sometimes I saw her and her face was sad, with lines drawn in from all those long hard days watching me struggle. Yet I groaned at the weight of her concern and did everything I could to evade her gaze. I knew that if I at least seemed to be doing well, it would release her from worry.

I didn't feel afraid, at least consciously, of physical harm. I had survived the trauma, and each day I was getting stronger and doing more. Unpacking a box of books myself and organizing them on the shelf. Cooking for friends who had always brought me food in the hospital. Deciding whom to see and when. I still couldn't bend over too far, or twist, or lift or . . . walk. When that thought stalked me, I ducked it, sought refuge at my new desk, sharpened my pencils, made a phone call. I distracted it, until it rested off on the side. I became adept at such evasions, too adept. I even found clever ways to have outbursts about anything but my losses, to suffer the pain of others.

Over all these months, Rick had kept my cat, Poozle. The first weekend I spent in the new apartment, he brought her down to New York. They arrived late at night. I told Francine I would get the door. I heard Poozle's meows out in the hall even before the bell rang. Rick carried the travel case in, set it down, and opened it. Poozle crouched down in the case, whimpering and squeaking. Slowly she rose up, put her paws on the edge of the case, and scanned the place. She set one paw, then another, on the newly polished floor. I sat there, poised above the surface she touched. My own feet don't touch down, they sit up on foot rests five inches above the ground. I watched how her paws splayed out on the cool surface, and I could feel in my mind the sensation of toes on wood, heels in wet grass, and the balls of my feet touching down in hot sand.

Poozle circled the room, checking behind the couch and under the table. She pawed open a closet door, and walked right in over the shoes and stuff on the floor. She sniffed her way through the kitchen, the back bathroom with the litter box I'd put out for her, and the pile of boxes still in the living room. I sat there watching her, tears streaming down my face. Rick stood behind me, his hands on my shoulders. Everything that was significant about this moment he understood. That she wouldn't come near me, that she walked and I sat, and that she was still there after so much else was lost. When Poozle had made her full rounds, she walked right over to me and rubbed her body across the wheel of my chair, just like she used to rub across my leg when I was standing, only this time she threw her head back and let out a piercing yowl. I reached down, scooped her up, and buried my face in her neck.

Rick spent the night. With me. In my bed. He had been visiting me in the hospital and then at the rehab center. At the center, when we were finally alone in a dark corner of the roof, we talked softly, all four of our hands held tightly together. During the months that I was there, he would drive down from Boston whenever he could, and bring me presents. We'd go out for coffee, or to a park nearby, and sometimes he would come upstairs and hang out with the gang on the roof. I was too scared at first to realize what this meant, to understand it as romance.

It seemed natural that he should be there in my new home. A lot of it was familiar to him. He had sat on the chairs many times, he knew the Jimi Hendrix poster that had hung in the kitchen, and now was over the mantle, and he had listened to the records on the very same stereo. There was a different bed, though, not the one John and I had shared. Someone had decided, my mother-in-law in Boston or my mother here in New York, not to send it ahead to this new house.

Rick started to come down from Boston for one or two weekends a month, and then, as summer came, more often. We went to the park across the street. We went to the movies. We went up to Broadway and bought vegetables, and cooked them up in my new kitchen. There was a steep hill getting to Broadway, to the grocery store, and Rick had to push my chair to the top. Coming back, I could speed down, out in front in the race to get back home. And we made love. After the first trial runs, it was not as complicated as it seemed it would be. There were awkward moments, sad, lonely moments for me when I felt ashamed of my crumbled body and my unwilling legs. The free spirit in me fought with the embarrassed me, each winning some of the time. Over time, though, I learned that the parts fit like they had before, and the pleasure was the sweeter after the long absence and for the tenderness and love we found with each other.

Those were the moments that seemed innocent of our shared history. Moments when it felt like we belonged together, not just that we had been thrown together by circumstance.

The first couple of months I was home I had to go to the hospital every day for physical therapy, but right after that I started classes at the New School for Social Research in Greenwich Village. The first semester I began with a French conversation course and Intro Psych. It went well enough, and so the next semester I took a full load. I was going there three or four days a week. A taxi service used by the state agency that was funding my education picked me up at my house and delivered me to the school. The drivers were experienced in these matters and handled my wheelchair easily, and gave me a hand getting up the curb and into the building. The main building had no steps going in, and there were elevators to most of the classrooms. On the third floor, there was an overpass that extended across an interior court-yard to the other building where classes were held. I found only one bathroom in the school that I could enter easily and, with some maneuvering, get to the toilet. It wasn't an official wheelchair stall, and it wasn't deep enough, once my chair was inside, for the door to close. When women would come and go, I just sat there, exposed, as they stood around talking or fixing their hair or sneaking a smoke. As unpleasant as it was, I always hoped my classes were scheduled near that bathroom.

One semester I had an early-morning class scheduled in a room in a back section of the building usually reachable by one set of steps down and then another, a few yards away, of equal height, back up. I found out from the security guard about an alternate route using the back elevator that bypassed the first set of steps. So when I came in the building in the morning, I first had to find the maintenance man who could work the back elevator. Then, when he left me off at the floor, there were still ten steps to get into the classroom. The solution that the teacher offered was that two of the male students would carry me up. So, when I arrived on the floor, I would wait at the bottom of the stairs till I got someone's attention or until someone showed up for class, then they would find the two lifters, and with one at the front and one at the back, heft me up the stairs. When it went smoothly everyone appeared congenial, but some days I was late, either because the car service hadn't shown up when it was supposed to, or because I couldn't find the man to operate the elevator, and then when the teacher noticed that I was waiting at the bottom of the steps, she would stop the class and instruct the guys to put down their pens and come down the stairs to carry me into the room. The other students turned to the back of the room and watched it all. The teacher never offered to have the class moved, so I assumed she liked that room and wanted to stay there. And I was inexperienced in these matters and felt guilty asking people to move because of me. I absorbed the awkward-ness and unpleasantness, because to protest it, I thought, would be making too much of my disability.

I made a few friends, and we'd meet after class to hang out and to study together. The only outdoor space in this city school was the inner courtyard, a pleasant enough spot. From the main building, there was a set of steps down to it, but from the other building the way was flat. If we decided to go to the courtyard after class, I'd tell everyone to go ahead, I'd meet them there. I didn't want my friends to have to go the way I did; it seemed to call attention to how hard things were for me. For me to catch up with them, I would first take an elevator in the main building to get to the overpass to the other building. I'd go across the bridge, look down, and see my friends already outside. Then, in the other building, I'd wait for the elevator to go down to the first floor and out the big door to the courtyard. Sometimes I would need to make a detour in that route to get to the bathroom on the fourth floor, and that would require waiting for one more elevator.

I always tried to appear upbeat; I guess I was trying to convince people that disability is no big deal. Also, I learned that if I said out loud that I was angry that there was only one bathroom I could use, or that I had a class scheduled in an inaccessible location, people would look sad and say things like: "Oh, that must be so hard," "Oh, how terrible, you must feel awful." But it was more complicated than that. They felt sorry, I felt angry.

It was 1972 when I went back to college, and in the two years I spent at the New School, I was just feeling my way with the disability thing. I hadn't yet learned how to raise my voice about the discrimination I faced or to look outside my own personal solutions (or struggles) to try to change things. There was a dean I recall, who was very nice and offered help, but anything I asked for seemed to be for me, not for a wider purpose. I felt alone in it, and it seemed the honorable thing to bear my burdens silently. The stink that I had been making about the war in Vietnam had to do with broad political issues of national importance. I could articulate how race and class played a part in who was fighting and who was not. I could make a case for the illegality of U.S. aggression in Vietnam. I knew of the lies and the cover-ups. I knew who was at fault.

Here, though, it didn't seem to be anybody's fault that a doorway was too narrow, or there were steps, or there was no way to use public transportation; these seemed to be just facts of life, random incidents, not governed by any principle. The size and shape of things appeared to be fixed and unchangeable. I had a feeling it could be different, but didn't know where to begin. I was having enough trouble just getting around, figuring out each step in my complicated life, and I couldn't see beyond that. I think if there had been other disabled people around, I might have recognized that they were entitled to get on the bus, to get to class on their own, to use the bathroom, and to have teachers provide reasonable accommodations in the classroom. I would have felt outrage on their behalf, and then, by extension, for myself.

The trips from home to school in the chartered car service were, at least initially, my major outings. But soon I started to move out in broader circles, going to the movies, my friend Judy's house, my sister's, my mother's, downtown for some shopping, going with Rick to the Village for music, the Mid-Manhattan Library, the museums.

When I left rehab, I got a bright, new, shiny chrome wheelchair. Compared to the lightweight, manual model I use today, which is sleek and black, the old chrome models looked clunky and were harder to push. They look like the wheelchairs you see in hospital corridors and at airports. I chose brown Naugahyde rather than the hospital-issue pale blue, and figured out that I only needed to use one of the metal side pieces (like armrests on an armchair) which frame my lap. I made no other modifications to the chair, nor did I decorate it the way some do. No decals or orange plastic reflectors. The chair had for me a purely utilitarian function.

When I went down the street in this machine, wearing some of my clothes from the "before" era, the people I would want to take an interest in me ignored me, but the stiff upstanding ones, the sort who used to bristle at the sight of my hippie rags, Janis Joplin sunglasses, and wild frizzy hair, now would go all soft at the sight of me, and bend at the waist to breathe their kindnesses on me. "Oh, I admire you so much," they clucked. On any given street, a woman was bound to come through the crowd to coo: "What a brave girl you are." And she would mean well, of course. Some days I would hear my favorite: "Oh my dear, what a shame, and you're so pretty, too." The logic of that was so incomprehensible I could find no way to refute it.

I felt bowdlerized, expurgated; the juice drained out of me. No matter how rough I looked, they saw me as smooth and clean.

But the interesting others, the happy hippies, loping along to some party or other—the woman with arms full of books, in denim overalls and sandals; the guy in tight jeans and a leather vest, carrying a load of lumber to his red pickup; the tall gray-haired woman, wearing copper jewelry and a long flowing skirt—those people would pass me by. Some people on the street did stare, of course. If I was up to it, I'd stare back, and they would look away, or, to compound the insult, they would mistake my glower for a plea for help and come to my rescue.

When I was on the street, I rarely stopped moving. I found that if I did stop, to look in a store window, or just rest my arms, someone would come up to me and ask if I needed help. Even if I was going along, pushing my chair, and I would casually look at someone, or smile, they would rarely just nod, or smile back, or say hello, but instead say: "Do you need a hand?" or "Can I help you?" If I paused anywhere near a street corner, a man or a woman might come up behind me, take hold of my chair, and start to push, saying, "Here, I'll help you across the street."

I tried to shift my behavior so people would leave me alone. I'd sit up tall, push my chair with authority, try to look like I was fine, not in need, not in jeopardy, but I was always being read that way. The dilemma was that I did need help with some things, like getting across the street or into a store that had a step outside. In those days it was extremely rare for there to be a curb cut on the street corners. Without them, I would have to stop someone on the street, explain how to tilt my wheelchair back, take it down the curb, and lift it back up on the other side. I found, though, that if I had the chance to pick someone out, rather than go along with the unsolicited offers of help, I could decide when I was ready to go across, and I could pick the person who seemed most likely to do it without fussing over me. Then, as now, many of the people whom I do ask for help are easygoing and take to their task with good humor. I explain what to do, they give it a try, I get to the other side, and we wish each other a good day.

Time passed like this for a couple of years. I was doing well in college, excited about it, and making new friends. I was healthy and strong. Without my back brace I was lighter and less constrained. Francine was there only three afternoons a week, and I had to do a lot more work just to manage the house. I continued to work out in physical therapy and later on my own, and I developed my arm and wrist muscles so I could push my chair up the hill to Broadway, shop for food, bring it home, and cook dinner without help from Rick, Francine, or, most important, my mother. I was getting As in my psychology and art history courses. For one course, I nixed the usual library research paper and went the extra distance to write on a hot new exhibit at the Museum of Modern Art. I liked being there so much, I went back several days in a row and interviewed the guards and incorporated their opinions of the paintings into my paper.

Rick and I took a couple of trips. We visited my cousins in North Carolina, and then went for a week to Virginia. One of the motels we stayed at had a pool right outside our room. We were sitting outside in our shorts eating sandwiches, and Rick spontaneously scooped me up out of my chair and jumped into the pool, convincing both of us that I could float. When he let go of me, I turned over and my new strong arms began to paddle. At first, little puppy strokes, just to keep my head above water, but then I put my head down and my right arm lifted, reached and scooped, pulling back as the left thrust forward. One after the other. My body rose up to the surface, my legs followed, and I was off across the pool.

We took one trip to Boston to attend the wedding of my friends Sam and Jane. They had visited me often in the hospital, had helped me move into my new apartment in New York, and I was so happy they were getting married and that they wanted me to be there with them. I was scared for many reasons to go to the wedding. We managed to lose the invitation with the directions and time on it, and so we arrived late, causing even more attention to be drawn to us. We even missed their march down the aisle, to the Chambers Brothers' song "People Get Ready."

Sam's older brother had been John's best friend since grade school, and I hadn't seen or spoken with him or any of John's circle since the accident. I would be arriving with Rick, everyone would know about Rick's loss and mine, but I didn't know if anyone would know what Rick and I were now, to each other. I had bought a long purple dress for the wedding, that was, I thought, a bold statement of the new me. The me that was living in New York now and more mature than the hippie chick I had left behind in Cambridge. It was a sleeveless dress, with a plunging neckline. It revealed cleavage, and it also exposed the long scar that runs down my right arm, from my shoulder to just above my elbow. I rarely showed that scar in public in those days, and I don't know why I chose to do it there, when so much of me was already on display.

I did want to look sexy, and for them to see Rick as my boyfriend, lest they think I was no longer capable of being someone's girlfriend. Yet once I was there, it seemed rude, a slight to John. I wanted them to see I was OK, lest they feel sad for me. Yet in that setting, it seemed disrespectful. I hadn't anticipated just how many people I knew would be there and how strange it would be for Rick and for me. We were both barraged with people's condolences and their feelings of grief. We were at a wedding, people shouldn't be looking sad, people should be paying attention to Sam and Jane. I was embarrassed.

The next day, before driving back to New York, we went to the cemetery to visit John's grave. It was just over a year since he died. I cried so hard, I could barely see. I was relieved that I cried that much. I knew then that I missed him. That I hurt. I hadn't yet cried just for him; I cried when things piled up, when it was all too much. He deserved this, and I felt closer to him than I had the whole year. A year in which I had to forget a lot of things in order to concentrate on how to make my life over.

Rick walked away and left me there for a little while. I stared at the ground. I remembered that John's mom had said that they buried him in his favorite bell bottoms and flowing white cotton shirt. With my eyes, I traced his body in the dirt. I started with his long, brown, kinky hair, his high cheekbones, his thin, tight body, and sought to remember the shape and feel of his hands.

I had an impulse to wave goodbye to him. To say: "I'm going home now, back to New York."

More and more I seemed to absorb disability. It's not that I was at ease. My mind darted about and I was rarely calm, but disability seemed, even in those first few years, a given in my life. I sometimes felt sad not to walk or run or dance, but I didn't argue with it, or bemoan my fate, or desperately look for cures. My frenzy, it seemed, was about making it on the road I was on. I did fear the collapse of my social world and worried most that I would fail at my plan. I had decided to go back to school and told everyone I was going to be a psychologist. Once said, I had to do it.

There was denial mixed in all this, I can see that now, but there was also acceptance. A recognition that I had been able to incorporate this massive bodily change and emerge a substantial person, not a flaccid or diluted version of me.

So I hurtled through my days, devouring each event, each class, each person I met. I couldn't rest with it, though, and always needed more. I filled in the squares on my monthly calendar, obsessed with making more dates, more notes of people to call and things to do. Stopping scared me, going didn't, or at least not as much. I did worry before each new semester, about how the students would react to me. Each social engagement seemed dangerous. Could I get in the door, go to the bathroom there? How would people view me? Could I pull it off—being a disabled person in a sea of nondisabled people, asking that nothing much be made of the fact, that we could all just get along and have a jolly time?

There were so many times, entering a party, a restaurant, or a grocery store, when people startled at the sight of me. People I'd never met sometimes got so exercised about it all, like I had fresh bleeding wounds all over my body and they must stop them up. If I was upbeat and outgoing, I was sure they saw me as putting on a brave front, as merely compensating for my pain. Someone was bound to come up and utter a long sigh, or tell me I was brave, or start pushing my chair across the room, uninvited. And, of course, it wasn't everybody, usually just a few, and that's what made me keep going out. I met many people who seemed to take me on my terms, who could ask what I had done that day or what my major was or what I thought of a movie or could begin a conversation with something other than "What happened to you?" or "Can I help you?"

I was in my twenties, and eager to meet people. I learned to make judgments about whom to move toward and whom to push aside, quickly developing the sorting skills of a seasoned minority group member. Of the people to avoid, there were the clearly hostile types, those who expressed annoyance at my presence in their otherwise pristine lives. Those who, it would seem, thought that people with impairments were best kept out of sight. The larger portion of the people to avoid could be categorized as the condescending, sympathetic, oversolicitous, intrusive, or anxious types. And though I developed mechanisms over time to deal with them, and some tolerance for their foibles, it cost me a lot to go along with them. I tried to resist, usually by diverting them from their single-minded pursuit. Of course, I wasn't always up to the task, and found myself smiling wanly as they clucked over me.

I encountered obstacles every day and new frustrations, people insisting on telling me what they thought of my sad state or people insisting that I was in a sad state and that I was to be commended for my courage in the face of it. No matter how I was feeling about life in general or my disability in particular, someone in the course of a day or maybe a week was sure to pronounce it a tragedy. God appeared in many people's declarations either as an end point, a parting "God Bless You," or as the premise of their thinking about my fate. Religion did not factor in my thinking about my disability or indeed anything. I was, from an early age, mistrustful of organized religion and its claims to guide people through rough times or be the premiere course of action and thought for people to follow.

While all of my grandparents had been observant Jews, my parents didn't pay much attention to things religious. In fact, the only time I remember hearing my mother talk about God was when she told me that my father had died. I was eight. She said, "God took Daddy away," and went on to give a philosophical reason for it. Even at the time, I remember being stunned to hear her invoke God; it made her news seem even more unreal.

God as intervener hadn't helped me then, and God as idea was not going to make one bit of difference in my life now. I saw the struggle in the details. If I left class and was waiting outside for the taxi service in the cold, God wasn't going to make the taxi come any sooner or redesign all the buses whizzing past me so I could get on them. If it was a sunny day and there was an ice cream truck across the street, but no curb cuts on the corners, and I had to decide whether to ask someone to help me with the curbs, deal with the helper, find someone else once I got my treat to help me back to the other side, calculating whether it would melt during this transaction or should I instead stay on the other side till I finished and risk missing my ride—well, this just didn't seem like God's work. God wasn't going to help me deal with the shame of my weak bladder or the old-lady swollen feet I get on a hot day. And as for comfort for the larger, more existential pain of my crippled state, the loss of John and Carol, and the trauma—I needed something more direct, more tangible.

I found Sarah, my therapist, when I needed her most. I had in these two years put together a life that had activity and direction. People around and places to go. It took all that for me to be able to fall apart.

It happened like this: A friend of mine, a guy named Vic, had been having a rough time. He was very depressed, had been fired from a job he liked and was scared he wouldn't find something else. He was gay, and I think he was both exhilarated and overwhelmed by the club scene in the mid-'70s and all the men coming out so boldly all around him. He came to live in my apartment for a while after Rick went back to college. When Vic left and went to live on his own in a rented room, I became increasingly worried about him. He seemed to have no life in him, he wasn't going out at night, and he made jokes about hemlock. Sure enough, one day I tried to reach him on the phone and the line was busy for a long time. I got the operator to check the line, and she told me the phone was off the hook. I called the police, who bashed in his door, found him on the floor unconscious, and took him to Bellevue. I met them in the emergency room just as Vic was coming to and thanking everyone around for saving his life.

In the course of checking him out of there, into another hospital, and, a few weeks later, out of that one and into a third, I spoke with several psychiatrists. I was startled when I heard a doctor say that Vic was depressed because he was homosexual, and that the way to help him would be to cure him of this affliction, but that it would be a long and difficult process. I remember arguing with one pompous resident, holding my own in the conversation despite his assured manner and fancy jargon: He wasn't to cure Vic of his homosexuality, I told the creep, he was to help him not be depressed anymore. I'd known him when he wasn't depressed, but he'd always been gay.

There was one guy (they were all men) who tried to reason with me, and gave me the benefit of the full extent of his knowledge. He knew I was studying psychology, and I think he believed he was doing me a favor by giving me this extra private lesson. He carefully explained that Vic's homosexuality was a product of Vic's domineering mother and passive father (he had it backwards), that it was evidence that he had not reached full maturity, and that finding love and companionship with a woman would be the answer to all his problems.

I had the sense that the doctor was sizing me up—would I be able to deliver the cure? He didn't seem to think I could do the job, because he looked me up and down and said, "Well, not you, of course," but asked if Vic had ever expressed interest in any of my friends. Afterward, I took Vic to the back of the visitors' room to relay this little talk we had had. We laughed till tears were streaming down our faces, and a nurse came out of her office to shush us. When we calmed down, we went to his room and wrote a dark and dirty little story that we called "The Paraplegic and the Fag." Now that was therapeutic.

Despite the doses of bad medicine he received at these hospitals, Vic started to come back around, and several months later he was back in his own apartment, employed, and in a relationship with a very sweet man.

What a tumultuous time this was for me. I was so glad to help Vic, and also pleased to find that I understood a lot of what was going on. I went with him to speak with doctors and social workers, and took care of things he wasn't able to handle. When I had been the patient I wasn't able to do much of that, nor be as insistent as I was here, and it all gave me confidence in myself. While I had already learned a great deal about the power relations between patients and doctors, this was a vivid new lesson. I saw how these doctors attempted to reach into Vic's sexual life and turn it into a medical condition, complete with diagnostic codes and pathological indicators. I told them they were wrong, and the telling felt good.

Yet as I checked Vic in and out of each hospital, brought him a new toothbrush, spent time there visiting with him, and meeting the other patients, I became increasingly disjointed and morose. I had been hanging on, dealing with all that was happening to me, moving fast, but not really talking to anyone. In the last few months Rick and I had broken up, and I was trying to prove myself as an adult, as a woman, as a student. I saw Vic and all the other sad strangers shuffling around the Day Room in their baggy clothes, and I got scared I would wind up there.

That's when I found Sarah.

I asked friends if they knew a good therapist, and the ones that they suggested all had inaccessible offices. I scheduled a couple of appointments with others I found, but there was no one I wanted to talk with. My biggest fear was that I would start working with a therapist and would find that underneath her professional accepting veneer she would be like the people on the street that I loathed, that she would see me as an unfortunate. An object of pity. She would make me smaller, not bigger.

I don't know what it was that turned me off to the first few, I just ran. Maybe I was afraid of upsetting them, telling them my saga, as I had been afraid of upsetting my mother by talking about my father after he died. When my father died my family went on as if nothing had happened. My mother never talked about it, and I always felt that I shouldn't either, it would make her sad. When my grandfather died a year later we did the same, and so I learned to bury loss inside me.

One therapist I saw was a disabled woman that someone recommended. Before I even met her, I felt protective of her. I was nervous too that all we would talk about was disability. While I worried that the nondisabled therapists would be overwhelmed by my disability, and not be able to see the perspective I put on it, I feared the disabled therapist might be so focused on my disability that she wouldn't see the whole me either. I saw her only once.

By the time I went for my appointment with Sarah, I had done this enough, and I dreaded going through the recitation again, saying all that had happened, and then leaving. I began in rote fashion, giving her the basic outline of the accident, John, Carol, etc. I didn't see the need to go any further back than that. I told her that I'd had a hard time with my mother growing up, and still did and I needed some help with that, but my father, well, he died when I was eight, I don't really remember him, I said, so he wasn't the problem. Except for the stuff with my mother, I had been fine before the accident, I told her, and then my life got derailed, and all these terrible things happened and that's why I'm here. I ran away from home when I was eighteen, dropped out of college, got married, wasn't doing anything with my life, but I had been just fine, fancy-free, unencumbered.

I slowly began talking about my present life, about men and relationships. "Rick and I split up," I told her. "We had too many sad things, too many things to break free of." I did tell her I missed him. "But," I said, "I've got a career now, I don't want to be tied down to anyone or anything," and, as I said it, I doubled over, my head dropping on my lap, my arms hanging down, draped over my legs, and I started to sob. Sarah got up from her chair, put one arm around my shoulders, and patted and soothed, patted and soothed, till I stopped. I remember her saying, "Talk through your tears," a phrase I would hear often.

So I began to talk to Sarah. Two or three times a week. She dug deep, but always shored me up, patted me down before I had to go back out on the street. For years, I would come to her office, slide out of my wheelchair, and lie on my back on her brown leather analyst's couch. She sat behind me taking notes, asking questions now and then. Sometimes she would make suggestions about how to look at something in a different way. Sometimes we argued. Even when we did, I knew she was on my side.

When I found Sarah, I found someone who could bear my weight, and I leaned on her.

3 *Coming Out in the West*

My mother was looming much too large in my life. In her worry that I would get hurt again, she saw danger in everything I wanted to do, from learning to drive a car to going back to college. I overheard her say to a friend, "We have to give Simi the feeling that she is independent."

There seemed to be no part of my life she didn't touch: She knew all my friends' names and phone numbers, my class schedule, where I had been for the weekend. She would sometimes drop packages of food at my house, because, as she would say, "I know you're having company." I was twenty-seven and had reverted to lying and acting out as a means of keeping some distance between us.

I got the idea to leave New York for a while. I told Sarah first. "Berkeley, I'll go to Berkeley," I said, making it up as I lay there on her analyst's couch, gazing up at the pale yellow ceiling. "I'll spend the summer, take courses at the university, try it out. There will still be hippies there, and I will be at home among them, recapturing the '60s."

I don't think I said out loud that I hoped they would recognize me as one of them, not just see some woman in a wheelchair.

Within a week, the trip was scheduled and airline tickets purchased. A few clothes and books were selected. Travel light, I told myself, and let your California self emerge.

I contacted the disabled students' office at the university for help in finding an accessible apartment near the campus. The request seemed natural to the woman I spoke with; she did not startle when I said I was in a wheelchair, and asked me some practical questions, like "How wide is your chair?" which reassured me she knew what I was talking about. She found a place that had no steps going into the building, and doorways that were wide enough for my chair to get through, but warned me that the bathroom and kitchen were very small. I also located a place to lease a car with hand controls for the summer. These arrangements for the apartment and the car were the only concessions I made to my disabled state, and I took pride in how few I had to make.

Each thing I could do without accommodation, I reasoned, indicated how unfettered and normal my life would be.

I began to let people in on my plan. I practiced a nonchalant recitation of the facts. It was no big deal, I would project, for me to get on a plane, move to a strange city, and make it on my own. I can go anywhere, you see, I can do everything.

A friend in New York who used to live in Berkeley said to me: "It's different out there. There are a lot more handicapped people, it's like a center—you'll really like it." I brushed that comment off, it was not what I was looking for, and when I told friends about the trip I didn't tally that in my list of reasons to go there. People might think I did everything because of disability, that it ruled my life.

I saved the hardest recitation for last. No need to tell the family until everything was in place for the trip. Resist all offers of advice or visits "to help you settle in." Turn down a ride to the airport. "All planned," I said. I wound up accepting the money that was offered, since I still hadn't figured out how to earn my own.

I craned my neck to look out the window as my plane was landing in San Francisco. I had been in my seat for almost six hours. My chair was down in the luggage hold in the belly of the plane, and I was beached here, my legs unable to lift me up and carry me away. A simple act, standing, walking two or three rows down to the bathroom, going in, turning around in that tight space, and closing the door. An impossible act. I could no more walk than I could fly. At times like that, I long for my chair. I've never fully understood why I don't pine for my legs instead. I can't explain why, even so early in the game, I let go of my walking self. I never chased after cures, it was so clear these legs would not hold me up.

Even my dreams, at least the ones I can recall, don't reveal to me an underlying longing for my lost walking self. There were recurring dreams in those first few years where my body would suddenly rise up and take off, but it was always in an implausible act, like floating above ground or ice-skating down Broadway. And while those moves may be mere substitutions for the act of walking, those dreams were optimistic; I'd wake up feeling hopeful, not jarred by the reality of the morning's paralysis. I felt that in this body I could accomplish what needed to be done; I needn't wait for a walking body.

The dreams that debilitate me are the ones where I am frightened and in danger, and when I open my mouth to scream, no sound comes out. I am helpless to save myself at night, and the fear lingers into the day. In my dreams, it is the inability to shout out, not the inability to walk, that defeats me.

There, in the airplane, I couldn't shout out. What would I say? That they should have a little chair on board, so I could get in it and go to the bathroom? I didn't even imagine that. The airline wouldn't go to all that trouble for me and the few like me who need it. It would take years for that to happen, and a federal law to mandate it. In those days, you just had to tough it out. I hadn't had anything to drink for many hours and had taken a pill that I use to keep my bladder in check. Fortunately, it had worked. I distracted myself by watching the skyline come and go as the plane banked. The dark green trees and the brown hills that surround the city had an exotic look. A slice of the gray ocean appeared, disappeared. A rocky cliff. The flat bay. Parallel rows of houses rode the crest of a hill, streaming down one side and disappearing into the valley.

I had only been to California once before, when I was nine, a trip to visit family in L.A. with a promised excursion to Disneyland, all given as salve for a sad little girl whose father had died a few months before.

So this view was all new, and I was excited about it, but I couldn't afford to get excited just then. My bladder couldn't be jostled, not one little bit.

I watched all the passengers get off the plane, silently urging each to move faster. Finally, an agent brought to my seat the small metal chair used on board to get me down the narrow aisle of the plane. I then transferred to my wheelchair, and he escorted me to the far end of the terminal where he assured me there was an accessible bathroom. Relieved, I was then able to focus on getting my three months' worth of luggage and me into a taxi.

I got to Berkeley by late afternoon and found my apartment building on Haste Street, only about eight blocks from the campus. It was a little box of a place, with moldy beige carpet, and well-worn furniture, but I claimed it happily. The bathroom had just enough space for me to get inside, but I couldn't turn my chair around, nor could I close the door. With considerable effort I could get onto the toilet from that angle, and I would learn to brush my teeth riding sidesaddle. The kitchen was no better, and I had to parallel park at the stove and reach my arm across to boil and fry, stir and flip.

This was an apartment designed for walking people, and in the course of that summer I would grow increasingly impatient with the effort it took to squeeze myself into their world. I found in Berkeley spaces designed to accommodate me, where I could fit comfortably and thus breathe more easily. Places where the provision of ramps, wide doors, grab rails in the bathroom stalls, and the like meant I could do things in the same place and in synch with others. These weren't "special" places, set-apart places, but open, public sites. As time went on, I wondered, might I play a part in reconfiguring the world to let me in?

After sniffing out all the corners of my new space and unpacking a few things, I went out to find a grocery store. When I reached the corner, I saw to my astonishment that there was a curb cut. All four corners had them. I whisked down one, crossed the street, and slipped up the other side. At the next corner, more curb cuts. Whoosh. Turn right, go a block. Whoosh. Another. Another. I was wandering. I never wandered in New York, where I calculated each move.

My new neighborhood was much lower to the ground than my block in Manhattan. There were mostly three- and four-story houses, and they exposed the more intimate details of life. I could see into living rooms and kitchens. People came and went, in and out of their houses. They sat on front porches and ate in their yards. The few low-rise apartment buildings teemed with students, and they moved about in groups of two, three, six. The young predominated in Berkeley, and I was ready to ride with them and catch up on my lost youth.

Each street offered something to look at: amusing lawn ornaments on patches of brown grass, ramshackle old houses with Victorian bric-a-brac, signs in windows declaring allegiance to the Green Party, or the Hemp Party, or the house party. Most of the houses had two or three steps to the front porch, off-limits for me, but on that first outing to the grocery store, I saw two that had wooden ramps going up the side. One of my kind must live there, I thought.

I had gone about ten blocks, zigging and zagging, when I found a store. It occupied the ground floor of a small apartment building. The front windows were filled with displays of paper towels and pyramids of canned fruit, a round tin Coca-Cola sign hung over the entrance, and little bells jingled against the glass when I opened the front door. As I pushed my cart down the aisle in front of me, picking out the ingredients for this new life, I realized that no one stared at me. Even the grocer ignored me. As the people had on the street. Might I be inconspicuous here? Could I escape people fussing and fretting over me?

The grocer packed my bag, and, when I asked, reached over the counter and placed it on the back of my chair. I put my sunglasses on, and donned the leather gloves I'd need for the push back home with the groceries adding extra weight to my chair. I swung the door open and went outside. But I stopped short. There on the corner, facing me, was a man sitting tall in a sporty black wheelchair. Wavy blond hair fell down his bare back. He wore only tattered jeans and leather sandals. He was not alone. Three women swirled around him, dancing and skipping. Each woman held a container of yogurt, and each, with gusto, was throwing handfuls of the stuff at him. He answered them. He scooped up the cream from his naked chest and off his sun-burnished shoulders, and lobbed it back. There was yogurt in their hair, running down each and every chest, dribbling down one woman's thigh, another's forearm. It lingered in bellybuttons, between toes, and in the spokes of his wheels. White, wet yogurt pooled on his lap.

The women frolicked and romped on their long, nude legs. They leapt about on their bare feet. He swivelled his chair back and forth, doing a kind of wheelchair twist. He snaked in and around them, and they jumped to get out of his way. The California sun was streaming down on them and they were laughing to beat the band.

Maybe this was routine California street-corner fare. I seemed to be the only one to take notice. The grocer had stayed inside, and whoever else was out and about just walked by, as though nothing marvelous was happening. I stayed till the last minute, drinking it all in, and watched the merry band go off down the street, turn, and proceed up a rickety ramp onto the front porch of a brown house with missing shutters and twirling lawn ornaments.

Yes, I thought, if that's disability, I can do that. He made it look fun and sexy. Not woeful and sick-like.

I wended my way back home through the Berkeley streets. My apartment was still and quiet. I put away my groceries, save for a bag of Oreos. I wheeled my chair up next to the sofa, put on the brakes, and slid over onto the ratty tweed cushions. I stayed there a long time, eating cookies and watching the sun go down. I had no one out there, no one at all. I hadn't really talked to anyone all day, not even the yogurt people. I watched them from the sidelines, an interested observer, but they hadn't even looked my way.

This seemed like the first time I'd ever really been alone. When I was growing up, I had family, then, for those brief few months, I had college roommates, and then I had John. In this new life-after, I had kept myself surrounded by people. I was always making plans, having people over, going out. Except for the hours with Sarah in her office, I mostly kept moving or working. In her office I could cry, I could be afraid, but she was there and she would somehow pull me along. Maybe this was why I had come out here, to face myself in a small dark room. With nothing to do, and no one to distract me, I could find out if I really was OK, as I'd been telling myself and everyone around me I was.

It was dark outside now. The sounds of rock music and cars going by on the street below began to break into my thoughts. Here I lived on the third floor, in New York on the seventeenth. I could hear people talking on the street. In New York I only heard the heftier sounds, like trucks and buses revving up as the light changed, or jackhammers breaking up the street on an endless construction project.

I thought of the blond man in the center of a circle of frolicking nymphs. How did he get there? Where was he now? Was he OK? Not just today, afloat with the pleasure of the yogurt affair, but day to day, week to week, year after year. Could people like us survive? I had witnessed him laughing and carrying on. I had witnessed myself, over these last four years, going to college, making parties, making love, flirting, taking care of myself, and also, those other times, withdrawn and scared, when I had to struggle to rouse myself and move on. I had no guideposts for this life, no one who had done it before. He became my first mascot.

I yawned and stretched out on the couch. My plane had left New York early that morning, and I had dragged suitcases across my New York apartment and then this one, had gotten myself in and out of airline seats and taxi cabs, and then once I arrived on the Berkeley streets had pushed my chair further than I ever had before. I closed my eyes and lay there for a while, but I couldn't sleep.

I demanded of myself that I get up and pull my denim jacket out of my suitcase. I prodded myself to find my keys and go out the door. I exhorted myself to keep moving. If I didn't, I might not succeed at this California mission and be forced to go home, weakened by my failure.

This time when I left my building, I turned to the left instead of the right, heading down to the main drag, Shattuck Avenue, which I'd seen from the taxi when I first arrived. It was a long hill down, and I worried as I went how I might get back up, but I did not turn back and take an easier course. It was as if someone was always watching me, judging my capacity.

Once I got to Shattuck, it was flat and easy going, and it, too, had curb cuts on every corner. I passed some crowded bars and restaurants with clusters of people talking at tables, no one sitting alone. I would be conspicuous there. People would look at me and feel sorry for me. I chose instead an empty Chinese food takeout place that had a couple of Formica tables up front. My seat by the window showed me a good piece of the late-night Berkeley street life, and I could watch it, even if I couldn't yet have some of it. My food arrived. The man behind the counter nodded appreciatively as I picked up my chopsticks with one hand, with the other brought the bowl up to my chin, and shoveled thick slippery noodles into my mouth. He seemed glad to be feeding me. His little daughter peeked out from behind a curtain and watched me too. Then the cat. I waved at them, and she smiled up at me.

I got lost in thought for a while, and when I looked up again, the girl had disappeared, and the chef was busy in the kitchen washing the metal cauldrons and big woks of his trade. I balanced my bowl in my hand and picked off each vegetable, and slurped down all of the hot broth. What mattered most to me at that moment was that I hadn't curled up in a ball on the couch in my new apartment, hiding out till daylight made it easier to get lost in the crowd.

As I paid my bill, and prepared to leave, the chef called to the girl, and she came out from the back to present me with a drawing she had made on a white paper placemat. Swirls of shiny Crayola colors tripped across the white bumpy paper. I leaned down so that we were eye to eye, and I thanked her. In a whisper meant only for me, she explained that it was a picture of the cat sitting on his blanket.

The next day I went up to campus. It was hard pushing up the hill to Telegraph Avenue, but then it was pretty flat, and I wove in and out of the crowds, and the vendors selling tie-dye and hippie beads. On through the main gates I had seen in a picture of Mario Savio leading a Free Speech Movement rally in front of Sproul Hall. An old boyfriend of mine was in that picture, up in front with Mario, and I had it pinned to the wall over my desk for years. The campus spread out before me, bigger than I had imagined, with imposing buildings and towering trees. After my years at the New School, housed in two buildings in the middle of a city block, this seemed like a real college, a permanent place of great authority.

I registered for a film survey course and a literature course. The next day I went to my first class, but fell asleep halfway through. I stayed awake in the other class, but stared out the window. I never bought the books or did any of the assignments, and withdrew after the first week. I wanted to be outdoors, on the streets, not indoors watching people, listening. It would be harder for me without these activities, without the regulated contact with people, but it made me feel like the trip was an adventure, not something safe and managed.

I went up to the campus almost every day anyway. I hadn't returned my student card, so I could use the library or go to the student union and hang out, playing the role. Maybe I had come to Berkeley to get away from the constraints of my family, and to prove something, but I discovered a wonderful place, and I took pleasure in the parade of students and Berkeley characters who strolled around campus. There were even days, or parts of days, when watching satisfied me. Other times, when the delight of that slipped away, and it felt like depression would descend and lock me in the house, I wound myself up into a frenzy of activity, sailing about, losing keys, toppling over vases of flowers, calling people I barely knew, like the guy I sublet the apartment from, and asking him to dinner. He declined.

One day I was sitting out on the plaza, just inside the gates. A woman who had been in my lit class saw me and came over to ask what had happened to me, why I had disappeared after the first week. She sat down on the steps next to me, and we stayed there a long while, watching the musicians and jugglers and such who played for spare change. She went to get us some coffee, and when she came back she found me talking with a group of guys from Oregon, waiting their turn to perform on the plaza. By the time they went on we were all fast friends, and my new chum, Barbara, and I cheered for them, calling to passersby to come and take a look.

That's how I got to spend a couple of raucous weeks with a band of traveling street actors. They incorporated me into their pantomime of the imperiled Pauline tied to the railroad tracks by the wicked villain, and then saved by her brave suitor in the nick of time. Though I was the only woman in the troupe, I never got to play Pauline, she was played by one of the men in a frowsy blond wig. I was instead the train coming down the tracks at full throttle, my wheelchair outfitted with a bell and a cut-out cardboard panel painted steam-engine gray. I wrestled with this casting decision, fearing I was no longer damsel material. Ultimately, I triumphed, even though I was never Pauline. In enacting the train I got to show off, and to create a spectacle using my chair. All my efforts to that point had been to minimize the chair and the impairment that occasioned it, but those July afternoons on campus and in Golden Gate Park the crowd watched me come chugging out, ringing my bell and calling considerable attention to myself and my wheels. The audience could make of us what they would. And later, when it was my turn to pass the hat after the performance, if that ol' chair caused them to cough up more change to fund the troupe's dinner and evening revelries, so be it.

I spent nights with the young actor playing Pauline. I liked him more in his day job, helpless on the railroad tracks, but I wanted "bad" in my life as much as anything. It was part of what Sarah called my "counterphobic behavior." Like driving way above the speed limit, picking up hitchhikers, and inviting rogue actors back to my house. I never did get hurt, but I posed a danger to myself and probably others as I gave myself almost daily tests of my invincibility.

Not listed on my California itinerary for that summer of '75 was the lure of other disabled people. As my friend Susan had told me, Berkeley was indeed a hotbed of disability activism, and it was, as I had predicted, a hotbed of hippies. I was so wedded to a particular image of hippies, and to a particular, yet very different, image of disabled people, that it had never occurred to me that they might share the same bed. Hippies were those with lithe bodies and keen eyesight; disabled people were crouched and bent, and too beleaguered for pot-smoking and free love.

The abstract category "disabled," or in those days more likely "handicapped," that I had grown up with carried over even when I got tagged to be on the team. Except for my Uncle Sonny, who had lost a leg in an automobile accident, I hadn't known any disabled people up close. And anyway, he was just my uncle, he didn't count. I thought them to be flat, reluctant people, not the sort to stir up the pot, to be juicy and interesting. I urgently hoped that I was all those things, and standing apart from the group, I reasoned, was my only way to prove it. I was determined to stay myself, this disability thing wouldn't bleed me dry, I would remain the daring, crazy person I wanted the world to know. I would dress like I always had, only more so. I would go to California, live on my own, and get the lead actor in the troupe.

Berkeley may not have had significantly more disabled people than other places, but it seemed to. Maybe it was because I was out on the streets more than I was in New York. Disability appeared ordinary in Berkeley; it even seemed to have some cachet, some exoticism.

I saw people acting out the daily routines of life—going to the supermarket, school, or their jobs—using wheelchairs or crutches, carrying white canes, using sign language and all of the other indicators of membership. There was my neighbor, the large-breasted blond woman in the peasant blouse and dangly earrings, with the guide dog, and no dark glasses hiding her pale blue, blind eyes. At the health food store I'd often see a burly guy with a red bandanna tied around his neck. He was a friend of the owner, and hung out there a lot, sitting on a high stool by the counter. One of his legs, the shorter one, rested on the top rung; the other, straightened out, touched the floor and kept him balanced. He always greeted me with a big smile, like we'd known each other a long time. Then there was a very small, pert woman, always impeccably groomed, who used a motorized scooter to get around the campus. We never talked, she always seemed in a hurry. I also frequently saw a man, part of the vagabond crew that occupied the corner outside Cody's Books on Telegraph Avenue. A scrawny guy with a lot to say, he held forth on the sidewalk, waving his thin metal crutches around for emphasis as he spoke.

These people were part of the Berkeley tableau. There was one, though, who stood out from the crowd. Seated, like me, in a chair with wheels. I met him on campus when we were both pushing up the ramp that leads to the cafeteria. We nodded at each other, an acknowledgment of our common bond. The ramp was wide enough for us to go up side by side, look at each other, and say hello. As we hit the top, I reached for the door with one hand, held the rim of my wheel with the other, pulled back on both, and opened the door. He nodded again and smiled as he went by me.

On line for sandwiches, we invited each other to share a table for lunch. I had a good time. He teased me about my New York ways, but his generous smile told me he liked me just the same. Our talk rambled. Movies, the courses I had dropped, his work—he constructed wooden models for an architectural firm. I told him that seeing all these disabled people in Berkeley was startling, that it was very different from New York. It was the first time I'd said that out loud. We talked some about disability, not our bodily states, but the way people stare at you, the inaccessibility of most of the campus, that sort of thing. He told me about the evolving disability rights movement, something I'd never heard of and, at first, didn't quite understand.

Philip, his name was, and he had a wry take on the peculiarity of our lives. He described dealings with nondisabled people that were so similar to my own experiences, I thought we must be running into the same people.

I thought about him for days after our lunch. Meeting a disabled man head-on, and being attracted to him, confused me. I had grown up thinking that disabled people are the unfortunates of the world. While I refused to believe that I was an "unfortunate," and I did everything I could to keep people from seeing me that way, I hadn't fully let go of the idea that others were suffering, and that their lives had fixed boundaries and held few pleasures. Yet Philip couldn't be one of them, he was too much like me, and so I had to exempt him too. But then, what about my neighbor, the blind woman with the cleavage, and the smiley guy in the health food store, the gorgeous blond yogurt tosser, and my friends from the roof at rehab? Maybe I was like them, and they were like me, but we were not like we were supposed to be.

Unsure of where I was heading with Philip, I drew in closer for a better look, stopping by the coffeehouse he'd told me about that was right next to his office. But then, when I did see him again, I balked. I had a vision of both of our wheelchairs, side by side at the movies, across from each other at the kitchen table, parked at night on either side of a king-size bed. I feared that "we" would double the jeopardy, and I would lose my footing in the nondisabled world. Even out here in California, with no one around I knew, little risk that anything would be permanent, I got scared to even make a date. Told him I was going to Oregon for a while. I say now with much shame and with regret, that I ran from him much like some men have probably run from me. Worried I'd be a burden, worried that it would be strange to have sex with me, worried about crossing over into the land of the other. Anticipating everything before knowing a thing.

Throughout that summer, I moved tentatively toward various disability encampments. I remember the first time I visited the disabled students office at the university. It was off-campus in one of the low-slung cement buildings that line the side streets off Telegraph Avenue. Down a driveway and around back was a long, steep ramp that I could barely get to the top of on my own steam. When I came in the door a vague collection of lean young men were sitting around a table, not doing much of anything. They were dressed in the lighter shades of denim, accented by black and brown leather belts and vests. Most of them were quads (quadriplegics), who had, even back then, souped-up motorized wheelchairs. These guys might eventually be cast as extras in an Oliver Stone film, but on that day they were unoccupied. No one seemed to register that I'd come in the door, and only a couple of guys nodded to me when I gave a big chirpy hello to the assembled group.

One guy, sitting in a well-worn wheelchair with bumper stickers protesting this and that across the back, did turn toward me and say "Hey" and ask where I was from.

Mistaking the question for a real social overture, I responded eagerly. "New York," I said.

The group around the table did stir, turned to look at each other, and one of the roughriders said with a sneer, "Oh great, another crip from New York."

Was he allowed to say that? Crip? You talkin' to me?

I hadn't realized I was a trend and Berkeley a mecca.

Any worthwhile retort would come to me too late to use it, so I left them to find someone who worked there. I had come to find out if they could give me some help putting a piece of plywood in the back of the car I had rented to go up to Oregon and visit the acting troupe. The plywood rests on the floor, and makes it easier to pull my chair into the car. An assistant in the back room directed me to the Center for Independent Living, or CIL as it is called, further down on Telegraph. They would be able to do that.

CIL isn't a place, it is a universe. Entering the door that summer day in 1975, I discovered a disability underground. Everybody I saw on my first look around the office had a significant impairment: people who were answering phones, typing, conferring around a long table strewn with papers, getting their wheelchairs repaired, repairing wheelchairs. I couldn't tell what everybody was actually doing, but whatever it was it created bustle and noise. I wandered through the office, peeking into cubicles, trying out the bathroom. This wasn't like the rehab center. That had a clear line of demarcation—the disabled people were the patients, pretty much everybody on the staff was nondisabled. There, if I left the patient floor, I found that the bathrooms were not wheelchair accessible—there was no expectation that disabled people would be using bathrooms on the floors with laboratories and offices, nor in the library in the medical school where I used to go to do my French homework.

I struck up a conversation with a woman in one of the cubicles who was eating a sandwich at her desk. Her crutches were propped up against the wall, and she wore metal leg braces with leather straps. "What is this place, what goes on here?" I asked. She took me around, told me about her work. As part of a team of peer counselors, she worked with disabled people in the community who were trying to live independently. CIL offered assistance in finding accessible housing, hiring personal attendants, securing employment, getting into college, and battling to get Supplemental Security Income, Social Security Disability Insurance, and health care.

She instructed me: "These are the needs that people have who want to move beyond the narrow lives most disabled people have had. For every one of the people who are working, going to school, living in the community, there are hundreds more living in institutions, or trapped in their families' homes, unable to live lives of their own making."

I left the next day for Oregon in my rental car. The board I needed was on the floor in the back, my chair sitting on it. As I drove up the coast on Highway 1, I weighed my freedoms and my pleasures against those who couldn't be where I was at that moment. I was living on my own, going to college, traveling, due in large part to the ability of my family to support me until I could support myself. Yet I also knew that in any town I drove through, if I were to try to find a motel room, or stay longer and look for a job and a place to live, I could face roadblocks. If I stayed, my new community might welcome me in their midst, but then might not want me as a teacher for their children, or a wife for one of their sons. They might not be willing to expend town resources for a lift on the bus, a ramp into the polling place, and curb cuts on the street corners.

What if I could slip by those obstacles? People with my brand of disability often encounter fewer social obstacles than others do, and we get folded into mixed company. Indeed, the town might find it wonderful to have a "handicapped" teacher, and the citizens might all pull together and build a ramp into the elementary school and a special back entrance into City Hall, invite me to their church suppers, and tell me they would wait for me out front to carry me up the steps. But what if they didn't, or what if my disability were a little different; what if my speech were affected, or I drooled a bit, or I used a motorized chair that they couldn't carry up the steps, or I refused to be carried up the steps into an inaccessible church? What if the local college had few accessible buildings and provided no accommodations to me? What if a landlord refused to rent me an apartment, and no one in town would help me expose him and force his hand? These are the thin threads on which my privilege rests.

I am like the well-heeled, elegantly dressed black man who tries to hail a cab in New York City on a winter's night. I can encounter good neighbors, as he can encounter a taxi driver who will pick him up right away and take him where he wants to go. But we may both find that our privilege doesn't help us, and we are shunned, discounted, and left to fend for ourselves.

The trip up north had some good times. Though the guys in the troupe, back in their hometown, seemed pretty dull and my rogue actor didn't even seem dangerous, just selfish, I got to see the giant redwoods and Mount Hood in Oregon. The rest of it was hard for me. I had to stop at many motels until I found one with an accessible room, and I couldn't find bathrooms I could use along the route. I would have to park off the side of the road and use a bedpan in my car when I got desperate. Truck drivers would stare in my windows and see me in there. I hated it. There weren't curb cuts in most of the towns I went to, and I had to always stop people to ask for help. It weakened me, and I was glad to get back to Berkeley.

When I got back, I attended an organizing meeting the woman I met at CIL had told me about. I traveled to a residential neighborhood about a mile from campus to a stucco house with a tangle of vines growing up the side and onto the roof. A long, low wooden ramp took me easily to the side door and into the communal kitchen of a group of hard-core disability rights activists.

People were busy stapling pamphlets, stuffing envelopes, talking about demonstrations, getting arrested, and mundane matters like kids and grocery shopping. Kids? The woman at the table with the slow, elongated speech indicating cerebral palsy, with arms and elbows pointing in various directions, using the back side of her hand to slowly press closed the envelopes she was sealing, this was the woman with a daughter entering kindergarten in the fall. She continued with her task as she talked. Finishing one envelope, she used her elbow to slide another across the table and position it with the flap open and ready. She then picked up a sponge by reaching down, sandwiching the sponge between the backs of both hands, her palms turned outward, fingers pointed down, and stroked the sponge across the gummy part. After flipping the top of the envelope down with an elbow, she dragged her hand along the V-shaped flap, sealing it shut. I imagined she would diaper a baby, zip up her daughter's jacket, or put away a roomful of toys as slowly and as patiently as she was managing this clerical job. Someone at the table told a joke and she erupted in laughter, her laughs coming out in short bursts, like little sneezes. She was the one, a few minutes later, who noticed me, asked my name, and introduced me to the group around the table. I hoped I hadn't been staring.

When an announcement was made that the meeting would begin, people started to file into the living room. The movement from kitchen to living room took about ten minutes. The blind people's guide dogs got up, shook, and assumed a forward position. People sitting on kitchen chairs grabbed crutches they had stored underneath the table, and slowly rose up from their seats, thrusting one hip out first, straightening a leg, locking a leg brace into position, then the other leg, the other brace, steadying themselves on the kitchen counter for support as they positioned their crutches. And, bringing up the rear, people with wheelchairs slowly pivoted around in the tight spaces to head out the door.

I watched this complicated dance, all accomplished with little verbal exchange. People left each other alone to do what needed to be done to get where they were going. No one rushed in to take care. People did help each other out, holding a crutch or picking up a dropped envelope from the floor, yet it was all so casual. Here, people could take their time—without someone standing over them saying "Take your time," as if time was the standee's to dole out.

I asked a woman along the way: "Where is the ladies' room?" Her disdainful look told me I'd made a mistake. "We don't have a *ladies'* room," she chided me, "but the bathroom is over there, behind the kitchen." I'd been put in my ideological place. I would need to be more careful.

I settled toward the back at the meeting, feeling somewhat guarded, still unsure of what this all had to do with me. They spoke of disability rights, and disability pride, power, activism. They said *crip* and *cripple* casually, and with fondness for the person described.

I had been so tentative about my disability, and had, up to now, only ascribed a very personal meaning to it—this is what happened to me, this is the effect on me—that their forthright ownership of disability and their drive to take action based on the collective experience set my mind racing. There was a fervor in that room, and I felt illegitimate somehow because I didn't share it.

I was inclined to believe what they said. My experience over the last few months had proved to me that disability meant something different here than it did in New York. Although I had initially idealized California, thinking it perfect, I had found over the course of the summer that the curb cuts were only in particular areas, that accessible bathrooms were not as plentiful as I thought at first, and that there was no accessible public transportation. Discrimination in education and employment was rampant, and there was no legal redress in most settings. And I learned that night, and would come to learn more precisely in the coming years, that each of the changes that had been made had taken enormous effort, and involved struggle and demonstrations and time in jail. I was struck by how I had been going along, accepting as my lot that I would not be able to easily find a usable motel room, get to all my classes at college, vote with my neighbors, take a bus to work, or any of the other activities that the people in this room were saying were attainable goals.

The problem, as I came to understand it, was not that I couldn't walk; it was that the society was configured for those who do walk, see, hear, etc. It would take me a while longer to learn how entrenched the patterns of discrimination are, and how solid and purposeful the disability community was.

That summer I began to recognize the whole me when I looked in the mirror. I was able to see my seated self and the chair I sat in as a unit. I didn't divvy us up, screening out the chair as I had previously done, with the hope that onlookers would do the same.

The summer was winding down. New York was more and more in my thoughts, and I called a few friends to tell them to look out for me, I was heading home. I had been accepted at Columbia University for the fall, and would start classes soon after I got back and finish up my last two years of undergraduate work there.

On a beautiful August day in my last week, I went to a Joan Baez concert at the open-air Greek Theater in the Berkeley hills above the campus. I went by myself and sat in the "Wheelchair Section." I had never before sat side by side in public with the so-called Handicapped. In the previous few years my triumph had been in transferring my body into a regular theater seat, my wheelchair whisked off to a rear closet, made invisible.

But here I was, hangin' with a bunch of other crips. I had by then adopted the word, though not the full swagger that goes with its use. We were all wearing our flimsiest summer clothes, letting our scars and our skinny legs out to air. Joan sang to us about organizing and activism, about love and longing. Her voice so clear and strong, her resolve so absolute, that equivocation was banished, nothing but full commitment to social justice and to lustiness was acceptable.

The stone amphitheater surrounded by swaying eucalyptus trees enveloped us and held us tight, Joan laughing down there on the big stage about all us crazy hippies. What would she do with us? She feigned shock as she pointed out a gangly, long-legged blond woman in the front row who had taken her halter top off and was waving her breasts and her arms in the air. "Well, good lord, she's nearly nekkid," said Joan, and picked up her acoustic guitar and sang:

> The night they drove old Dixie down, and all the bells were ring-
> ing,
> The night they drove old Dixie down, and all the people were sin-
> gin'.
> With Joan's prompting, we all sang: *Na, Na, Na, Na, Na, Na,*
> *Na, Na, Na, Na, Na, Na, Na, Na.*

4 *A Special Education*

Columbia University doesn't have the great sweep of the Berkeley campus, but it commands respect. The turn-of-the-century buildings that have earned landmark status mingle with the newer buildings. The additions sit down low with the others, and carry the same dustiness, so they don't seem at odds with their more venerable neighbors.

The wheelchair rider enters the campus through the main gates on Broadway and 116th Street, leaving the traffic and much of the bustle behind. College Walk begins there and extends to Amsterdam Avenue, a long city block away. The rider moves across the hexagonal paving stones, skirting past the stones that have heaved up from the swells of many winters. She pushes with a slight force on the rims of her tires as the walkway rises a bit in its procession toward the middle of campus. It levels off soon, though, and she sails along, proud to be going to college in such a serious place.

Stretching out to her right, to the south, is the lower campus, sitting a few steps below College Walk. A wide expanse of lawn is interrupted by pathways that lead to Butler Library, the bookstore, dorms, and some classrooms. To her left, a grand staircase about a half a block wide, and many, many steps high, rises up to Low Library, the administrative building, and behind that is the rest of the upper campus and the buildings that house the disciplines. Philosophy, psychology, music have their buildings, as does chemistry. There are the Schools of Engineering, Business, and Architecture, each with its own home up there.

But Low is the central architectural and symbolic fixture of Columbia. It is a big birthday cake of a building, topped by a round dome, and it is visible from most everywhere. The steps up to Low and the

56

terraces that punctuate its climb are the social center of the campus. On any reasonably nice day, people eat, study, sprawl, and kiss on the various tiers. The stairs are the main artery between College Walk and the upper campus, and people flow up and down the steps in between the eaters and the kissers.

My earlier body had been trained to walk such steps and my eyes to appreciate their grandeur. I grew up thinking, although I'm sure I never said it out loud, that steps are either a pragmatic solution, a means to connect spaces of different heights, or they are an aesthetic element, added onto a design because it makes the building more beautiful. But now, with their function lost to me, their beauty began to fade, and I saw something I hadn't noted before—attitude. Steps, and particularly these steps at Columbia, seemed arrogant. The big building sitting up on top said, "The worthy can climb up to me, I will not kneel down and open my doors to those below me."

The steps at Columbia didn't broadcast that message to me all the time. On a beautiful spring day, when people were strewn across the many levels, when I used the steps in some of the ways others did—to meet people at the base or head of the stairs, or to stop there to eat a sandwich—I read them differently. People sitting in bright clothes, with their backs to the high building, took some of the weight away, and on those days the steps seemed to join us all together.

I could see it both ways. Sometimes it seemed that the steps separated the upper and lower levels, moving up in precise increments that marked the distance between those below and the august building that crowned the top. Other times I could see that the steps connected the two domains, and unified them. The steps then seemed to invite the uses they were put to. I recognized that I read the steps as imperious because of their rejection of me. The design of steps forbids the wheelchair user, and the designer of these steps, deliberately or unwittingly, provided for us only a solitary and difficult route to get where those steps took all the others.

To get to the upper level, I would need to proceed to the end of College Walk, past the stairs, into a small, side door of Kent Hall. I went through the usually crowded bursar's office, saying multiple "excuse me's," down a corridor to a small, creaky elevator that went to the upper level, and then down a long hall to the back door of the building and down a narrow ramp. From there, I could get to some of the upper-level buildings. But after five o'clock and on weekends, when these special side and rear doors were locked, I had to go to a parking garage on the north end of campus, several blocks away, and down a steep hill from College Walk. It was dark in the garage, and at night there was usually no one around as I wove my way through the empty cars to a back elevator.

Some of the upper-level buildings didn't have ramps, and the alternative I discovered was through the chemistry building, where there was one elevator that took me to the subbasement. That led to a tunnel that wound under the buildings and could take me to classrooms and advisors and administrative offices. I hardly ever saw anyone else in the dimly lit, dank tunnel. It was my own special route, and I got locked in down there on several occasions and had to scream and bang on the gate to get someone's attention. It always took a while for someone to find me, and then I would have to wait there behind the gate till they found the security guard with the key to release me. I hated those times, and the fear that I would be locked in haunted me every time I used the tunnel.

Up above ground, my classes went well. I enjoyed most of my courses, and I was getting good grades. There was an old-fashioned air to the professors, even the younger ones, that spoke of something not stale but solid. They had faith in the benefits of a good liberal arts education, and they expected students to want the same and work hard to get it. There was an earnestness about Columbia, a sense that education was functioning here as the great leveler and the democratizing agent that it was supposed to be. While you would hear a reminder now and again that you were being given the privilege of learning at one of the world's great institutions, no one talked much about how that privilege was conferred on such a select group. It was assumed to be an earned reward, open to anyone with the ability to do the work. There was something so basic and wholesome about everyone there, students, faculty, and staff, seen in the clothes they wore, in the musty offices and bare classrooms, that I often lost sight of the elitism of the institution. The state was paying my tuition, under the provisions of the Department of Vocational Rehabilitation, and so I was spared the burden of the high cost of this special education.

The elegant architecture and the expanse of lawn in the middle of

New York City were relics of the gentlemen's college Columbia had been. Now the school was there for all, and the faded paint, dirty windows, leaking sinks, and elevators that regularly broke down seemed to herald that mission. It was the broken-elevator part of the philosophy that did me in. Getting from one part of the psychology building where the elevator was often out of order, to the other wing with the usually working elevator involved two steps. They were high steps, they were marble, and they were slippery. To get to class I would have to round up two lifters and instruct them in the technique—tilt my chair all the way back, I would tell them, with one person in front, one in back, and take the chair down, or up, one step at a time. People were usually polite, even when they were in a hurry, no one ever dropped me, even those that faltered and lost their footing on the marble floor, and I got where I was going, more or less intact.

It was never easy. I was haunted by bad dreams about the tunnel, I felt embarrassed and conspicuous when I had to interrupt people on their way to class to get them to help me, I put on a cheery smile as the two-step lifters pulled me up the marble steps, pretending I wasn't afraid they would drop me on my fragile spine. I would find myself sometimes in the middle of class rehearsing how I was going to get out of there if I had to get to the bathroom or if class went on a little long and the tunnel was locked.

I began to complain. First in a casual way to one of my advisors, then to the Dean of Students. I often thought of Philip and the people I'd met in Berkeley. What would they do?

The dean asked me to join a committee looking into what he called "these matters," and I went faithfully to their meetings. Everyone was very nice, and expressed concern for my well-being, but nothing much was done. There had been a few "handicapped" students at Columbia before me, I was told, and the people on the committee were quite sincere in their belief that we should have an easier and safer time of it, but the next step of getting the administration's commitment to make those changes never happened while I was there. Although I didn't realize it at the time, the committee had probably been formed in response to a law, the Rehabilitation Act, Section 504, that went into effect in 1973 requiring colleges that receive any kind of federal money to make their programs and facilities accessible to students with disabilities. These laws were largely ignored until the '90s, when the more rigorous provisions of the Americans with Disabilities Act (ADA) went into effect, requiring not only access, but reasonable accommodation to students and employers.

I tried to see the members of the committee as allies. They seemed genuinely concerned, and would express outrage at my stories of being locked in the tunnel, or the problems I had with elevators that were broken more often than not. They were shocked to hear that I regularly had to go through the back of the deserted garage to get to the library and to class. They agreed with me that it wasn't safe. They commiserated with me when I told them there were courses I couldn't take and evening events I couldn't attend because they were held in inaccessible buildings. They already knew, and said they were trying to do something about the fact that the bookstore and parts of the library were inaccessible. And the bathrooms, they knew about that too. They were apologetic that there was no one at the university specifically assigned to help disabled students and that I had to figure out most of the solutions on my own.

The committee, and me along with it, didn't fully understand what we were doing and why. I had been to Berkeley, where the principle of the matter drove the actions. It was easier to see a principle when there was a group of people for whom the changes would matter. Here, I was relying so much on my own experience to tell me what was wrong, and, again, I seemed to be asking for things to make my own life easier. I felt shame in that because, it was implied, each ramp, each security guard who was needed to keep a door open in the evening, each accessible stall in a bathroom, each elevator repair, came at the expense of a scholarship for a needy student, or another "worthy" cause. I had fought the "zero-sum" argument when it was posed about other issues—public education, health care, etc.—when the needs of one group were pitted against the needs of another. Here, when I was fighting for what seemed like my needs alone, I sometimes caved in to their logic.

There were no other disabled people on the committee, and only rarely did I see people in my travels around campus the way I had at Berkeley. There were, I was told, those few disabled people who had over the years "made" it at Columbia, and they told me I would make it too, because they knew I would persevere even in the face of these obstacles. Their faith in me was no comfort.

I was reluctant to approach any of the disabled people I saw on campus. I would often see a woman walking with a cane and could see that she had difficulty getting up the stairs, and I wondered if she wanted to join forces with me. But I talked myself out of speaking to her. There was an unwritten code I had grown up with that said you don't acknowledge a person's disability. Here, even when I had reached a stage where I should have reevaluated all those poorly written codes, see if they were ones I still wanted to live by, I didn't act. What if she was offended that I thought she needed help, that I had presumed she was like me—a wheelchair user, a paraplegic, which, I thought, put me lower down on the hierarchy, rendered me the more helpless creature? Maybe she liked walking up the steps. I feared I would do to others what so many meddlesome strangers did to me, barging in, assuming I needed help. There were a few other disabled people I saw from time to time, but I didn't look their way, and they didn't look at me. That was the way things were done back then.

What I didn't understand at the time was that there was a filtration system that allowed so few of us to breathe in this rarified atmosphere. It hadn't occurred to me in elementary or high school that disabled kids existed somewhere out there beyond my life. I never thought about them or where they went to school. I didn't think about the children with mental retardation who never had any formal schooling. I didn't know that most children with physical disabilities were in special education or received home instruction. That included most of the kids who contracted polio. When it came time for them to return to school, many didn't go back to their same classrooms; they were sent to different schools or to other classrooms with a teacher who would "understand" them and help them with all their difficulties. It slowly dawned on me that the small number of disabled students in college was due, in large part, to the fact that those who had been in special education would not be among Columbia's or other schools' first choices. I had always assumed that anyone in special ed was not and never would be college material. I learned how the American school system took that chance away from so many.

I was at Columbia from 1975 to 1977. Public Law 94–142 was passed in 1975, the legislation that mandates a free and appropriate education for all children. It specifically outlines how disabled children should be folded into the general education classroom whenever possible. It was the beginning of a long slow process, still largely incomplete, to integrate the public school system along disability lines. With as much optimism as the moment when *Brown vs. Board of Education* was signed into law, and with as much disappointment twenty-five years after its signing, PL 94–142 remains a mixed blessing. While more children are receiving educational services and a broader range of children are incorporated into the general education classroom, segregation and marginalization of disabled children are still the norm.

I had a few friends at Columbia, people I'd have coffee with or meet to study for an exam, and then another few whom I saw outside of school. There was one man I dated for a while, a woman from my biology class who became a good friend, and a couple I invited to a party and later visited when I went to Paris. Mostly, though, I socialized with people I met in other places.

I was seeing Sarah often in those years, two and three times a week. It was a rough time for me. As much as I was growing, it all hurt like hell.

I don't think I told friends how scared I was, how unprepared I felt for all that was ahead of me.

I could tell my friend Christa some of this. She was a constant in my life in those years, and still is. I had met her shortly after I got out of the hospital, when I was still going back almost daily as an outpatient for physical therapy. Her husband was, at the time, in the rehabilitation institute, following a serious illness and surgery. She watched from the hall every day as all of us struggled with our exercises in the gym. Mine were mostly on the parallel bars, where I was trying to learn to use braces and crutches. It was a short-lived experiment in a frustrating and cumbersome method of getting around. I took the braces home with me, after my months of therapy, but I never used them.

Christa and I began talking one day in the hall, and I always looked forward to seeing her there. I visited with her sometimes in her husband's hospital room, or we would have coffee in the cafeteria. One day she invited me to her house for dinner. She and her husband, Ham, short for Hamilton Armstrong, lived in a beautiful townhouse in the Village, with dark wood paneling and fireplaces in the living and dining rooms. It was Ham's family home, and they had lived there together for over twenty years.

Over that dinner, and hundreds since, I learned about her life. Christa grew up in Germany and lived there through World War II. She harbored a Jewish woman and her daughter in her apartment in Berlin in the last years of the Nazi regime, escaped from Berlin the night before the Russians closed in around the city, and then came to the States and began a career as a photojournalist. Her life with Ham was rich with travel and friends, many of whom I have gotten to know over the years.

She is about thirty years older than me, and she was, at the time I met her, almost the age I am today. I had never been comfortable with a woman older than me. Maybe it was a resistance to anyone who reminded me of my mother's strong influence, or maybe my hippie cautiousness about trusting anyone over thirty. Yet I liked being with Christa. We could talk about sex, pain, and love, and I could curse and be bold with her. I was startled that she seemed interested in me, and it made me feel like a grown-up to be with her.

Ham died a few months after I met her, when we were just getting to know each other, and there we were, two young widows, confused and sad, starting solo lives. Christa moved to an apartment near Washington Square Park, and, like me, was trying to make some new friends to fill this unknown space. I was struggling to succeed at Columbia and learning to live on my own. We were both in need of each other.

Over all these years, we have become wonderful friends, sharing many secrets over long dinners in that apartment near Washington Square.

The last semester at Columbia, I took a course across the street at Barnard in the psychology of women. When it began, I assumed it would be about women's "problems," but as the course went on I questioned my automatic connection of the word "problem" with women's issues (it then occurred to me that "disability" might not be a "problem" in the way that most people view it). It was the first and probably the only course I ever took that was taught from a feminist perspective. The course demonstrated the ways that psychology as a field has historically distorted and misrepresented ideas about

63   A Special Education

women's needs and experiences. We examined the myths inherent in the so-called objective knowledge base. That was the lesson that most intrigued me. The idea that every one of the courses I was taking—from history, to biology, to art history—might be faulty; a lop-sided presentation of material tilted toward men's perspectives and accomplishments.

I decided to apply some of the ideas I had learned in the course in a paper on the psychology of disabled women. When I went to do the research for the paper, I found absolutely nothing in the women's studies literature on disabled women, and the only other material I was able to find were a couple of slim articles in the rehabilitation literature. They framed disabled women's behavior and needs largely in terms of deficits or pathology. Unlike the readings we had been doing for class, which challenged traditional conceptualizations of women's roles and framed issues from an insider's perspective, the rehab literature recounted clinicians' views about disabled women's needs and experiences that seemed far removed from the way that I and the disabled women I had been meeting actually felt. It looked at us and, it felt, through us, and I mistrusted all of it.

Here was something I might do. I could write these missing pages. The professor, Mary Brown Parlee, shared my outrage that there was no literature on this subject, and spent a fair amount of time showing me how to extrapolate from related work some ideas that were relevant to disabled women's experience. We both quickly recognized, though, the limitations of such extrapolation.

She asked me questions about the perspectives I thought were missing or misrepresented in the material we had read for class. She listened with a curiosity and interest no one had ever shown in my opinions. In telling her, and later writing about it, I found I had acquired a fair amount of knowledge and had started to put the pieces together in a way that seemed to make sense to her, and to me.

I told her that there was hardly a subject that was discussed that semester that would not benefit from a comparison with disabled people's experience. As an example, I explained the parallels between depictions of women as passive and assumptions about the passivity of disabled people. In focusing on the forces that create passivity, rather than assuming it was inherent in the condition of "woman" or "disability," we developed a foundation for the paper I would write.

It was the first time I had the opportunity to put together the various lessons I was learning along the way, the insights I had had at particular moments in the hospital and out in the world that were instructive. I told her about the often contentious relationship between disabled people and the medical establishment, how doctors presumed to speak for us and made pronouncements about our needs and experiences. They always spoke of medical solutions to our problems, whereas the people I knew spoke of political solutions. She said she had not previously understood the patterns of prejudice and discrimination I was describing and encouraged me to write about these matters and continue conducting research and speak at conferences.

I told her she was one of the few people outside disability circles who had granted me the authority to speak of my own experience. It felt so good to have an ally, one who showed me how I could use my experience of disability in fruitful ways.

As there was no existing material to base a paper on, she agreed to let me conduct a series of interviews with women who had been disabled since they were young, to learn more about their experience.

The women I spoke with had all had polio in grade school, and left school for long hospitalizations. As with other children I've read about, they rarely returned to the schools they had gone to; they either were placed in special education classes in a different school or had home instruction. One of the central questions in my interviews was about how they felt disability had affected their sense of autonomy. Consistently, in those interviews and in many conversations I've had with women who became disabled when they were children, they spoke about the way they were treated in the hospital. They said that they only got to see their parents once or maybe twice a week for an hour, and were left alone for long periods of time in a crib. Several women said that they learned if they were cheerful and cooperative they would get more attention, and so they learned to be "good" patients. This is strikingly familiar to the ways that women talk about having been socialized to be "good" girls.

Two of the women talked about being touched inappropriately by men fitting them for back and leg braces. I remembered my own experience in the hospital when the man touched my breast repeatedly while he was fitting me for a back brace, and I could only imagine how confusing and frightening that must have been for girls who were then twelve or thirteen. The women also talked about being touched by many hands—by doctors and nurses and physical therapists—in ways that they had always been taught were unacceptable. Here, their mothers sometimes stood by and said nothing to stop the touching. In fact, they often encouraged their daughters to be cooperative.

One of the other questions I asked was about the messages they had received about their sexuality when they were growing up. Several women spoke about how, in their teens, they noted that their parents spoke differently to their siblings than they spoke to them. Again, this is something I have heard over the years from other disabled people, particularly women: that parents would often speak to siblings about future romance and marriage, but never mentioned that to their disabled children. Instead, they were told to do well in school and work toward a career. Their sisters' clothes were, they remembered, prettier and more feminine than theirs.

When these women were released from the hospital or institution, after months, or in some cases years, they resumed their education, having missed many lessons. They recounted the deprivations and degradation they experienced in their new classes, how they longed to go to school with the other children on their block, but were relegated to the special education classroom down in the basement of a school miles from their home, in small classes with women hovering over them all day. They wanted books and spelling tests and, most of all, the opportunity to hang out with other children after school. But the school bus came and swept them away, just as the bell rang and the other kids came crashing through the double doors and out onto the playground. The bus dropped all of the disabled children off at their own homes, and they were stranded there with their mothers. They all said that it was hard to get to know the neighborhood kids, because the others went to a different school and got to stay after school and play or do activities, and the disabled children were usually taken right home. The disabled children didn't even get to play with each other, because transportation was difficult, and even getting in and out of the house was difficult. Many were carried up and down steps into and out of the house.

One of the women I spoke with never got to go to school; she received home instruction because the local school had steps going in, and they wouldn't put in a ramp for her. Another woman had a similar story—this time there was no accessible bathroom, and the school wouldn't even put a grab bar by the toilet which would have made it possible for her to use it. Another woman, now a wheelchair user, was able to walk with a brace on her leg when she was young, and so she went to school with her neighbors. Most years she had to climb up a long flight of steps to the second floor to her classes, and then down again for lunch, and then up, and then down to go to the auditorium, and then up, and then down again to go home in the big yellow bus with the three steps up. She bore the strain in silence, she said, because otherwise she feared she would be sent to the special education classroom and bring shame on herself and her family.

I understood her fear. I had been walking a tightrope since I entered this world. Here I was for all the world to see a disabled person, and there was a certain pleasure I took in demanding that the world accept me on my terms. Also, there were the people I'd met—the gang on the roof at rehab, the Berkeley crew, the women I interviewed— whom I liked. When I attended meetings with them, I witnessed a purposefulness about them—a sense that what they were about, and what I was increasingly about, was important. We were seeking fundamental change that could bring about greater equity and justice. But I was afraid to linger too long with them, afraid I would be tainted by disability's ugliness and shame. I'm not like them, I would think, as I saw one of those vans loaded with tired, sad-looking disabled people go by. They're riding in an "Invalid Coach," and so they must be going to their sheltered workshop or doctors' offices. They need special supports and services. I go to Columbia, I'm going to be a psychologist, and all I need, I foolishly thought, are a few ramps.

I couldn't initially see how close I was to them. There were differences, but they weren't the ones I assumed. I could be riding in one of those coaches with the big letters spelling "INVALID" on the outside if my disability were a little different—for example, if I used a motorized chair instead of a manual push chair, which folds and fits in a taxi. And I would be in the coach if I couldn't afford to take taxis to get where I was going, and had to rely on the state to send the van for trips they sanctioned. And I might look sad and tired if I had to pay forty or fifty dollars per trip just to go to the movies and could rarely leave the house. Or if I wasn't going to Columbia University and didn't have the support I needed to live in my own apartment.

One day during my last month at Columbia, my mother said that she had just seen a program on television about research on cures for spinal cord injury. She was reluctant to bring it up, she said, because she didn't know how I would feel hearing about it, and she didn't want to upset me. The research was at a preliminary stage and so everyone was quite cautious about it, but they did show people who were able to walk a few feet with the aid of a type of electrical stimulation to their legs. She wanted to know if this was something I might like to look into.

I told her it didn't upset me to talk about it. I knew about the research, but it wasn't something that I thought much about. If I had to go through a major medical procedure I wasn't interested, I'd had enough of hospitals. If they ever perfected the method, I would think about it.

I meant what I said, but the telling of it surprised me. It made me realize that I had made a commitment—to live this life the way it was.

It seemed strange—why wouldn't I wish to trade in this condition for a pair of worthy legs capable of transporting me out of the tunnel? It would seem, on the surface, a straightforward, uncomplicated improvement. Like when I was young and I used to dream of my father coming back, years after he died, and everything would be set right again. Nothing but good could come of his return. But the prospect of cure, of being re-abilitated, does not feel like a simple gain. I was reminded of this one day when I read in the paper about a man released from prison after new DNA evidence had cleared him of a crime committed many years before. He was asked by a reporter: "What do you want for your first meal?" He answered: "Whatever they put on my tray." He quickly realized that the answer revealed how different this new life would be, how ill-prepared for it he was, and said, "I guess I will have to make a lot of decisions now." Another news story, a few years back, profiled a man who had been blind most of his life who underwent surgery to have his sight restored. He spoke of the difficulties of sight, how overstimulating it was and how cumbersome to have all that information. I recall that he said he found it unpleasant.

I am not these men, and our experiences are vastly different, yet what is striking is that each of us views the almost universally assumed more desirable state—free, sighted, walking—as foreign, and the road back to it, when such a road exists, as difficult, with losses as well as gains to be contemplated.

And of course, there is no cure for this condition I have. A real cure hasn't been found even in the thirty-some years since. Not a get-up-out-of-bed, stand, get-dressed, walk-to-the-supermarket kind of cure. Not a Christopher Reeve kind of cure, which he told the public would be right around the corner if we just donated enough money.

I suppose then I wasn't rejecting "cure," I was choosing not to participate in the quest for one. Maybe it was because I didn't want to stop what I was doing or risk losing this new vantage point on the world. Maybe I was, and remain, just too frightened to think about what might have been or what might be—how I could still be a high-heel wearer, a step climber, a waltzer, an upright citizen.

Whatever my reasons, and I still can't say with certainty what they are, I am more interested in finding a way out of the tunnel, doing away with tunnels, building accessible campuses and laws to insure them, than intrigued by finding a way to get my legs moving.

There were things I didn't like, things I hated about this new state, but there were and are things that work well. My body works well. It gets me places, it affords me and, I dare say, others great pleasure.

When I told my mother that the quest for a cure didn't interest me, she shook her head. She told me that a few years before, a short time after my accident, she was talking with her brother about me and her fear that my life would be hard and I would never accept being disabled. She told me that my Uncle Sonny, the one who had been in an accident in his twenties and had one leg amputated, said to her: "You know, Simi will get used to it long before you ever will."

5 *Going Away*

I finished up at Columbia in May of 1977, and was to begin a doctoral program in psychology at New York University in the fall. I would turn thirty that summer and decided it was time to go to Europe. By myself. I didn't necessarily desire to go by myself, but I had mostly been living and traveling alone since Rick and I split up. I spent a lot of time in those years leaning toward men and thinking about them. There were other comforts and pleasures in my life, and I was getting smarter and more clearheaded, but I couldn't seem to rest with those gains. And so I vamped and cozied up to men, and I did go out some, and had a few longer relationships, but I always had my eyes open, looking for what would come next.

My cousin Scott planned a party for me in early June, knowing I would be away for my July birthday. Scott was my steady date in those years. He didn't live in New York, his real home is in North Carolina, but he had a key to my apartment and would show up at improbable hours, stay for a day or a month, and then move on. If I was planning a party or had tickets to something, I would call him and he would get in his truck, drive the fourteen hours to New York, and show up looking like he'd just breezed in from across the street. As always, his long black hair hung down almost to his waist, and his red suspenders held up his skinny jeans. Even in the first months when I was just out of the hospital, my back still fragile, and my little body not quite ready for it, when he arrived he would jump on my lap and give me a big fat hug and a juicy kiss.

That party, like all the others in those years, sent me into a manic spin. I had such a strong need for activity, and the idea of a party, building up to it, calling people, and cooking for it, made life seem full. I made so much of it.

70

My trip to Paris was different from all that. I was going alone, and except for booking my flight and a hotel for the first few nights, I had made no other plans.

I asked my friend Diane to give me a ride to the airport. We parked and Diane came in with me so I could check in and see if the flight was on time. I went up to the first available agent at the airline counter. Diane followed and stood a few feet to the side as I gave the woman my ticket and passport and asked about the departure time and gate. While she processed my ticket and checked my bags, I turned to talk to Diane. We chatted about her summer plans.

When I moved back to the counter to retrieve my ticket and passport, the woman behind the counter did not meet my gaze. Instead, she turned away and walked down to where Diane was standing to hand her my papers. The woman said, "You can take her down to Gate 14. They will be boarding her in an hour." I moved quickly to where they were standing, reached up, and snatched the tickets. "Oh, you'd best speak to me," I said. "My friend doesn't speak English." The ticket agent blurted out an apology, but we were off, laughing as we went.

Why would I choose that retort? The woman was polite, her insult so slight, the erasure so subtle that it would not seem to warrant my sarcasm. I could have let it slip by, or I could have used the moment as a didactic opportunity—carefully explaining that I am the one to be addressed as I am the passenger. I am going to Europe. I bought the ticket. Talk to me.

I get tired, though, of being talked of in the third person, of being polite in the face of rudeness, and of being ignored.

There are the waiters who ask my dinner companion, "What will she be having?"

There was the woman who answered the door when I arrived at a friend's party, who, upon seeing me and my date (standing), said "Hello" directly to him and introduced herself, shaking only his hand, and told him, "Oh, you can put her over there."

The usher (many different ushers) at the theater who speaks to the person I'm with, rather than to me. "Will she be transferring out of her wheelchair?" And "Will she want to go out at intermission?"

The owner of a restaurant in upstate New York, who, when I mentioned to him in a friendly way that a small ramp would convert the one-step entrance to an accessible one, offered in an equally friendly tone: "Well, yes, but we don't get many of your kind in here."

Then there was the father of the bride at a friend's wedding who came out to the driveway to greet me and my date. The man smiled down on me, told me how pretty I looked, and then walked around me to shake my friend's hand behind my back and to say in a conspiratorial whisper, just loud enough for me to hear, "Ah, yes, we were warned she'd be coming."

These moments slip by so quickly I sometimes don't notice that I have been taken out of the conversation. I have been made to go away. My reinstatement depends on me, or maybe a friend, redirecting the action back to me. I did that at the airport, but did it at the woman's expense, mocking her and putting her at a disadvantage. I felt remorse, though, at leveraging my advantage—her action so casual, and my sensitivity so heightened by the impending trip. Further, she had surely endured moments when she had been "melted down" by an imperious man, or had a boss who had rejected suggestions for changes in procedure she made, but implemented a male colleague's proposal based on the same suggestions. Also, had this trip occurred in 1997 rather than 1977, she would have received the systematic training that most airline employees now receive, teaching them to directly address disabled people if they are the customers. It takes lessons to learn these things.

On my flight over I worried a great deal—would Paris reject me, would I be able to move about there, would I find obstacles everywhere, would I go home defeated, afraid to travel? I knew that Europe had even fewer accommodations in place for disabled people than the United States, and that the atmosphere was less hospitable. I got my first whiff of this when I was met in the lobby of my hotel by the manager, who told me in no uncertain terms that I would not be allowed to use the main elevator because I was an "insurance risk." Instead I had to wait in a back hallway for the service elevator operated by the sullen bellhop, who begrudgingly moved valises and bags of garbage out of my way so I could get on. I vowed to leave the hotel as soon as I could find another that was accessible. That took a few days, and it became a test of wills between me and the recalcitrant bellhop.

The first night in Paris I set off with trepidation, but once outside things went pretty well. I was interested in everything around me. There were only a few high curbs and lots of alleyways, so I was able to travel in a wider arc than I had expected. I wandered into vestibules of buildings, entered some shops. I felt less conspicuous than I thought I would in prissy Paris. I think it helped that my French was coming out with some clarity and fluidity. Barbara's lessons while I was in rehab and my classes at Columbia had given me a new language, and I loved to speak it.

I ate dinner that night in a Vietnamese restaurant, sitting alone and feeling somewhat self-conscious, but generally glad I'd taken the risk I had—glad I'd ordered the delicate fish with the sweet sauce, glad to be just where I was at that moment, and pleased that I had understood and accepted a passerby's offer to help me up the steps to the restaurant.

After a while there was a flurry of activity at the front door, and several waiters rushed forward to help a man in a wheelchair up the steps. He arrived with a group of five or six people and sat at a table not far from me. Evidently he was a regular customer, and all the waiters stopped at his table to say hello. After a few minutes he spotted me sitting at my table, reading a book. He greeted me and waved me over to join his group. It was hard to say no to him, and in my best French I thanked him and accepted the glass of wine that was offered. He had already had a few, I think, and put his arm around my shoulder and told all around that we were kindred spirits, we *invalides,* and we should stick together. He was a veteran, wounded in World War II, he said, and you, what happened to you? A long story, I said, and was relieved to find he went easily to another topic.

The next day I visited the Jeu de Pomme Museum. A guard came out to greet me and, with considerable effort, and some help from another visitor, pulled my wheelchair up the few steps to the entrance. I went up to the admissions booth and asked for a ticket, but the woman behind the desk silently shook her head, eyes cast downward, her signal to me that I was to go ahead in and would not need to pay an admission fee. Ah, the dubious perks of crippledom.

I toured the first floor, taking my time, absorbing room after room of paintings I'd seen only in textbook miniature. When I arrived at the end of the last room, the friendly guard who had helped me at the door suddenly reappeared to escort me to the staff elevator. I thought

I had been alone, an anonymous visitor, part of the crowd. But it seems I'd been watched, and followed. And now my very own guard was there to show me the way. He was so pleasant, and stood far back from me, lest he seem intrusive. We chatted about his job, and his favorite paintings, and he complimented me on my French. He took me to the second floor, where I was let loose to wander. This time, I was conscious that he was always nearby. In the last room, he waited to take me back downstairs. When he realized he did not have the key he needed for the elevator, he left me unguarded in the storage room, where for a few dazzling minutes I was alone with the left-over Manets and Renoirs.

The trip had many of these wonderful moments. There was the afternoon at the flea market at the edge of Paris where I bargained with an old Russian woman for a beaded necklace from the '20s that I still treasure. We bargained hard and each of us put on a very stern face, but when it was all over we both burst out laughing. There was the reunion with two friends from a French literature class at Columbia, now married and living in Paris. When my taxi pulled into their street, I was greeted by a band of their neighbors who had assembled on the sidewalk ready to hoist me up to their second-floor apartment. With great humor they bore me up, and then, several hours later, a bit less steady on their feet, delivered me back down to the street.

There was the conference on sexuality and disability that I went to in Brussels at the end of the trip, where I met disabled people from all over Europe, from Israel and the United States, speaking a jumble of languages, all eager to know each other. We talked through the night about our lives and the situations in our countries. On the first day, during the question-and-answer period, the Israeli physician leading the discussion misheard my name and began to call me Silly. Every time he said this the English-speaking members of the audience would start to giggle. I tried to correct him, but it was a lost cause, and the poor man didn't understand why people laughed whenever he spoke to me. For the rest of the conference, the group I was hanging out with called me Silly, and we had a grand time. I wish I could see them all again.

But there were the other times. Shooed out of restaurants in Paris because there's "no room for you here." In one place, when I was with a friend and we refused to leave, we were taken to the back, to an awkward little table they had set up for us behind a door, and we were ignored till we raised our voices and demanded service. There was the woman in the Luxembourg Gardens who saw me smiling at her daughter, and pulled her away from me just as the little one opened her face in a wide grin and waved. The woman glowered at me as if I might soil them just by my presence. There was the taxi driver who refused to take me to my hotel, snapping, "This is not an ambulance." There was the loneliness of traveling solo, the disappointment that the Louvre was not accessible, the hard work of figuring out so much that was new, and often difficult, about traveling when you are disabled. The hours without an accessible bathroom in sight. The time I couldn't hold out and begged a man to let me in to a toilet in his building, and, shaking and in pain, hung precariously over the communal *pissoir,* a hole in the floor in a back vestibule, clinging to my chair to keep from sliding into the muck.

I've been back to Paris since then. The Louvre and the new Impressionist museum are now accessible, and I can travel unescorted, at my will, through the treasures. And for better or worse, I did pay to get in this time at both museums. The new entrance to the Louvre, through the glass pyramid in the center court, has a beautiful unenclosed platform elevator that descends along the same wall that holds the stairs. The open design gives you a full view of everything as you travel a route parallel to the one used by those going down the escalator. In fact, it is the most outstanding example of accessible design that I have ever witnessed.

The hotel and airport personnel are more casual now about my traveling, and seem, in general, somewhat indifferent to my wheelchair. And the sprightly flight attendants seem less inclined to chirp at me about how independent I am and talk to me as if I were a nine-year old with one of those destination tags pinned to my blouse. I am more experienced too, more hardened to the slights, and better prepared for the difficulties. I've laughed off some outrageous examples of Parisian rudeness that were so omnidirectional that I got a kick out of being dissed along with the rest of the tourists.

In the intervening years I've witnessed tremendous change in the opportunities and freedoms available to disabled people, yet most days it seems that the glass isn't even half full. Disability still marks me and others in most places that we live and travel. Particularly outside the United States, but here as well, accessible theaters, museums, hotels, and bathrooms are rare. I always have to calculate how far I am from a usable bathroom before I order a cup of coffee. In New York City, where I live, most restaurants and theaters do not have accessible bathrooms, and many don't have accessible entrances. My local post office and library are still inaccessible, and until a few years ago, so was the polling place where I was to vote. For people with other types of impairments, there are different and equally problematic access problems. TTY telephone communication systems for deaf people and sign language interpreters are mandated by law in many public institutions, but often even the most minimal provisions are not put in place. The availability of materials in alternative formats for people with visual impairments or learning disabilities is limited, even in places where such forms of communications are required by law.

While the United States now has the most comprehensive laws governing discrimination on the basis of disability, and ensuring access, the legislation is recent, its goals and timetables not fully achieved. Even with it, I am barred from many places that I need or want to go. And I recognize that I am, of my fellow disabled travelers, enormously privileged. I am privileged by a career, and opportunities most disabled people are denied. I am uneasy with the gains in freedom and access that I have. My presence in airports, in shopping malls, and in front of the classroom may lull the public into complacency. It may lull me into complacency. It may appear to signal disabled people's liberation and integration. But it only signals the gains of the more assimilable of us. We are the tokens. We can go places that disabled people in institutions and nursing homes, those who get stuck in special ed, those who work in sheltered workshops, those denied employment, and the many who have inadequate health care and inadequate in-home attendant care cannot. We can go away.

6 *Pleasures and Freedoms*

Everything I know about dancing I learned from a quadriplegic. His name is Glenn, and when he swerves and shimmies, when he bobs and lists—his head, that is—you must pay attention.

Glenn is a big guy, and he carries his size well. He sits tall in a large motorized wheelchair that he propels with a mouth stick, a plastic tube that is used to control the movement of the chair. Though they are officially called "Sip and Puff" chairs, Glenn refers to his as "Suck and Blow." His forearms rest on the side pieces of the chair, his long fingers curve down, draping over the rounded front of the leatherette pad under each arm. He usually wears chinos and leather boots, and has been known to sport a tie when he needs to look serious. If you have a chance to meet him, he will come to greet you, stretching his lips out, wrapping them around the plastic tube and blowing a precise stream of air, just enough to whir him across the room and right to you.

A mutual friend introduced me to Glenn and his wife Myrna when I was in my second year of graduate school, in 1979. Life was slowing down and heating up. I wasn't as frenzied, there were fewer big parties and less urgency to my social life. My courses were not as interesting as they had been at Columbia, but there was a great deal of work, and I was going full-time because I was eager to finish.

When I first met Glenn and Myrna they spontaneously invited me to a party at their house way out on the North Shore of Long Island. I was in the early stages of a relationship with David, the man who would become my husband, the man who would become my dearest love and my best friend, the man who would, over time, come to call me Snugs, Bunny, Poochie, and, in my sillier moments, Chucklehead, but we at that time were still on a first-name basis. I told David about the party and said they'd asked if we wanted to stay over. "Sure," he said.

David hadn't met many of my friends at that point, and I felt nervous about this introduction. I thought that if David saw me with Glenn, and others who are disabled, the reality of my disability would hit him. He would be scared off. Every time I had that thought I told myself to shut up, to trust David and to trust his feelings for me. In my worry about pleasing him, I lost track of how I felt about the party, about whether disability, mine or others, scared me, or whether I even wanted David to stick around.

We spoke of none of this, only the practical matters of whose car we would take, when we would leave, whether we would stop for lunch. We talked on the way out about different pieces of our lives, filling in the spaces. At the time, David was teaching at a high school on Long Island, and we passed the exit he got off at every day when he went to work. He had lived out that way until a couple of years before I met him. He had gotten married to his college sweetheart, and when they divorced, David moved to Brooklyn. We had both married young.

We arrived at Glenn and Myrna's by late afternoon. Their house was a pale gray cedar-shake bungalow and sat among oak trees and dogwoods on a narrow street that led down to Long Island Sound. Over time, the four of us would take many walks down that road, Glenn leading the way in his power wheelchair, me hitching a ride by holding on to the back of his chair with one hand, weaving along the road behind him, David and Myrna, both walkies, bringing up the rear, and their big shaggy dog, Mischief, running in circles around us, herding us down the street.

On the bright fall day of our first visit, Glenn and Myrna came out to greet us. They stood at the top of the ramp that leads to their front door. Myrna is tall, and Glenn, seated, is almost as tall. A robust couple. They ushered us into their house and introduced us to the dog and cat. I'd not yet been in the home of anyone else who used a wheelchair, and easily wove through the house, enjoying the wide doorways and the extra space left between pieces of furniture. The house was all on one level. The living room, dining room, and kitchen melded together, with only a kitchen counter cordoning off what was definitely Myrna's domain, the place where the heat and the rich smells were coming from.

Over the years, we went to many parties there, and I don't remember if that night was the Indian feast, or the Greek, or the Mexican, but whichever it was, the ingredients were precise, and the menu elaborate. The food may be served in big pots, and ladled onto paper plates, but the curry is blended by hand, using packets of spices imported from the wilds of Queens or Brooklyn. There are courses. There is a specific sauce for each dish. There is a cake, or two or three, each distinct, and you must taste them all.

That day, with only a couple of hours to go till everyone was to arrive, things were in disarray. Myrna and I set to chopping, and David and Glenn to organizing the house. David did the moving, and Glenn directed, gesturing with his head to a hiding place for this or that pile of papers or clothes. Once David and Myrna had rolled the rug up, Glenn got to move some of the furniture about. He came up in front of or behind a piece, maneuvered his chair into position so that the tips of his hard-toed boots were in the center of the object to be moved, and, with a slow steady stream of air into his mouth stick, steered a bureau across the floor, landing it against the wall. David stood back, admiring this advanced tool use. They were laughing, this was a game.

Myrna had to make a run to the store for some last-minute supplies, and David offered to drive her into town. She jumped at the chance to ride in David's cute little Honda, as she always drove a lumbering blue van with a wheelchair lift and a raised roof to accommodate Glenn's height. Glenn and I took some time off to talk about a project we had drummed up in a recent phone conversation.

His desk, Myrna's weaving loom, and her easel occupied most of the front room. These had not been moved for the party, nor had the piles of books and papers that filled up the top of the desk. Glenn showed me his computer, also operated by mouth, and programmed to accomplish multiple tasks with a minimum of key strokes. To use it, he reaches his head down, bares his teeth, and plucks a plastic wand from a bracket on the desk.

I watched as he moved the wand over the keyboard and struck a few keys to bring him to the file he wanted to show me. It contained notes he'd made since our conversation. We wanted to establish an organization that would gather and disseminate information on the sexuality of disabled people. It would be an organization run primarily by disabled people and would serve disabled people, through education and advocacy.

When I was in rehab, and got the idea to go back to school, become a psychologist, and return to the rehabilitation center and set up sex education programs there, I wasn't able to even imagine anything like what Glenn and I were planning. The world I had inhabited those many months was the only one I thought would have a place for me. There were two groups of people there: the patients and the staff. When I was on the patient side, I could only see far enough to seek a position for myself on the opposite side. As there were only five people I'd seen in that group who were disabled, three secretaries who used wheelchairs, a lab technician who used crutches, and a psychologist I met with once who had very short arms, my plan to secure a place for myself as a psychologist in a rehab center seemed ambitious enough. None of the physicians were women, although a couple of the psychologists were, and none of the professional staff were wheelchair users. Partly because I was naive and partly because my mother was a strong businesswoman, I had never seen my gender as an obstacle to anything I might want to do. I was certain that my disability would be.

The further I was from the place, though, the less appealing such a post seemed. I became more interested in working outside the rehabilitation system, and as the years went on it seemed likely that I would be able to do that. While I did hold some grandiose dreams about the ways I could have an impact on an institution, my more realistic side recognized that physicians would remain in charge, and they would support only modest change.

At best, whatever program might exist within an institution would be most effective in enhancing the personal sex lives of the people the institution served. Glenn and I were aiming at a broader range of people and ideas than would fit in such a place. The focus of most rehab centers was on intervention with people with spinal cord injury, stroke, brain injuries, or other types of mobility impairments. One of the lessons I had learned in Berkeley was that coalitions of people with all types of impairments had strengthened the disability community and helped to reveal the commonalities in our experience.

Discrimination in employment, housing, transportation, and education, including sex education, is experienced by people who are blind, people with cerebral palsy, and people with mental illness. Beyond the common political struggle, we all share what I like to call "the vantage point of the atypical," the perspectives gained from negotiating a world configured for nondisabled people.

Glenn and I recognized that there was a similar commonality of experience and outlook in discussions about sexuality. Time after time people with many different kinds of conditions revealed that negative messages about disabled people's sexuality, the lack of sex education and reproductive health care services, and constricted social opportunities were what marked all of our sex lives. These factors, more than the specific conditions we were identified as having, influenced our sexual activity and feelings. We wanted to set up an organization that would address the imposed social restrictions, and inadequate sex education and counseling.

The other important lesson I had learned in Berkeley was the importance of disabled people speaking for ourselves. Although we hadn't yet heard the phrase "Nothing about us, without us," which would become the rallying cry of the disability rights movement, Glenn and I knew that we wanted disabled people to be at the core of the leadership of the organization.

Functioning outside of a rehabilitation setting would allow us to critique practices that undermined our goals, and to work to create integrated sex counseling and sex education in the community. When the field of rehabilitation medicine developed following World War II, it was able to provide better medical care and more effective treatments than people with mobility impairments had ever had, and it also provided job training and other skills that were enormously useful. The field fought for many years to gain legitimacy in the medical profession. Its focus was not on curing, but on maximizing function. Because doctors worked in teams with psychologists, social workers, and occupational and physical therapists (methods that seemed unorthodox to traditional medicine), rehabilitation did not initially have the status of other fields.

Rehabilitation professionals made possible some types of job training, and they increased employment opportunities in a few areas. Simultaneously, their technological innovations increased mobility and comfort. These people made a great deal of difference in our lives. Yet the error that they made was to speak for disabled people, which undermined the autonomy they claimed to promote. The doctors who ran these institutions were almost exclusively male and nondisabled, and they set out to define for the public what disabled people needed and wanted. In those years, rehabilitation professionals tended to call all disabled people "patients," whether we were in their care or not. That designation was replaced in the '80s by the term "consumers," as in consumers of their medical services. That has not changed; it is still as if our only identity is in relationship to them.

In the '60s and '70s, and to a certain extent today, rehabilitation institutions often didn't work actively to address discrimination and problems in the environment; their focus was on helping the individual adapt to and fit into the existing social structure. While a number of individual members of the rehab profession were dedicated to such causes, those were personal commitments outside the boundaries of their work lives. Rehab emphasized regaining function and focused on what used to be called "normalization." Other organizations geared toward the welfare of specific groups of disabled people, such as the American Foundation for the Blind or United Cerebral Palsy, also set the agenda for their constituents. Once the various groups of disabled people began to break down the barriers these organizations had erected and find common cause, we could work together to address the social-justice issues that many of us were concerned with.

When Glenn and I set off on this plan, we had an inkling that teaching about sexuality would be controversial. I had seen, back in the rehab center, when a group of us tried to get the doctors to show some films and talk more actively about sexual concerns, that we were entering a forbidden zone. Like kids who latch onto the one thing that unsettles their parents, we pursued the doctors and kept demanding they pay attention to us and to our sexuality. Over time, I came to understand that linking disability to a robust sexual life is among the more radical ideas that one can put forth. It is radical because it debunks the myth of the long-suffering disabled person, but is even more disruptive because it challenges accepted ideals of sexual prowess. We were saying that pleasure isn't dependent on certain standards of performance, and on intact bodies. If disabled people can invent new definitions of sexual ability, the cultural norm is called into question.

When I met Glenn, I met someone who thought the same way. He also enjoyed the prospect of rattling people by talking casually about disabled people and sex. We learned from other people we were meeting, sex educators and therapists as well as psychologists, rehab counselors, and, primarily, disabled people who talked with us about their experience.

The scant professional literature that we found on sexuality and disability was focused almost exclusively on men's needs and performance. Many of the articles concentrated on men with spinal cord injury because erection and ejaculation, seemingly the most important components of sexual function, were often affected, although not in the simple way that many might believe. Authors may have included some throwaway line like, "It's easier for women to adjust because of their more passive role," as if that fully explained the omission and justified their bias.

While I was critical of many of their ideas, particularly the notion of the "passive" female, I sometimes caught myself buying into the idea that adjustment is harder for a man because he is expected to be the breadwinner, to be in charge, and to get an erection. Maybe my own needs factored in here too, that that was what I needed, or thought I needed, in a man. Maybe I was denying my own struggle and projecting it onto Glenn or other disabled men that I knew. It was easier to say that they were having a hard time, not me.

Being with Glenn made me question these assumptions. He is a fullfledged quadriplegic, moving not a muscle below his neck. He's not one of those almost-but-not-quite-quads who can manage the throttle on a power wheelchair or can hold a fork well enough to eat solo. Yet he rejected the social presumptions about the limits of his body, leading me to do the same.

When Glenn and I worked together, usually making presentations at a college or medical center, I learned from his laid-back humorous approach. While he cajoled his audience, I was a more strident speaker, yet we were a seamless team. Although we were there to talk specifically about the sexuality of disabled people, the implications were much broader. We were encouraging people to use disability as an opportunity to think in new ways about sex and what is important to them. We had become versed in anatomy and physiology and so were able to talk the talk with physicians, but our favorite audiences were other people with disabilities. We suggested trying oral sex, or, indeed, sex with noses, ears, elbows, or toes, if that was what was available and usable. We de-emphasized the importance of genital sex, saying it was just one option. We talked about heterosexual and homosexual couplings as acts with similar properties, fulfilling similar needs. We urged people to redefine "orgasm," suggesting that it should be considered the peak of sexual excitement however they experience it.

We tried for a balance between an upbeat, matter-of-fact approach, and a sensitive, concerned one. We recognized that some people would find our suggestions offensive or upsetting, and didn't want to be overbearing. Neither of us would deny that there is pain and struggle in the lives of disabled people, and there is loss. We never wanted to sound like we were above the struggle; like we had conquered the shame, doubt, and sadness and had uniformly successful sexual experiences.

The project that Glenn and I were scheming about that day in his living room would develop into the National Coalition on Sexuality and Disability, and it would become quite a healthy organization. It certainly didn't arrive fully grown that afternoon; it would take a few years and many talented people for it to emerge. Myrna worked with us. She had been an occupational therapist—in fact, that is how she and Glenn had met back when he was in rehab—and she offered a critical analysis of the ways that medical institutions exerted control over disabled people and shaped how the public understood our issues.

The Coalition aimed at a broad range of targets. The Board wasn't always in agreement, and we didn't get to do half the programs we thought up, but we sketched out an interesting platform. It wasn't just the private pleasures that sexuality affords that we advocated. It was integrated sex education in schools, meaning the incorporation of disabled children in those classes and the development of a curriculum that represented their interests and experience. We advocated for sexual health care services and full reproductive rights, including family planning, birth control, and abortion services available and accessible to all in the community. We spoke out against forced sterilization of women with mental retardation and other women who were in institutions. We talked about sexual abuse and the need to educate people with disabilities so that they could protect themselves against exploitation. We emphasized that disabled people's right to a sexual life is as essential as the right to an education or the right to vote. After all, weren't we guaranteed life, liberty, AND the pursuit of happiness?

By the time Myrna and David returned from the store, we had a couple of pages of notes for a grant proposal and we were ready for a party. I had just enough time to put on my red glass beads and fluff up my hair before the guests started to arrive.

An early guest, who sported a full black and gray mustache that curled upward on each side, said, upon meeting me: "Now I hear you're in the sex business with Glenn. Is it true?"

"Well, yes," I told him, "but he is much more highly paid than I."

As far as I could tell, Glenn and I were the only disabled people there, but I knew right away that I wouldn't have to fend off intrusive questions or strike that pose that tells people they mustn't treat me with kid gloves. This was a well-schooled group; Glenn had already broken them in.

Both men and women kissed Glenn hello and wrapped their arms around his big shoulders. There were no macho handshakes possible here, and a hearty clap on the back would discomfit Glenn greatly.

People greeted and gathered, hugged and kidded. I moved through the room visiting different clusters of people. After a while, Glenn asked someone to turn up the music and, with Glenn in the lead, a group of four or five headed toward the living room to the space that they had cleared that afternoon.

Dancing? It had never occurred to me. Dancing was for standees, not for the likes of Glenn and me. It would be unseemly for us to cavort and frolic. Wasn't that true? I could laugh, and tease and joke, but not shimmy and shake, at least not in public. I could snap my fingers or clap my hands at a concert, but not raise those arms up over my head and twist and twirl them about.

When I pictured Glenn and Myrna's party, I saw people talking and eating. That's what we did at the parties I'd been having. There was always music of course, and sometimes people would dance in place in different spots about the room, but here people were clearly revving up, and Glenn was right in the middle. I watched him intently, although no one else seemed to; this was clearly not his first time. Big bad Glenn, out there on the floor, rocking his head slowly to the music. He was just warming up. As he got looser and moved his head more, the rest of his body seemed to go along with it, like waves of electricity coursing down a wire. He twitched and shouted. He rocked, and, every once in a while, he rolled. Back and forth, in and out, in circles if there was enough space. Women shimmied up to him, and he, eye to bosom, turned to give them his full attention.

So this was why the furniture was moved. I thought it was just to give Glenn, and me as well, room to circulate and talk to everyone. That's what I'd been doing, circulating.

Bluesy rock prevailed. My favorite music. I edged in closer, part of the circle around the dance floor, clapping to the music. Oh my god, David is a great dancer. People moved back to give him all the space he needed. He kicked off his shoes, worked out. Crouching down, springing up, twirling, his footwork is a cross between Chuck Berry's and Baryshnikov's.

I hung on the edge for a long while, talking myself into and talking myself out of moving into the circle. Glenn and David were whispering on the side, near the stereo. They nodded in unison, and David changed the record, carefully placing the needle on a particular groove.

It was Aretha Franklin who finally got me on the dance floor:

What you want
Baby, I got it

As if I had been holding my breath for a very long time, my mouth popped open and a loud whoop came out. It was a call to action that even Myrna heard on the other side of the big room, and she came out from behind the kitchen counter to join me on the dance floor.

This dancing was the public equivalent of what Glenn and I had been saying at the desk that afternoon. If sexuality is the individual expression of any person's desires and needs, not bound to a particular set of people who possess physical or psychological traits deemed worthy, and if sexual activity needn't follow a measured recipe of arousal, intercourse, orgasm, in more or less that order, engaged in only between two people of the opposite sex, then dancing shouldn't be restricted to people on feet, people who can see, people who are young, and thin, and popular, or people who can perform all the moves.

I had been managing the private expressions better than the public ones. I had more readily understood that pleasure and intimacy were not outside the limits of what this body offered. Whatever shame I felt in intimate moments about my scars or my floppy legs, I had seen slipping away over the years. The feelings may never disappear entirely, but when they did emerge I could often tag them as demons, as unnecessary baggage. I couldn't always reason with them on the spot and make them go away, but over time I had had enough successful experiences that I recognized it was possible. And, of course, when I was successful, the rewards were so clear and palpable.

Here, on the dance floor, with no warning, the rewards came showering down on me. My weighty body found rhythm it hadn't really lost, just misplaced. David was clearly happy to see me out there, and that made a world of difference.

After a few songs, those of us still left on the dance floor were hot and sweaty, and moving in very slow motion. We were "doin' the Glenn"—standing or sitting stock-still, bobbing our heads on our loose necks. The rest of the party was relaying platters of food from the kitchen to the table and serving it up. The smells revived us dancing fools, and we queued up for our share.

The party drifted on for a while, and when everybody left, there were just us four. We hugged and went off to bed. Glenn and I couldn't figure out at first how to hug, but we have figured it out since then. I can't reach across his lap when we're knee to knee, so we sidle up to each other, wheel to wheel, facing opposite directions, and I wrap one arm around his chest, the other around his shoulder, and kiss his hand or his arm. He moves in, tilts his head down, and gives me a sweet Glenn kiss. It has taken years of practice to perfect this technique. That night we were only at the hand-kissing stage.

David and I slept on a pull-out sofa that marked the border between the dining room and the living room. Late the next morning we began to stir with the smell of coffee. Myrna was up, padding about in bare feet, wearing a loose Japanese kimono. Glenn was still in bed. It takes at least an hour for him to get up and ready for the day, and no one wanted to rush into anything that Sunday morning. We were invited into the bedroom for breakfast. Glenn was spread out in bed, reading, his head and shoulders propped up with multiple pillows. A shelf was suspended over the bed with a reading stand on it. He had a different plastic stick in his mouth, this one with a rubber tip on the end that he uses to turn the pages.

Myrna and David carried in trays with mugs of coffee and rolls. "Walkies are so useful," Glenn said. "Yes," I added, "and so clever too, getting around on those funny little feet."

7　The Design of My Life

David and I met at the end of my first year of graduate school. I had been in psychoanalysis for several years by then, and Sarah had been shoring me up and fortifying my borders. I no longer said, "I don't want to be tied down to anyone or anything." It still seemed dangerous to rest with someone and love him, but I could wish for it now out loud. At the same time, I feared loss, and erosion of the place I held in my own household, the voice I had developed.

Growing up with a mother who was a businesswoman and a tough broad, I thought I had mastered the independent-woman thing. I thought of myself as assertive, a free thinker and a loose talker. I thought I was unafraid of men, and that seemed all that there was to being a feminist. I didn't understand how I used men as a mirror to better see myself. I existed more fully when they were looking at me than in my own conscious mind.

So I lunged toward boys, and later men, too needy by far to ever be fulfilled. In my adolescence I was boy-crazy, as they used to say. Bent on pleasing, being attractive. Often subverting my own needs and satisfactions for those of the object of my interest. I had met John in my first week of college, right out of high school. We got together, and by Christmas, much to my mother's dismay, I had dropped out of college and moved to the East Village. John followed at spring break, and a year later, on a whim, with a promise of a honeymoon at the Bronx Zoo, we got married at City Hall. We brought along two friends as witnesses. One was my neighbor Delia, the friend whom I would call some four years later from a phone booth in the hospital to say how, tragically, our marriage had ended. The other was a guy that John hung out with at the corner bar in Little Italy, where we were living.

After the ceremony, we had pizza and champagne back at our apartment, and then we all boarded the subway for our trip to the zoo.

Suddenly at nineteen, I was a wife. Sure I wore miniskirts, swore, and started hitchhiking everywhere once we'd moved up to Boston. Yeah, I understood some politics, and had quite a few independent ideas. I even auditioned for a job as a DJ at a progressive radio station, the first woman who would hold that job, but when I thought I might get it, might move past where John and I were, taking turns working temp jobs, I fled, scared I would wound my husband with my success and destroy the marriage.

Here, on the other side, breathing on my own now and moving toward a career, I valued the whole me and feared I would have to give a piece of it up if I became seriously involved with someone. I had a number of relationships in those years. At the beginning, after Rick and I split up, I carried over some of my adolescent cravings. It was in part, I think, a reaction to my fear that I would not be able to gain the attention of men now that I was disabled, and in part a reaction to marrying young and missing a critical piece of my life as a single woman. In my newfound single life, I had some good times, and I also got tossed around as I tried to find my way. There were fallow periods and loneliness. More shoring up. "There, there," Sarah would say, "talk through your tears." And so it went.

Longing for a relationship and fearing it were the dual themes throughout my analysis. I think there were many reasons. The loss of my father at an early age, then John's death, confirmed for me that any man I depended on would leave me unprotected and alone when I least expected it. I was also afraid that I would lose myself in the company of a man, having so often pushed my own ambitions aside in my marriage to John. I realized after the fact that I had barely thought about going back to college in those years, let alone pursuing a real career. At the time it seemed such an act would be a betrayal of my hippie vows, but I think I was more guided by my womanly vows, unspoken, to let the man set the pace, to not race out ahead. And then, with disability in the picture, I was also afraid that ultimately my chosen man would reject me, that despite how much I had grown and strengthened myself, I was too small, and I was in disrepair. I could not stand by my man. I could not stand up to his scrutiny. I could not meet his standards.

When I heard such riffs going through my head, I would admonish myself. Smarten up. Don't decide what others will think of you. Go by the experiences you've had, the relationships that have worked. Don't take all the various insecurities you've been cultivating since childhood and bundle them all into the disability package—it is too simple and it makes no sense. And when I caught myself, I more or less listened.

In 1979, when David moved in, we changed some furniture around, and fixed up a closet and a work area for him. He held onto his apartment in Brooklyn, subletting it for a year as we made our way in the relationship. Slowly we made more changes, deeper commitments. He let go of his apartment and we repainted, bought a couch, renovated the kitchen. We got married. We traveled. Made friends together. In the first three years of our marriage, we nursed first his mother and then my mother through terminal illnesses, and watched them die. We not only cared about our own mothers, but had come to care deeply for each other's.

I became a caretaker, after such vast experience being a caretakee, preparing food, calling doctors, and keeping track of medicines. While David could do the work of lifting these women into and out of wheelchairs as they each, in turn, became frail and could no longer walk, I could figure out how a ramp could be built into my mother-in-law's Victorian home, so that she could more easily get in and out of the house, and so that I, finally, could as well. David could calm my mother and distract her, in a way that was harder for me to do, and I could make his mom smile. There were rewards in doing it well, a sense of competence and maturity, a quieter and more private resolve than I had ever exhibited. It was a struggle. I tried to resist taking over, and speaking for these strong women, and when I wasn't patient and gave in to those impulses, I felt a sharp, precise kind of guilt.

David and I each had fears and needs that kept us from truly feeling safe with each other. We fought a lot in the first few years, although we also had great times, and slowly, and with much doubling back, we moved toward each other, toward friendship and love. Sarah helped me through the crises, urging me to look forward and choose the path I wanted to take, and to look back to gain insight into the conflicts that weighed me down.

In all the years of therapy, I was only able to recapture the wispiest of memories of my father, but even now, many years after she died, my mother stands out in my mind, larger than life. Her full name was Augusta Chaiken, but most everyone called her Gus. She was Aunt Gus to many, and came to be known in the family as Auntie Mame, after the Rosalind Russell character in the movie. At work, she was called Miz C., a cross between Miss and Mrs., long before the term "Ms." had been invented. She could be seen by day at the warehouse, out in the back talking to the drivers, a cigarette dangling from her lips, a pencil behind her ear, and then appear that evening in a long black skirt, a brocade coat that she probably had made herself wrapped around her shoulders, on her way to the opera. Though a mighty figure, she was slight and rail thin.

She would be driven to the opera by one of the guys from the warehouse, usually Avery. "A good soul," my mother would say of Avery, and he would smile broadly and take her anywhere. He drove a beat-up Mercury, which was the office car by day, mostly used to carry boxes and packing crates around. By night, it was my mother's limo, and Avery, still in his scruffy green work jacket with the company insignia stitched on the back and a wool cap on his bald head, sat up straight behind the steering wheel, his round belly out in front and the long hood of the American car stretching out in front of that.

At the end of the performance, my mother would emerge from the doors of the grand old Metropolitan Opera Building on Fortieth Street, or from Carnegie Hall or a Broadway theater, and Avery would wave his big arm in the air, shouting for all the coiffed and tuxedoed crowd to hear: "Hey, Miz C., over here." The liveried chauffeurs stood at attention beside their shiny black vehicles and silently opened the back doors for their patricians to slip into and out of sight, but Gus would usually open the door herself, ride up front with Avery, and roll down the window so she could have a cigarette. She knew the smoke bothered me, so each time she took a drag on her extra-long Benson and Hedges, she would turn her head all the way toward the open window and lean out before exhaling.

On the trip back home, Avery would often have a woman friend along. So, as Mom, and often Mom and I, had been inside watching Carmen or Mimi or Madame Butterfly die an awful death, Avery had gone to the Bronx to pick up his date. We would get in the car and

Avery would say, for instance, "Janine, this is Miz C., and this here is Cookie." Avery kept calling me Cookie until I was well into my thirties, which is when I last saw him.

Wherever Mom asked Avery to take us, he would say "Good, good," in a double burst of quick, breathy syllables, then ratchet the gearshift into drive, and off we would go. We would head uptown, Avery piloting the two-toned Mercury up the broad New York avenues. He could not seem to drive more than thirty miles an hour, even on the highway. City driving required an even slower pace. Taxis and trucks whizzed past, and Avery would just keep creeping up Sixth Avenue, his eyes straight ahead, narrating to Janine the wonders of midtown New York. Any time my mother opened her mouth to speak, Avery would quickly move his foot from the gas to the brake in anticipation of a command from Miz C. He didn't bring the car to a full stop, but he did give us a bit of a jolt as he leaned on the brakes, regardless of the traffic behind us. Exasperated drivers honked their horns, but my mother, oblivious of her impact, went on to describe the beauty of the tenor's voice that evening.

I had not learned to drive when I was a teenager growing up in the city, nor during the years with John. We couldn't afford a car. I learned to drive after the accident while I was still at the rehab center. They had cars set up with hand controls, and the instructor took me out just a few times and I easily got the hang of it. I didn't have to unlearn using my feet on the gas and brake, so it was natural to me to use my left hand to push and pull on the lever attached to the steering column that operates the pedals, and to steer with my right hand. I began driving about the same time as I was becoming more expert in maneuvering a wheelchair through tight spaces, and learning to back up and gauge distances, and the skills are complementary.

When I left rehab, I wasn't ready to buy a car. There was already so much that was new and difficult, I put it off for a couple of years. My mother would offer to send Avery to my house to take me places, and as much as I wanted to move about without notifying her, at the beginning I gave into it.

I bought a car after I got back from Berkeley. I had leased a car out there and gotten used to the pleasures of it, and the freedom to spontaneously go places on my own. My cousin Scott went with me to the car dealer, and we tried out many kinds. We finally chose an American Motors Pacer, a funny squat little car, with wide doors so I could fold my chair and pull it into the back seat easily. I always get into a car on the passenger side, then lean out, fold my chair, move over to the driver's seat, push the back of the passenger seat forward, reach across, and pull the chair onto a board placed on the floor well in the back. Once I mastered it, I managed the whole business, from unlocking the car to turning on the engine and driving away, in three to four minutes.

I started getting out of the city as often as I could. If I told my mother I was going away for the weekend, or, indeed, going anywhere, she would urge me to have Avery drive. Before I had the car, I once made the mistake of having Avery take me to visit friends on Long Island. It was a mistake that revealed itself very slowly as I watched the hands of the clock on the leatherette dashboard of the Mercury go round and round. The appeal for my mother, of course, was that she knew where I was, even had the phone number, and I had to check in with her about my comings and goings. She also, I think, believed that driving with Avery was safe because he went so slow.

I had struggled with my mother since I was a child. She seemed to push into every corner of my life and leave behind some evidence which would stare at me even after she'd left and gone back home. Yet she loved me and encouraged me, and that counted for a whole lot. She had been forced to leave school in the sixth grade and go to work. In her family, she and her older sister, my dear Aunt Selma, were expected to go out and work so their younger brother, my Uncle Sonny, could go to college. It was a lesson about gender that she learned very early and very cruelly. She loved learning, and taught herself through years of careful reading about literature and history. When I floundered in high school, and then dropped out of the only college I got into, she was deeply disturbed. I am sure that failing in school was my adolescent weapon of choice, though I didn't understand it at the time. After the accident, when I went back to college and then went on to get a Ph.D. and become a professor, I knew my academic success made her very proud, and I was finally old enough to enjoy the pleasure she took in that.

My mother loved David, thought him smart and fun, and I think appreciated that he married me, that disability didn't stop him. And he loved her too. They bonded and always had a lot to talk about. I sometimes felt jealous of the attention my mother showered on David and how she'd ask his opinion about world events and political candidates. I am generally lively and engaged in social situations, and I was most of the time when I was with Mom and David, but there were times that I felt extraneous and I'd get quiet.

Mom died of cancer in 1986. She was seventy-six, and for as long as I can remember had subsisted largely on a steady diet of cigarettes, coffee, cottage cheese, and Special K cereal. She was occasionally observed eating other foods, but only in little bites, and then she would pick up her plate and shovel the remainder onto everyone else's plates so they could get fat, not her. She went to work five days a week until just a few months before she died.

There was so much about her that I admired and loved. To both my mother's and father's credit, they were equal partners in the moving and warehouse business. After he died, she ran the business, and the company flourished. She respected the people who worked for her, and, unlike many bosses, she supported the union. I think she went to the opera because she genuinely loved the music, not because of its cultural status. She chose exotic places to travel, ate at good restaurants, and chose beautiful things to have in her home because they appealed to her, not because they conveyed to others her worth or her wealth. Indeed, they were often not worth much money. I attribute my love of flea markets to her early tutelage. Once, she bought bolts of inexpensive paisley fabric at a rummage sale and covered the walls and the furniture of our large den. She did it all herself, sewing the slipcovers and pasting the fabric on the walls. We called it the Red Room, and it was a grand place.

Because of the warehouse, Mom had access to people's furniture and household possessions. I would hear stories at the dinner table about how a customer hadn't paid the bill to keep her things in storage and the company had to auction off her belongings. It seemed that Mom gave people many extensions on their bills and bent over backwards to help them get their furniture back. I believe that she was compassionate, and felt badly when this happened, yet some of these things eventually found their way to our house. We had bookcases filled with used books, and we had chairs, rugs, picture frames, and lamps that some family had, of necessity, forsaken. My mother took these objects in and gave them a home, but I always thought they looked sad.

When the show *Funny Girl* came to Broadway, and I heard Barbra Streisand sing "Second Hand Rose" I felt she was singing just for me. As with all Broadway shows that I saw, I bought the cast album and played it over and over, till I knew every word and had choreographed a dance to go with each song. My rendition of "Second Hand Rose" stayed in my repertoire for many years. The little number I worked up had me flitting from room to room, caressing the backs of the chairs and running my hand over the shelves of orphaned books with split spines, singing: "I never get a single thing that's new!" I tried not to think about the families and their lost possessions.

In my family, a common Sunday outing was a trip to the Lower East Side with Aunt Selma to shop in discount stores and buy sheets from vendors on the street. We would have hot dogs at Katz's world-famous deli on Houston Street for lunch, and then dinner at a crowded family restaurant in Chinatown, and we would rave about them like we'd eaten at the Four Seasons. I remember an early lesson from Mom given in a novelty store in Chinatown. I said out loud, "Let's have Chinese for dinner." Once outside my mother said you should say "Chinese food," not just "Chinese," because that is the name of the people, not the cuisine. I understood that I had been rude; I didn't want to be, and I paid attention to what she said.

Gus wore dark glasses everywhere, even to the opera. At my sister's wedding, in my mother's first year of widowhood, she appeared in an emerald green strapless chiffon gown, and in all the photos she is wearing sunglasses and smoking a cigarette. I'm sure these emerald touches in my life helped me when I became disabled to see the exoticism in disability. I had become the "other," but I was determined to be an other with a feather boa and my own dark glasses. And because I had learned to laugh at anyone who looked down on us in our Mercury, I would eventually be able to laugh at people who looked down on me in my wheelchair.

My sister Chick lent her own air of "You Can't Take It with You" to my life. Hers is a charming eccentricity, warm and generous. In the ups and downs of our lives, we have more often than not been good friends. In adolescence she was a needed ally. She is sixteen years older than I, and left home to go to college a couple of years after I was born. She lived with us only sporadically as I was growing up, but then when she married, her apartment was my home away from home. Now we are closer than ever. We go to the gym together twice a week, vying for who will wear the floppiest, most frayed, and most unlikely outfits. We swim, but in different lanes, otherwise we would gab the whole time about our family and friends. We save that for the bus ride home.

Chick is given to weaving stories about the mundane and critical events in her day that loop around and through many subplots and minor characters' lives, and then, when you least expect it, will loop back to the main plot and carry the tale along to its tidy conclusion. The stories are fancifully told, and she has an eye and ear for colorful detail.

Her philosophy of life can be summed up in three of her favorite sayings. I was fortunate to have learned them when I was young and to recognize their utility in my disabled state. For instance, "If you can't convince 'em, confuse 'em" and "Public opinion no longer bothers me" served me well, particularly in the early years when I was given to bouts of shame and fear. When people didn't pay attention to me or take me seriously, I might say something implausible or outrageous to throw them off guard. Having gotten their attention and tripped them up a bit, I didn't care as much that I had been ignored. When one of my feet went into spasm, making my leg jump about and setting table tops or coffee cups in motion, I could conjure up a vision of my sister holding her head aloft, closing her eyelids halfway and pronouncing her indifference to the judgments of others. The third famous Chick saying was ultimately the most useful: "Don't let the bastards grind you down."

Chick had a handle on the social-justice issues from the beginning. When I was first able to leave the rehab center and we would go over to Second Avenue to find a place to have lunch, she declared her offense at being shut out of places that were inaccessible to wheelchair users. This wouldn't be a source of shame for our family, this was an outrage, an injustice. She felt this viscerally and transmitted to me how unacceptable it was that THEY didn't have a ramp, or a bathroom I could use. There was something wrong with THEM, not me. It was a position that would take me years to fully comprehend and assimilate, but it was a stance that I could at least outwardly adopt.

As I was growing up, my sister helped me to understand my mother's potency and find humor in the way that the world seemed to go along with her.

One time, a year or so after the accident, we went together to the local bakery where my family had always shopped. Nettie, one of the women in crisp pink uniforms who seemed to live behind the display cases, greeted us when we came in the door. She cast sad eyes at me, and said, "Ah, my dear," but rustled up a big smile and offered us each a cookie. My favorite. The square cookie with pink, green, and white stripes of marzipan surrounded by a chocolate border.

Nettie asked, with hushed voice, "So how is your mother?" We responded that she was fine. "What a mother you have," she said. We silently nodded our agreement. My mother was held in high esteem in the bakery, because she regularly called in huge orders—three rye breads with caraway seeds, four raisin pumpernickel, a dozen bagels, four pounds of rugeluch, two babkas etc., etc.—and also because every Friday she would send one of these orders to my grandmother in the Bronx. The women at the bakery thought Mom was a saint because she brought such a large quantity of baked goods to her aging mother. My grandmother, like my mother, fed everybody in sight, the immediate family and neighbors up and down her block, but barely ate any of it herself. Mom usually sent Avery to pick up the orders, and deliver them to friends and family around the city, or pack them to ship to our cousins in North Carolina. When Mom went into the bakery, all the pink ladies would flutter about packing everything up and making sure it was all done just right.

When my sister stopped at the bakery a few days after our visit, Nettie, without even saying hello, said to Chick: "That was your sister, right?"

"Yes."

"So what happened to her?"

Chick, making every effort to appear casual and not wanting to get stuck in a position where she would have to reveal more than she wanted to, said, "Oh, she was in an accident."

Nettie didn't stop. "How?"

"In a car," Chick said.

Nettie threw her hands up in the air and in a very loud voice exclaimed, "You see what I mean!"

That line, "You see what I mean," can always send Chick and me into fits of laughter. It came out of left field, and we are still not entirely certain what she meant. We use it to comment on any ridiculous situation or just to make each other laugh. When my sister first told me the story, right after it happened, she was showing me how to find humor in all the catastrophizing about my injury.

There was something else that Chick offered, although I didn't fully understand it until many years later. She refused to accept the unspoken rehab ethos that walking was the *only* really successful outcome to this long-term hospitalization and intensive therapy. It was implied that everything else was a compromise. In the early hours and days after a spinal cord injury, the usual question the family asks the doctor is will she/he live? Then, once that is clear, the question is, "Will she ever walk?" It is totally understandable that families and friends ask that, and fear the answer is no—for so many reasons, not the least of which is that they probably never knew anyone who had a good life that didn't include walking. But my sister saw me, saw the wheelchair, and felt optimistic about my life in a way that it would take others around me several years to feel. Chick hated seeing me in pain or scared, but she could imagine me in this life and for her it wasn't a compromised life.

Later, after I had sat in this seat for a while and gained some perspective, my sister taught me other lessons. She had become interested in disability issues before I became disabled. She is a writer and was putting the finishing touches on a book called *Help for the Handicapped Child* at the time of my accident. As my family was struggling to get information that would help me, she was simultaneously reviewing the galleys of a book that gave parents the kind of information that would help them negotiate difficult systems. She remained interested in disabled people's lives and well-being and participated in disability rights demonstrations in Washington a few years before I began to do so. In 1986, she published *No Apologies: Making It with a Disability,* a book ahead of its time. She interviewed disabled people and compiled that material into a beautiful book filled with pictures and words of people often not seen or heard from.

Chick is my connection to my father. He died when I was eight, and since Chick is older, she had more time with him. Our father is just a memory for me, rather than a real figure in my life, and she has helped me fill in the blanks with old stories. In photos he is often smiling and is always handsome in a 1940s movie-actor way, his hair parted on the side and slicked back with a little wave in the front, and a prominent cleft in his chin. In my favorite picture of him he is kneeling, resting both his hands on his left knee. He is wearing saddle shoes. When I was young, I made up names for what I would call him if he were there. I had daydreams and night dreams about him. Somehow he would return, using a mysterious route, explaining his absence in a perfectly plausible way.

But he didn't, and so it was just me and my mother. It was a time when most of my peers lived in intact families, with siblings, with mothers who stayed home and daddies who went to work every day.

David grew up in rural western Pennsylvania with his mother and father, and his brother Bill. He received an undergraduate degree and a master's from a state college not far from his hometown. He was raised a conservative Baptist and in college, in 1960, campaigned with other Young Republicans for Richard Nixon. He began his career as a high school English teacher, and married a woman he met in college. When I met him, his father had recently died, he had been divorced, and he was living in Brooklyn and working on a Ph.D. at New York University in communications theory. At N.Y.U. he led a group of graduate students on a study tour of Cuba. He was a union officer and strike leader in the school district on Long Island where he was teaching, and was an early supporter of Jesse Jackson. He had traveled a long distance to get there.

At our wedding, our families and friends came from many places to join us in what was the greatest party I've ever been to. For our entrance music, we played Al Jolson singing "The Bells Are Ringin' for Me and My Gal," and at the ceremony's end, as we went back down the aisle, I plucked rose petals from a pink silk sack tied to my wheelchair and showered them on the guests, while we listened to Jolson's "Sittin' on Top of the World" (just rolling along).

Our mothers were very different people, but during the ceremony they sat side by side, holding hands. David's mom was a nurse who had been born, lived most of her life, and then died in the house built by her parents in their small Pennsylvania coal-mining town. My mother had been raised in various Bronx enclaves of immigrant Jews, stayed on in the Bronx for almost twenty years after she married, and then moved with my father to Manhattan when I was three. At the time of my wedding, Mom was living in an apartment overlooking Central Park, and that was where, three years later, she died. Our mothers were both happy for us, and both were relieved, each for her own reasons.

When David and I first called our mothers to announce our wedding plans, each expressed joy, and love for her new daughter/son-in-law. Afterward, as we heard later, my mother called David's mom, and asked in so many words whether it was OK with her that David would be marrying me—my mother was worried that she would not want her son marrying a disabled woman. I had the sense that for David's mother, my disability was irrelevant. She was a devout Baptist, and was just relieved that we were getting married and would no longer be living in sin. Our mothers and other family members never expressed any concern that we were of different religious backgrounds. Neither David nor I have an interest in religion, and there were few expectations that that would change.

My extended family welcomed David with open arms. The only test they put him to, he passed with flying colors. It was the first time they met him, back in 1979. We had all gathered for the birthday of my cousin Alan at a restaurant in New York. There were about twenty of us sitting at a long table. Harry, Alan's brother, had ordered the wine and, as an inside joke, chosen something from the Simi Winery in California. When the first bottle arrived, Harry instructed the waiter to take it down to the other end of the table, to make sure the gentleman saw the "Simi" label, and have David be the one to taste the wine. Everyone got quiet at the table as the waiter poured and David slowly held his glass up, sniffed the Cabernet, took a long sip, and, knowing he had everyone's attention at that point, took another. He raised his glass and, in a reverential tone, with full appreciation of both the drama and the humor in the moment, proclaimed: "Great body!"

8   *I Sing My Body Electric*

David's toast to my "great body" fleshed out our love. A public dec-laration of my body's appeal in front of the most important people in my life, it sealed my cousins' affection for him and had a marvelous effect on this body that he loves. An effect very much like the moment, just a few months before that, when I rolled out on the dance floor at Glenn and Myrna's party and saw how happy David was to see me there.

I had much to tell him about my body. Its history. Not just what had happened *to* it, but what my body had yielded me. For instance, it had been instrumental in two encounters with celebrity, something I thought David should know about. It could only, I reasoned, enhance my appeal.

On an early date with David, I mentioned that when I was sixteen, Salvador Dali swept up behind me at a cocktail party and goosed me. I did not, however, divulge exactly how my body gained entry to the party where I received his attention.

My friend Lucy and I were both in our junior year of high school, and fancied ourselves very sophisticated. Lucy called me to say that she had met a man at her drama school, an older man, and that he and a friend wanted two glamorous young women to escort to a fancy evening on the town. She was assured, in some form of coded message, that there was to be no sex involved. I immediately agreed, provided some elaborately crafted lie to my mother, and packed my red silk sleeveless "special-occasion" dress and black patent-leather high heels into a suitcase. I had to sneak it out the door when my mother wasn't looking.

The evening began at the New York Yacht Club, where I drank

champagne (the red dress made me look at least eighteen, or so the waiter and I must have thought) and mingled with the elite. Someone pointed out Dali standing alone behind a tall carved pillar on a darkened balcony that surrounded the room. He stealthily moved from pillar to pillar, and as he bounded from one to the other he swirled his black silk cape in front of his face, lest he be revealed to the crowd below. I thought he was sneaking looks at me from his hiding place, but it was hard to tell, and I didn't want to get caught staring.

At some point when I had all but forgotten him, I felt my bottom pinched, and whirled around to see the black cape disappear in the crowd.

That gave me instant celebrity status, and as our group headed out to dinner at the King Cole Room at the St. Regis Hotel, there were many jokes about my "surreal" experience, and speculation about how I might appear in his next painting. A few hours later the group wound up in a discotheque, a dark cave of a room, with deep booths around a tiny dance floor. Lucy and I danced with everyone in sight. Our two gray-haired escorts, dressed in matching blue suits, sat together on the velvet banquette, saying they preferred to watch.

At three A.M. Lucy and I found ourselves at an all-night coffee shop where we were stranded until morning, having each told our mother that we were sleeping at the other's house. Despite our push-up bras and pointy-toed high heels, I am sure we looked like two bedraggled kids.

I told David that back in 1970, when I was a young, nondisabled hippie chick, albeit a married hippie chick, I usually wore either miniskirts or tight jeans. I would have denied any desire to allure men, as I was faithful to John and I wished to appear loyal—although not necessarily proper.

In those days, I was often torn between competing impulses—to be a "good" wife or to be a frisky girl. Although I knew how to buy a week's supply of groceries for fifteen dollars, and was adept at jockeying for machines at the local Laundromat, I realized that at twenty-two I had almost forgotten how to flirt.

I was aware, though, of my bare advantage, and of its usefulness. I donned my miniest skirt and most outrageous orange platform shoes when my old friend Lucy came to town and said she thought she could get us backstage at the Jimi Hendrix concert at the Boston Garden. It was a long shot, she said; she knew the drummer, Mitch Mitchell, but wasn't sure we would be able to get in, and we would definitely not be able to bring our husbands (Lucy was also a young bride). We dressed with great care, hitched to downtown Boston, and waited our turn outside the backstage door of the Garden with many other young hopefuls (none, probably, domesticated housewives like us) until the team of Jimi's bouncers could check us out. Lucy gave our names, and the big bruiser at the door checked his list. We were on it, but it was a long list, so a decision had to be made whether to let us in. The men behind the door looked us up and down, and after a long huddle, with finger-pointing and much guffawing, they admitted us to the long hall that led to the band's dressing room.

As our two designated escorts led us down the hall, there was small talk about where we were from, and serious talk about what we were doing after the show. We gave nothing away, but flirted like crazy, as one of the chaps hinted that he might be able to get us front-row seats.

Jimi's dressing room was the Boston Celtics' locker room. I had expected something glamorous, with couches and bouquets of flowers. But as I entered the cinder-block sweat house, the man himself was standing there, his halo of black hair floating around his head and his lean body sheathed in a purple haze of suede. Sliding down the inside facet of his sleeves was long fringe in Day-Glo colors that swept the floor as he moved forward to greet us.

I didn't go limp, but stood tall on my long legs and extended my hand to him. He bypassed my hand, took hold of my shoulders, and leaned in to kiss my right cheek. His full lips lingered on my face, and he whispered something to me I couldn't hear. I have washed that cheek since then, but always reluctantly.

David was witness to this body's next rock-and-roll adventure.

Some twelve years after my Jimi Hendrix Experience, James Brown kissed my left cheek. It was 1982, and David and I were graduate students at New York University attending a concert on campus. I was, once again, a married woman, but this time had David right next to me.

We were brought into the auditorium before everyone else, because wheelchair users had to take the service elevator, and the theater manager let us in through a special locked door. We also sat in the front row, not because I had flirted with the staff, but because that was the only wheelchair location. My spot allowed me, once the concert had heated up and people began to surge forward, to muscle my way up to the front. David was right behind me. I positioned myself at the feet of the hardest-working man in show business.

It was a great concert, one of those that go on and on. People were dancing in the aisles. Mr. B. had moved downstage to meet the crowd clustered below him. He grabbed the mike placed at the edge of the stage. He was standing just above my head. His lips almost touching the shiny metal, he began in a slow, deep rumble: "Please! Please! Please!" I thrust my arms in the air and swayed with the crowd. He looked down and saw me there. In an instant, he let go of the mike, and it rocked back and forth on its stand as he jumped off the stage. The crowd parted as he moved toward me. Mr. Brown arrived in front of me and I looked up at his wide-open face, perfectly coiffed hair, and his teeth, I remember lots of white teeth. He leaned over, just a tad, his sweat raining down on my face, and shouted in that famous James Brown screech, "You havin' a good time?" I squealed back, "I'm havin' a great time!"

He planted a wet, juicy kiss on my left cheek, jumped back up on the stage, steadied the mike, and went on with the song. The band never skipped a beat.

My left cheek was now sanctified, by the Godfather of *my* soul.

James's question, "You havin' a good time?" was rhetorical—he knew I was. He wasn't worried about the poor handicapped girl at his feet, he was reveling in me, and I did not feel patronized or demeaned, I felt welcomed. Jimi's kiss, too, had been welcoming, and I felt like a woman standing there, not an insignificant groupie.

At the Jimi Hendrix concert, after our visit with the band in the dressing room, Lucy and I did get escorted to front-row seats along with the other VIPs, although afterward we slipped away, leaving our bodyguards in the lurch, and went home to tell our husbands about our fabulous night.

Both James and Jimi changed their clothes before coming on stage. David and I had a private viewing of James before the concert as he and the band came on stage for a sound check before the auditorium's main doors were opened. We were the only ones to see him in his day clothes—an elegant tan silk tailored suit. For his performance, Mr. Brown wore black silk pants with a contrasting band of shiny satin going down his leg. His steel gray cutaway jacket had spangles on the lapels. Jimi abandoned the suede jumpsuit with the fringe of many colors after Lucy and I left the dressing room, and donned a long black jacket that flared at the waist, like a pirate captain's coat, with stripes of gold braid on the cuffs. Underneath, a flowered shirt was unbuttoned to his waist, so I could see his smooth chest every time he lifted his guitar up close to his face to find and hold a particular note for a long, slow metallic wail.

I don't remember what I was wearing the night of the James Brown concert. It was not a miniskirt, I had stopped wearing them after the accident. I did wear short skirts sometimes, but not ones that might, in my seated position, reveal underpants and the tops of my thighs. Whatever I did wear, I assume it was racy. I have retained that impulse, and now more readily take pleasure in its impact.

It was, at both these concerts, my body that gained me entry to these blessings. Jimi's henchmen reviewed my body, its sportiness and promise, and gave me leave to enter the inner sanctum. It was this body, or more likely the wheelchair that signaled how this body functions, that got me into the James Brown concert early, positioned me in the front row, and it was surely this body that prompted James to jump from his stage and confirm that I was pleased by his "Please!"

Yet my body wasn't only instrumental in these events. In its receipt of the kisses and its glow in their aftermath, it also gave me pleasure. And while the young, lithe, nondisabled body is so often depicted as inherently pleasurable, the disabled body rarely is.

As wondrous as these experiences were, they didn't completely surprise me. I learned in my teens how I could parlay the physical charms of my body to gain favors for all of me. When I was young, I didn't know enough to be afraid of objectification. I convinced myself that whatever slights I experienced by the whistles of men on the street, the leering at the beach, or the come-ons of men much older than myself were flattering, even when they felt unpleasant. I sought men who ogled me, rather than seeking out boys and then men I found appealing. When I met John, at eighteen, I had recently ended a relationship with a thirty-seven-year-old married man. John didn't ogle, we laughed a lot together, and we talked about politics and people we met. In some ways, it was a relief to be married and to be faithful.

Even as a novice disabled person I understood the (mostly negative) consequences of being seen as "woman-in-wheelchair." It was probably because I had a great deal of prior experience writing off disabled bodies that I knew that few people would see Simi as *Simi*. I knew how prominent *Simi* had to be—assertive, imposing—to be seen. In the early years with disability, when shame and denial were at their peak, I doubted that people would pay attention to the *me* in the wheelchair. When I got certain favors—such as exemption from waiting in line at a movie theater or a reduced-price ticket at the box office—I resisted them because I felt so conspicuous and exceptional. It didn't seem like an accommodation, it seemed I was being patronized.

The first time I was reasonably comfortable with using my disabled body to gain favors was the time in Berkeley when I was traveling with the street theater group. I was always the one to pass the hat after the performance, because we all recognized how such a spectacle would stimulate people's charitable impulses. It was a conscious decision. In the years since, other such decisions have rested on the degree of pleasure gained and the degree of compromise necessary to accept such favors.

Now, at fifty-something, my body remains an icon to many and the site of much pleasure for me. A couple of years ago, David was standing at a bar, the Pog Mahones Irish Bar, in a small resort town in the south of New Zealand, and he struck up a conversation with the drummer of a local rock band. The young man was impressed that we were from the United States, a place he held in high esteem, and as New Yorkers we were even more exotic, but David really scored points when he revealed the rock-and-roll history of my cheeks.

The lad went back to the bandstand, where the group was preparing for their next set. There was whispering, and nodding in my direction, and soon the entire band was lined up to kiss the shrine(s). The bass player, long a fan of American R & B, chose the left cheek. The younger guitar player, very much into the recent Jimi revival, decided on the right. The poor drummer was beside himself with indecision and seemed so relieved when I granted him dispensation to kiss both sides. We treated each of the charming, talented, and handsome Stoutfellows, named for their love of Guinness, to a round of their favorite brew, and they began the second set with an original song, dedicating it to their new American friends.

9 *What I Learned*

I have become a disabled woman over time. I certainly would have rejected such a title in the beginning. It could precipitate my death. Consign me to an itty-bitty life.

And I was never a joiner. I would have been describing myself as part of that group—the ones whose lives are measured out by others.

It took many people to bring me into the fold. To help me move toward disability, carrying myself in the upright posture of a newly enfranchised citizen. My advancement was due to other disabled people and, significantly, to the times we were living in.

I came of age as a disabled person as the disability rights movement was evolving into a recognized political entity. In the years from 1971, when I left rehab, to the present moment, I have witnessed the passage of legislation aimed at integration and equity in education and employment, and the emergence of many disabled people from sheltered dwellings and workplaces. In recent years, I've observed the backlash against that legislation and the people who fought for it.

This new cadre of disabled people has come out of those special rooms set aside just for us. Casting off our drab institutional garb, we now don garments tailored for work and play, love and sport. Indeed, as an indicator of our new social standing, the high-toned among us even appear in television commercials wearing such finery.

While many of us have obvious disabilities—we wield that white cane or ride that wheelchair or limp that limp—we don't all necessarily, as I didn't in my early years, ally with the group. And all the others, those whose characteristics are more easily masked, come to the surface even more gradually, determining how, when, and to whom to declare their membership.

For me and other disabled people, the process of claiming disability as an identity and the disabled community as our own is complex. I crept toward it, then skittered away. I remained for a long time an eavesdropper, a peeper.

In that first year after the accident, there was so much to learn. Ostensibly we were at the rehab center to learn to use our changed bodies. To strengthen the muscles we could use and to adjust psychologically to our new states. This was aided by the rigorous program of physical and occupational therapy, and the sessions with psychologists and social workers. That covered the curriculum of this institution. But there was another curriculum we needed access to—we needed the tools and knowledge that experienced disabled people have. We were novices, and we needed to learn how to get better at being what we now were. Where do you find the motivation to get better at being "disabled"? What does that mean?

Whom could we learn from? Was it the doctors, physical therapists, and nurses who tend to refer to all disabled people, whether in their care or not, as patients? Was it our family and friends, probably even more ignorant than we were of the ways of this new world, and many still in despair that they couldn't have us back the way we were before? It was, of course, our fellow travelers, but the only ones we had access to were maybe a month or two ahead of us in the game.

It was clear from our experience inside the rehab world that people like us were not in charge. It was clear from our memory of the outside world, and from our few forays beyond the walls of the institute on day passes, that people like us were largely invisible.

It is not surprising then that when I first came back out into the world using a wheelchair, I sought to minimize the outward signs of my impairment, and to downplay its significance. This encumbrance, this paraplegia, would not weigh me down, and the social role assigned to me would not script my life. Afraid of being engulfed, made invisible by the label, I sought to maintain as much of my individual identity and as much of my former lifestyle as possible. While there is merit in the impulse to be active and to think of oneself as an individual, I mistakenly thought that alliance with the group would be my downfall, that it would consign me to perpetual group-travel, all of us strapped down in the "Invalid Coach," bumping along Second Avenue on the way to see our rehab counselors.

So, in those early years, I tended to describe the disability elements of my life primarily as the results of an event that occurred in one moment in time, "I was in an accident," and to present my current situation in the most concrete way, "I'm in a wheelchair."

During my initiation at the rehab center I only hung out with the young people with mobility impairments. We avoided the other major cohort, the older people who had had strokes. I tentatively grouped myself with my buddies, yet I don't think we had a word for ourselves. I rejected the more inclusive term of the '70s, "handicapped," used to describe either the individual, as in "she or he is handicapped," or the group, "the handicapped." There was something static and absolute about that language. It was an institutional term, not one chosen to describe a neighbor or friend. If I were to say, "I am handicapped," I would be saying, I am one of them, not one of me.

So, whether catching up with an old friend, or responding to inquiries in social situations, or writing an autobiographical essay for my creative writing class, I spoke of the critical incident and the functional consequences, but said little about the ideas, still barely formed, buzzing in my head, about the social significance, the politics, the meaning of "handicap" and all the cultural uses of the image of disability seen around me.

When faced with intrusive inquiries from strangers that began, "What happened to you?" or "What's the matter with you?" I usually answered (and still do), "It's a long story," or "I was wounded in the Battle of the Bulge," and move away as quickly as possible. Sometimes it is hard not to answer. A long taxi ride, and the question asked in a concerned voice by a man who doesn't seem so much rude as mistaken. With only the bits of information I give—yes, an automobile accident; oh no, it was a long time ago; no, I wasn't driving; yes, too bad—the man will nod and commiserate and act as if he now knows what is important to know about disability—its genesis.

I did not yet have a precise language to describe the other parts of the disability experience—the kinds of obstacles or the intrusive people I encountered every day—nor had I found a way to talk about my new situation as a natural state, my wheelchair as a convenience, or my experiences in ways that would be interesting to anyone besides myself and a few like-minded people.

In the same way that I reduced my disabled state to its most elemental form, I was only able to talk about these encounters in the world as individual moments, isolated from one another. Although I sort of understood that there were connections among them, and I knew that other people encountered similar impediments, it was hard to see the pattern. And it was harder still to fathom the root cause of the problems we were faced with.

In the beginning, of course, the accident was still fresh and its relation to my current state the clearest, so it is understandable that I would present that as explanation. Yet even if I had been further along in my personal history with disability, in the early '70s there was little I could read that would help me frame my experience in a different way. And even ten years later, I had not found a community like the one I encountered on the West Coast. I wish I had. I could have learned from them, and tried saying "cripple" out loud as I had begun to do there. It would be some time until I did. And even longer until I understood the many things that keep disabled people apart from one another.

I began to get wind of an entity called the disability rights movement in the mid-'70s, shortly before I went to Berkeley. But it wasn't until I went out there and saw the effects of activism and a new way of talking about disability that I became interested in it. I had not labeled the problems I'd been encountering at school or in getting around town as discrimination, but once I heard people talking about it that way it made perfect sense. After I came back East, I was hungry for any news as I knew it could be helpful to me. Yet I was only able to get vague information from people I met here and there.

I couldn't find anything about disability issues in the publications I looked at. The mainstream press had little. There was the occasional human-interest story that told a tragic tale and described the plucky determination of the "handicapped" man or woman, the "sufferer," the "victim" of some tragic condition. The story's main focus was on what had already happened—the cause of the injury or condition. The agonizing birth, the catastrophic accident, or the family medical history. Yet to uplift us, to reassure us, the article would somehow demonstrate the triumph of the human spirit. We might be told of a young woman's or man's resolve to walk again one day, or of a woman "confined," as they would say, to a wheelchair, sewing aprons at home, and feeling good that she could contribute something. Another story would tell us of someone who had achieved something seemingly extraordinary—going to college, becoming a lawyer—accomplishments it would appear were reserved for more robust people. The story inevitably included the word "despite . . . ," followed by the name of the individual's condition, in the first sentence. We would also be told, implausibly, that the successful woman or man had "overcome disability."

By focusing our attention on the individual and eliciting sympathy or awe, these articles diverted us from thinking about how to change social conditions. There were no comments on the discrimination these people faced or the lack of transportation; instead the people interviewed were asked if they missed all the things they used to do. The articles didn't mention how federal monies dispensed to disabled people came with a set of conditions that made it impossible to go to work without losing needed health benefits. Instead these "news" items extolled the virtues of charitable contributions, both for the redemptive benefits to the giver, and for the salve they offered the givee. The people profiled were saddened, yet brave. No one was too angry. The papers would not display an angry cripple. They would neither burden us with the specter of an embittered man enraged at his fate, nor ask us to tolerate the rants of an activist who might expose problematic public policy or a corrupt state agency.

Some of the more progressive newspapers might give us a taste of this, but it was usually done to demonstrate how U.S. policy in Vietnam had damaged so many lives and how the government was not doing anything to help disabled vets. That was the story told in the films *Coming Home, The Deer Hunter,* and *Born on the Fourth of July.* Disability and death were portrayed as the costs, the effects, of foreign policy. In this way, journalists and filmmakers used disability without ever explaining it. The articles did not include the long history of such neglect, and the ongoing discrimination faced by all disabled citizens, not only the vets. They used disability as a metaphor to symbolize something terrible, but failed to depict the terrible things done *to* us.

Few of my college classes contained a word about disability. That didn't surprise me, nor did it bother me at the time. I was in college to get a solid liberal arts education—learning about disability would provide a marginal education, the type that would only prepare me to work in rehabilitation institutions or special education. The disability activism and pending legislation I would occasionally hear about outside the college seemed at the time to relate to practical matters, such as curb cuts and accessible transportation, not the sort of things you study. The significance of these changes seemed only for disabled people—for our comfort and convenience. College was a place of ideas, theory, metaphor, the history of important people and events. While I knew that these practical solutions could make a world of difference in some people's lives, it took a while till I saw their relationship to the study of history, anthropology, psychology, political science, and even longer till I made the connections to literature and to the arts.

As it is for most students, I guess, the college curriculum initially appeared to me as a natural formation. This is what there is to know. I took issue with many things, of course. For instance, I mistrusted most forms of empirical research and laughed at the notion that the two-party political system offered real choice in contemporary America, but I somehow accepted the idea that there was such a thing as The Curriculum. I didn't really know what women's studies or African-American studies were until I was almost through with my undergraduate work, and it would take more years for me to understand their significance. I fancied myself a pretty sophisticated commentator on racial politics in America, and I had a great deal to say about how few black students there were at both the New School and Columbia, and how the faculty was predominantly white and male. I can't remember, though, if it registered how closely the scholarship we studied matched the profiles of the faculty.

It wasn't until I became a professor myself that I noted that disabled people were rarely represented on the faculty. I could by then point out the impediments, the types of discrimination experienced, and the history of oppression that precluded so many disabled people from earning doctorates and getting teaching positions. I would later, in 1998, write a book examining how knowledge about disability is presented in the academic curriculum.

So much receded into the background and went unnoticed. At first, I even experienced the inaccessible classrooms as part of the natural landscape, like trees or rocks. It didn't dawn on me that steps or the width of a doorway were results of decisions made by people who didn't have my best interests in mind. The decisions they made were a sorting system; we let some in, we keep *you* out.

After I came back from Berkeley in 1975, things started to change, and by my last year at Columbia I scrutinized everything. When disability wasn't mentioned in class, I brought it up. Of course, I had a limited range of things to say, I was figuring it all out as I went along. I saw too that most of my professors and fellow students found these inquiries irrelevant, or particular to me and of little use to them, and that inhibited me. There were a few professors who encouraged me to do papers and research with a disability focus. They readily admitted they knew little about the things I wanted to explore, and when we found how few resources there were to draw on, their interest wavered.

It may seem strange that it was hard to find research on disability, but the material I found was almost exclusively in the rehabilitation or special education journals. This material focused on what to do to and for individuals. Once I began to think about ideas that now seem very basic to me (for instance, that there is a complex history to the societal response to disabled people, or that ideas about disability govern how characters are rendered in fiction and drama) I couldn't be content to study how to "fix" people and give them a "special" education. A few of the texts we were assigned in social science courses did discuss disability, but the topic appeared exclusively in chapters on abnormal psychology, or it was classified as "deviance" in sociology. With increasing confidence, I rejected these characterizations of my experience.

Questions floated around in my head, but I could never latch onto an answer. Are there countries in which infanticide is still practiced, and if so on which children? Are economic or mystical beliefs given as reasons? Are those cultures more accepting of infanticide based on disability than on gender? Do sociology professors view institutionalization of people with disabilities as a rational practice to protect a vulnerable population, or is it understood as a discriminatory practice? Is there research on disabled people that is actually conducted by disabled people? What functions do disabled characters serve in the novels we were reading in my English and French literature courses, or the films seen in my film course? Why are those characters so often sad or peculiar? These things were never discussed in class.

One of my psychology professors at Columbia was disabled, and he offered to supervise an independent study. We set up, but never carried out, a research project on health professionals' attitudes about disabled people. At our meetings, we would start off talking about my research, but inevitably we wound up sharing our feelings about the bleak picture painted by most theorists of disabled people's diminished capacity for psychological development and fulfillment.

It was in my last semester at Columbia that I took the course in women's studies in the psychology department at Barnard, the women's college across the street, and conducted the interviews with disabled women. I began to tie together the two seemingly disparate domains—scholarship and personal experience. I don't think I had yet heard the phrase "the personal is the political," and I had certainly not encountered the more comprehensive idea that the personal is not only the political but the scholarly as well.

The next year, 1977, I began a Ph.D. program in counseling psychology at New York University. Again, there was no mention of disability in any of my courses, and again I brought it into class discussion whenever possible. I was more convinced of its relevance by then, but still not very sophisticated or sure of myself. When I did raise questions, I was just responding to particular omissions, or errors in logic. I didn't have a framework to rely on that could provide an alternative to the depiction of disability in the curriculum.

I did latch onto the ideas and the language ushered in in the early '80s, known as "People First" language. If we use the term "people with disabilities," rather than "handicapped" or "disabled people," the reasoning goes, it emphasizes that we are people who happen to have disabilities, but that it's not our defining characteristic. It seemed logical at the time. I often embellished by saying "women and men with disabilities," particularly in my work in sex education, to point out how my description differed from the neuter term "the handicapped."

People First language served to minimize disability, keep it in its place. I think the idea was that if we sought to contain it, linguistically and theoretically, then the society would do that as well. This would facilitate integration and diminish discrimination. We would be seen more readily as whole, fully formed people with ideas and abilities, not just the weak who need care and services. Underlining our similarities would help erase our (all people's) differences and our (disabled people's) differentness.

Throughout graduate school I relied on this idea, and used it as the premise for the lectures and workshops I was giving on sexuality and disability. This was an idea that Glenn and I utilized when we did presentations together, that we are people who have, as only one of our attributes and often not the most significant one, a disability. When we addressed sex educators and counselors in general service, we emphasized the need to extend their practice to the entire community. We spoke of the similarities among people, and urged these professionals to use what they already knew to serve a broader range of people, adding specialized techniques and knowledge only where necessary. Yet despite our efforts, these professionals rarely went on to work with disabled people.

The omission of material on disability seemed particularly egregious in a doctoral program in counseling psychology. There were times that faculty members would actually say to me that if I was interested in working with disabled people I should be getting a degree in rehab. They didn't say it rudely or dismissively; they were merely echoing the idea perpetuated throughout the graduate and undergraduate curriculum that disability is a separator—its impact on people so unique, and the people who possess it affected in such specific ways, that only those specially trained in this area can work with us. I knew from my work with Sarah that this was not the case. Her understanding of my feelings of loss or my feelings of joy, or my irrational or clearheaded thoughts about my life as a disabled person, was not based on specialized training. She had none.

Shortly after completing my doctorate I got a full-time teaching job in the psychology department at Baruch College. I loved my three years teaching there and then the eleven years at Hunter. The students were wonderful, and I gained so much being with them. It seemed that no matter what was going on in my life, my outside world rarely intruded when I was in the classroom. I'm sure that my mood or fatigue got the best of me at times, but I was glad to be where I was.

At the beginning of my teaching career, I taught a range of general psychology courses, and in the last few years at Hunter, mostly graduate and undergraduate courses in child development in the teacher education program. I would bring disability subject matter into the classroom where I could, but I was rarely satisfied with my approach. Then, and even as late as 1997, the last year I taught full-time, the psych textbooks that I found rarely mentioned disability, or they presented it in a constricted way that only spoke of deficits or pathology. There was no social context, as was provided, although poorly, in discussions of race or gender. There was nothing to help students understand how particular physical, cognitive, sensory, and behavioral characteristics are interpreted and responded to. I would always add readings to my syllabus on disability and other relevant topics, but it often felt artificial, like I was appending something to an existing structure. I felt I had a limited impact on the way students were thinking about disability, or, for that matter, race, gender, or class. The multicultural/diversity movement was gaining attention by the late '80s, and I used some of that material in class, but almost all of the authors excluded disability from their analyses.

During the years from 1985, when I began teaching, until the early '90s, I let go of disability. Pushed away from it. I focused on teaching general psych courses, and conducting research in a serviceable domain, the sort that tenure committees might appreciate.

That changed when I encountered the field of disability studies. It is a social, political, cultural inquiry into disability, and functions very much like women's studies does to reframe the whole idea of "disability." Once I had learned about disability studies, it became, and has remained, the central focus of my work. I started to find answers for all those questions that had been buzzing in my head since I was an undergraduate.

In 1992 I began teaching a course that was supposed to be on social and psychological aspects of disability for prospective counselors. Over time, though, I broadened the scope of the course in order to offer a more comprehensive look at disability and, in a number of respects, a more fundamental one. The listed course was designed to teach students about how disabled people feel, what determines those needs and feelings, and how counselors can respond. The traditional approach in such courses was that it is the disability itself that causes an individual to think and behave in certain ways. Further, ostracism of disabled people was considered a natural response to something that reminded people of human vulnerability and mortality. Yet what

I felt students needed to talk about was how social structures, such as institutions, segregated special education and job discrimination bred antipathy and alienation.

By the last few years that I taught the course, I abandoned textbooks and drew on material in anthropology, film, philosophy, literary criticism, political science, and poetry, infusing it all with a strong social and political perspective. My students were assigned to watch movies such as *Coming Home, City Lights, The Men, Gattaca,* and *Twilight of the Golds.* We read poetry and accounts of infanticide of disabled infants in select cultures. Over time, it became a course in disability studies, grounded in the liberal arts.

It was around this time, somewhere in the early '90s, that I also began to use the term "disabled woman" to identify myself. I no longer said, "I am a woman with a disability"; instead I was likely to describe myself by forefronting disability. "I am a disabled woman," I would say, and then might explain to my students, "That means that I identify as a member of the minority group—disabled people—and that is a strong influence on my cultural make-up, who I am, and the way that I think."

In my years teaching, I'm sure my disability wasn't insignificant to students, but its significance seemed to have more to do with their wish to understand the meaning I put on it, rather than a need to impose their own. Maybe because we got to know each other in a context in which my role as teacher overshadowed my personal characteristics, they needed to focus first on whether my exams were hard and what I expected of them, rather than on why I use a wheelchair. I'm sure they were curious, and some were probably uncomfortable. I would talk about disability in class when it seemed right, although I rarely talked about the cause of my impairment—the medical condition and that history—but would readily discuss obstacles I'd encountered or experiences I'd had. What I said depended on which class or which group of students, as well as my mood.

In the courses I taught on disability, I did actively "use" my disability and talked more openly about my experience. I didn't start off with, and sometimes never mentioned, the reason I use a wheelchair, but when talking about the discrimination disabled people face, I would mention particular attitudes I'd encountered, obstacles to travel or access to the places I want and need to go and how that feels.

If someone asked me a direct question about my impairment, which they did sometimes, I answered it, but if I initiated the discussion, I was more likely to focus on my identity as a disabled woman, and my alliance with other disabled people and what that means to me. By the time we were talking about these things, I had already spent time critiquing the traditional view of disability: the idea that disability is a deficit, simply a medical condition best responded to in a medical context.

My focus in these courses was on the history of ideas about disability. What brings us to think about and respond to disabled people the way we do? Let's consider how the books we read, movies we watch, the news that is reported instruct us to think about disability. Let's look at how ideologies of the past continue to influence who is considered fit and who is not. For instance, have American notions of progress closed us off to the inevitability of human variation, fallibility, and imperfection? Did the advent of modernism make demands for certain kinds of rationality and order that privilege nondisabled people? Did that thinking influence the institutionalization and segregation of disabled people?

These were graduate students in counseling and rehab, mostly women, and anywhere from twenty-five to sixty years old. There were very few disabled students over the years, but they contributed a great deal to the class. There was usually a fair balance of African American, White, and Latino students and a smaller number of Asian Americans.

We talked a great deal about ostracism and segregation. As they were preparing to be counselors, we talked about how these experiences influence disabled people's sense of self-worth. But we would also talk about how ostracism is so often viewed as a natural, inevitable response to disability. It is said that disability makes nondisabled people anxious. Yet what is usually not discussed is whether those reactions really are inevitable. What situations allow those feelings to flourish? What is morally wrong with such ostracism, and what is undemocratic about such segregation? What can we do to change people's response, or show them it is unacceptable to act on such feelings? Can integrated communities, schools, and work environments alter such behavior?

It was often the students who made the connections among issues of race, gender, class, sexual orientation, and disability. Once I had proposed the idea that disability is best understood as a designation that has social and political significance, once we had explored the limitation of viewing disability simply as a medical category, they were off and running. I would say to them: If I want to go to vote or use the library, and these places are inaccessible, do I need a doctor or a lawyer? I might ask: What if Sandra—speaking of a student in the front row who is blind—was denied an accommodation by a professor? Let's say he or she refused to let her take an exam in a separate room with a reader. What good would a medical explanation of her blindness do for Sandra? The students easily recognized, and taught me a great deal about, how disability functions like race and gender to set people apart, to restrict opportunity, to designate certain social roles and obligations.

Those were exhilarating moments for me. The times when the ideas drove the class, not the procedure. I stopped lecturing, students stopped raising their hands to respond to a specific question, and I didn't need to call on anyone. They got heated up and argued, and went off on tangents, in wonderfully messy, chaotic exchanges that could sometimes bring me to the verge of tears.

I saw in those moments how big disability is, not the condition I or others have, but the elaborately constructed network of ideas and practices that keep disabled people in place. When the students shared my outrage, I felt at my most authoritative. What was important to me was, at least for that moment, important to them, and I had authority, not because I was the teacher and have a Ph.D., but because of my commitment to the position: "disabled woman."

I think, too, they could see that I had gotten to this place not by denying my disability or, implausibly, "overcoming" it, but by sailing headlong into it. Making sense of it had become the most meaningful thing I could do.

10 *Weddings and Marriages*

This is the story of three wonderful weddings and a hint of the marriages that followed.

The first is the wedding of two friends of David's from his roller skating circle. It took place at their favorite skating venue, the Roxy, a nightclub on Eighteenth Street off the Westside Highway.

David is an avid roller skater. He goes to the Roxy every Wednesday night, come hell or high water, and to the roller dance scene in Central Park whenever he can. There is little that will deter him from skating, and he has traveled to a number of the fifty states, and several countries in the world, carrying 20 percent of his weight in skate gear, in case there is opportunity to roll. His favorite mode of skating is on traditional "quad" skates, the two sets of side-by-side wheels below a black leather boot. He also often carries with him a pair of in-line skates for outdoor use.

In most places that he goes outside of his regular haunts, no one has seen his brand of skating before. It is not a straightforward path he rolls on. It is often a circuitous one, with dips and twirls. Imagine Michael Jackson's moonwalk on skates, or Mick Jagger's strut. Speed and distance are never the objective, funk is.

David's hair is long, and it is big. It curls and waves around his head and down his back. He wears a headband when skating, which only makes it flare out farther. His usual skate outfit pairs colorful pants with wide balloon legs and a tight tank top (in which, I should mention, he looks gorgeous). Once, at a rink in upstate New York, a meek, but frank, teenage girl came over to him and asked: "Aren't you 'shamed to skate like that?"

Friends from his roller skating circle are as zealous and outlandish as he is, and Lezly and Robbin are among the most committed. So, on a hot summer day David and I got into our 1984 white Cadillac El Dorado convertible and headed downtown. As we got near our turn onto Eighteenth Street, David pointed to the northbound side of the street, where, coming toward us, was the stretch limo that held the bridal party, escorted by a phalanx of Harley Davidsons. Thirty bikes, with Harley-size men and women on them, all from Robbin's brother's motorcycle club.

And it was those stalwarts who greeted us at the door and lifted me off the sun-baked sidewalk and up the long flight of stairs into the dark pleasure dome, lit by colored lights, and a spotlight aimed at the mirrored ball twirling over the large oval dance floor.

I had learned from David about the bride and groom, both star skaters at the Roxy. Robbin is a nurse, and her most recent job was treating young people with AIDS in their homes. She worked in tough neighborhoods and had to make house calls accompanied by a body-guard. She has a tough medical history herself. She has cystic fibrosis, and now in her forties has outlived every medical prediction handed her. Lezly, the groom, is a skate instructor and choreographer, and an elegant gentleman with a wicked sense of humor.

A colorful crowd was streaming in and taking their seats on the white folding chairs that were set up in rows on the polished wooden dance floor. Soon the lights dimmed. The ceremony began when the flower children rolled down the large center aisle to Michael Jackson's "Heal the World." Ten boys and girls, anywhere from six to twelve or so, all competent skaters. Half of the kids were Robbin's patients. They were followed by a sizable bridal party, women and men in elegant clothes, all created by an international dress designer, Elie Tahari—a fellow skater. Next, under an arch of purple balloons, came the rolling rabbi, and then four skaters each holding a pole of the huppah, the traditional Jewish wedding canopy that would be held over the couple as they took their vows.

Next was the best man, dressed in an elegant tuxedo. He was on skates of course, but carried a cane with a rubber tip, which he used to propel himself down the aisle. He clearly needed it, and leaned on it from time to time. I never got to see if he used it off skates.

And then Robbin, a medieval princess with her soft purple chiffon gown flowing behind her, followed by her courtly suitor in white tails with purple accessories. He wrapped his arm around her waist, and they waltzed out to the cheers of the crowd. We knew that Robbin had spent a good part of the past year in the hospital, fighting for her life, and the joy of this moment couldn't be silent.

The rabbi married these two lovebirds, joined them to each other, in all that is beautiful and whimsical about their life, and all that is harsh and painful.

After the ceremony and toasts, without being prompted to do so, the majority of the guests moved to the couches around the dance floor to put on their skates. A voice over the loudspeaker requested that everyone pick up the chair they'd been sitting on, fold it, and carry it to the back to be put away. That might be an awkward task for the novice rollerskater, but for this crew it was a cinch. Some picked up three or four at a time, snapped them shut, and, weaving in and out of the others, carried them to the back. The floor was cleared in minutes. I watched the skaters move chairs, climb steps to sit on the cozy velvet banquettes that surround the skate floor, carry their food and drinks across the room, and maneuver a baby stroller through the crowd. I almost said out loud, "My, you do that so well!"—the same words said so often to me by intrusive strangers as I carry out an ordinary task.

As the music began and people started to roll by around me I knew that I couldn't stay still and hang on the edges of this party. David, now on wheels too, grabbed my hand, and we began moving with the skaters that were circling the floor. The first song was kind of slow, and there weren't many people on the floor. We'd done this before, rolling along side by side in Central Park or on the boardwalk by the ocean, but never in such a big space with a great floor—smooth, no bumps. We went around a few times, the music picked up, more people came on the floor, and the pace quickened.

I let go of David's hand and went solo for a while, pushing faster and faster. As I picked up speed, I was sailing along, taking the curves, easing up as people entered the circle in front of me. I didn't realize what was making it so easy; my chair seemed to be moving on its own. I glanced back and saw that a lean, dark man with a gorgeous smile was pushing my chair. He must have been there for a while, but he hadn't interfered with my movement; he let me chart my own course, and just provided the extra juice to help me keep up with the skaters.

We rolled and rocked, going round and round and round again under the mirrored ball. Once, trying to avoid bumping into someone, I swerved to the left and my chair fell over, but he scooped me up, and quickly got us back on course. We couldn't be stopped.

Normally, I won't get out on a dance floor, in this case a skate floor, unless I feel comfortable with the crowd. I'm not sure what the elements were that spelled comfort to me in this place, but I was, throughout the day, both relaxed and excited. It may have been the age mix, or the racial mix—the skating community in New York is one of the most integrated I've ever seen. There appears to be an easy flow across groups; friends don't seem to cluster along age or race lines. A wide girth in a social circle gives plenty of room for me.

The master of ceremonies took the mike before the last skate, reminding all of us why we were there—to celebrate this joyous union. But he paid tribute to the event as well as to the marriage. "It is about skating and skaters," he told us, "and it is about these two people who met and fell in love on wheels. So, for people who roll on wheels and for people who hang out with those who roll on wheels, this is a beautiful day."

Some months later, when we were telling my cousin Alan about this wedding and mentioned that even the rabbi was on skates, he said, "Well, he must have been a reformed rabbi." "Maybe," said David, "but he was an orthodox skater."

Our friends' Barbara and Daniel's California wedding was filled with joy and love, dancing and celebration, and made remarkable by the fact that state and federal regulations are such that these two disabled people needed a waiver from the Social Security Administration in order to be able to marry and yet still receive the health benefits they relied on to keep them alive.

They secured the waiver, after years of protests and letter writing to state and federal agencies, and they did marry, but then, terribly, sadly, they died. Just two years after the wedding, Daniel died of an aggressive cancer that felled him within weeks of its discovery, and my dear Barbara just two weeks later, from an accident that quite literally took her breath away.

I had known Barbara for many years. In hard times and good times, but never as good as when she envisioned the promise of a life with Daniel. I wish everyone in the world had known her.

Barbara was elegant in appearance, maternal and nurturing with all her friends, but prone to talk dirty just to throw you off guard. She wore shoes that glowed in the dark on dainty feet with high arches. Her laughter would come out in soft waves; it wasn't shrill or staccato. I cherished her declarations of love for me, and the way she puckered her lips on the *p* in "Poopsie," her pet name for me.

We didn't get to see each other often, so when we did, we wanted to do everything, from the mundane to the special, to seal our love. We went on excursions to the beauty parlor together in her hometown of Tarzana, in the valley north of Los Angeles. We sat under adjacent hair dryers, having the same auburn dye baked into our bobbed hair. We ate tuna fish sandwiches and read passages from movie magazines to each other. And then we went back to her parents' house for a beautiful Friday-night dinner with Toby and Saul.

Barbara defied expectations. She would not live beyond thirty, they said. She would not have a full life. She would not go to college and hold a demanding job. She will / she won't / she will.

Her body became weaker over time. Spinal muscular atrophy will do that. Walking became less easy than riding, and so she rode a motorized chair, with a tall upholstered back. Over the years she added new levels of adaptive equipment to her arsenal. She put her mark on these tools, they didn't mark her. She affixed a portable respirator to her wheelchair. The breathing tube that came up from the back of her chair, where the store of oxygen is kept, was a long coil of clear plastic tubing, about an inch in diameter. It was a ribbed tube, and had at its tip a white plastic mouthpiece that looked like the stubby cigarette holders sold with cigarillos. Barbara would hold this mouthpiece between her lips, where it would hang at a rakish angle from the right side of her mouth. When she was ready to talk, which was often, she would whisk it out of her mouth with her thumb and forefinger and hold the tube off to the side. She would make her point—and declarative statements outnumbered questions or mere rambling by a goodly number—then return the tube to her mouth and take a long drink of air. Seated in repose in her luxe power chair, her head against the black leather cushioned back, Barbara resembled the Cheshire Cat pulling on his hookah.

The contented look on her face derived from her own certainty in the face of a complex moral or intellectual argument that might cause a more jelly-like creature to waver. In a crowded room she could make the seemingly offhand, but clearly calculated, comment that "Jack Kevorkian is a mass murderer," without troubling herself to add the cautionary prefix "I think" to her declaration.

Lest you misunderstand, this wasn't arrogance, but efficiency. There was simply too much work to do fighting for the most vulnerable, and Barbara would not waste your time or hers flopping about in moral pea soup when people were dying. She did, however, take more time than most crusaders do on makeup and clothing. I can see her now in a batik linen jacket, with kimono-type sleeves. Or in a bright, crisp red summer dress that set off her dark red hair. Her stunning hazel eyes were always outlined in black, her feathery lashes always coated with mascara. And then, of course, there were the shoes. Pumps with small heels in pink or green, or the ones with the leopard spots that she called her Pebbles shoes, named after the character in the *Flintstones*.

Barbara's life wasn't so much interrupted as punctuated by medical treatments and hospitalizations. Because she saw her life as a political act, lived outside the institutions society would shelter her in, and beyond the reach of the special education experts who were eager to stick her in their basements, each piece of her life was as deliberately focused on social change as any other. A trip to the hospital was an occasion for observation and intervention. "What," she asked, "is that procedure for?" "Let's look at my chart together and determine in what order the procedures should be done." "Patients can't see their charts, you say? Let's examine that policy." "How," she might have asked a young resident, "can you take a complete medical history without incorporating a sexual history?" "What is the hospital's policy on 'Do Not Resuscitate' orders?" "Have you examined the data on who is resuscitated and who is not, to assure that certain groups are not more vulnerable than others due to their gender, racial, economic, or disability characteristics?" And so forth.

Coming back home meant a return to work. Projects ranged from an initiative she authored and directed to make family-planning services in California fully accessible to women with disabilities, to the amendment she brought to Capitol Hill a few years ago in an effort to have disabled people added to the list of target groups included in the hate-crimes bill. And then there were the articles she wrote on sexuality, on violence against disabled women, and on prenatal testing and selective abortion.

Once she was home, she quickly returned to the kitchen. Poached salmon, fondue, little dumplings for the vegetable soup are pleasures she offered her guests. And, once they found each other, coming home meant a return to her beloved Daniel, a man as uncompromising as she philosophically, and as compromised as she medically. These were two people in love: a passionate Italian man, with a soft voice and dark curly hair, schooled in Ancient Greek philosophy and culture, and a smart-talking, intrepid vixen, who hailed from the legendary "Valley" north of Los Angeles.

They had wanted to marry for some time, but learned that if they did, the state would swipe from them the health benefits and Social Security Disability Income they relied on. It would have been difficult at that point in their lives to take full-time jobs to gain access to reliable health care, and they certainly could not afford private insurance even if they could secure it, given their medical conditions. Although they both worked very hard and accomplished a great deal, they were each prone to different, but equally dangerous, bouts of illness that would knock them about, take them out of the ring for periods of time. So they worked from home, Barbara on her projects and Daniel on his writing and activism.

There were few extravagances in their lives. They lived modestly, as Barbara was reliant on the fixed and very meager income allotted to her by the state, and Daniel did not earn much in his consulting work. In addition, Barbara and Daniel used the services of assistants to help them with their personal care, and these services are only partially paid for by the state of California.

When they decided to proceed with their marriage plans, they found lawyers willing to take on this complex case. They conducted research, they initiated a national letter-writing campaign to Donna Shalala, then the Secretary of Health and Human Services, and when it all seemed it would not work, they organized a sit-in at the Social Security Administration building.

It took years, and when they won, their unique prenuptial agreement was with the Social Security Administration, which finally agreed that their benefits would not be jeopardized by their marriage. Barbara and Daniel were at first reluctant to accept these terms as they were based on a special exemption for them, all others that came after them would still be denied, but they decided to proceed and to keep fighting for systemic changes in such policies. After they received the waiver, they quickly arranged a civil ceremony before any federal or state entity could renege on its promises. They continued to fight for changes in policy, and help other couples attempting to marry under these circumstances.

It was therefore on the occasion of Daniel and Barbara's second wedding—their real wedding—that we gathered in Los Angeles to celebrate. Our friend Corbett and her daughter Meecha came down from Berkeley; David and I, along with my sister Chick and my brother-in-law, flew out from New York; others came from near and far.

After so much that was difficult, their wedding was a joyous event. The late-afternoon sky was streaked with red and orange, as we all gathered on an outdoor terrace for the ceremony. The guests sat in a circle, three or four rows deep, around an open area set with two white chairs and a table holding a Bible and flowers. Over this area was an embroidered huppah.

The rabbi and rabbitzen, a husband-and-wife team who would officiate here, entered and sat in the two chairs, facing the path that Daniel and Barbara would follow to the huppah. Flower girls with baskets of rose petals came next. Meecha in her bright green wheelchair and her red sparkling shoes led the way, saying "whoosh, whoosh" as she flung handfuls of petals in the air.

I first began to cry when I saw Meecha. It was her delight in her role, her beautiful round face, and her assured place with the other children, the nondisabled ones, who pushed her chair and giggled with her as the procession went around the circle creating a petal carpet for the bride and groom. And then, there they came. Barbara in a dress that was a collage of colors and textures. The colors, all those of precious metals, copper, bronze, and gold. A tight-fitting satin bodice and scooped neck showed off her creamy skin and long graceful neck. The soft folds of the silk skirt flowed over her lap. Daniel was in an elegant dark olive green suit. They both wore, like crowns, short pill-box hats of gold brocade. Simple and artful. They proceeded down the aisle, side by side, Barbara in her tall motorized chair, and Daniel in his scooter, holding hands as they steered their chairs toward us. The crescendos of Lohengrin rose up into the sky, and all of us sat up tall, proud to be witnessing their commitment to each other, and their resistance to the forces that would keep them apart.

Woven throughout the ceremony was the tale of the struggle that Barbara and Daniel had to get to the altar. The rabbi had participated in the sit-in, spending the night camped out in front of the Social Security building, and he thanked the couple for the education gained in working with them.

Several people had been asked to speak after the ceremony. The testimony we gave was to Barbara and Daniel's endurance and vivacity, their purposefulness and playfulness. We blessed their union, and we cursed their oppressors. We championed their cause, and we decried those who would deny them happiness. And we spoke with delight of these two who had brought us all here and who had brought so much good to our lives.

After the ceremony, we all went inside for dinner. Round tables with colorful flowers were placed around a big dance floor. A rousing band played Klezmer music, and rock and roll.

There were two masters of ceremony—myself and a good friend, Paul Longmore. We introduced people who read poems, stories, and letters to Barbara and Daniel. Barbara's goddaughter gave us a dance recital. Many offered toasts. In between courses of our wonderful dinner, Paul and I kept the action flowing, and we all danced.

David and I, and my sister and brother-in-law, Chick and Dick, had planned a surprise event. We had brought with us long rolls of plastic bubble wrap, a case of light sticks, the tubes that glow in the dark when they are snapped and activated, and a tape of wild disco music. We commanded the stage, and had the lights turned all the way down. David and Dick rolled out the bubble wrap across the dance floor, and Chick and a team of confederates distributed the light sticks to the crowd. We then invited all people on wheels up to the dance floor. Corbett and Meecha, the bride and groom, and a bunch of other wheelers came forward as we pumped up the volume on the '80s disco hit "I Will Survive."

When wheelchair tires hit bubble wrap at full speed, the effect is of multiple firecrackers set off at once. The audience snapped their light sticks, and many spontaneously stood up on their chairs and waved the wands of pink, green, purple, and red in the air as we danced and popped down below.

Fireworks were a fitting celebration of the hard-won rights and liberties of Barbara and Daniel Fiduccia. This union was their Independence Day. That they didn't live longer is a loss to this nation. That this nation made it so hard for them to marry and live comfortably in the time they had is the shame of this nation.

The third wedding is David's and mine. It took place in December of 1981, on the coldest night of the year, in a health club on the top floor of a tall brick New York apartment building. Our invitation said "Bathing Suit Optional," and following the ceremony and dinner, many of the guests changed in the locker room and then jumped into the heated swimming pool, filled with rubber duckies and pool toys. Our wedding celebration set the tone for the marriage we would have.

It was a splashy party, and, as we were to learn in our life together, we love to give parties. This one was filled with family and friends, people who still remind us, nearly twenty-five years later, what a great day it was.

There were bumpy years to come, particularly the first few, as we strained against each other, and fought too much. But even in those times, we built the memories, the stories of the places and the people that make up our book, the lore of Simi and David. "Remember that woman who walked over to us in Central Park, sat down on the bench next to you, and said 'I have always been faithful to my husband' . . . the James Brown concert where he jumped off the stage and kissed you . . . the herd of somewhat tame, somewhat wild kangaroos on the beach in Australia that ate up all our crackers . . . the maitre d' in the restaurant in Florence who thought you were the attaché to the American embassy and treated us like royalty, until he found out he'd been 'misinformed'?"

We are proud of our stories, and we vie for center stage in the telling of them. It is not fancy clothes and the latest-model car that we crave, it is experience. And we milk those experiences again and again, performing them for any willing audience. We are both hams.

Maybe it was the potential for recountable adventures that motivated us to choose Cuba as our honeymoon spot. I can't remember which of us suggested it, but we were both eager. Ronald Reagan had just been elected president, but previously Carter had opened travel from the United States to Cuba, and Reagan had not yet had the opportunity to reverse that policy, so we were able to fly directly from Miami to Havana. We stayed in one of the former mafia resort hotels built by Meyer Lansky in the '50s, just before the revolution. We ate breakfast in the big dining room, selecting from the buffet of fresh fruit, biscuits, yogurt, and sweet bread. Our room looked out on the blue ocean, and you could get delicious rum drinks at the bar by the swimming pool. There were few other similarities to typical Caribbean resorts. Here, you weren't shut off from the rest of the island or the islanders. Cubans on holiday were as likely to be staying there as the Canadian and European tourists.

In Havana, where we spent most of our time, we wandered the streets, visited the university, attended a piano recital, ate in small family-run restaurants, browsed in bookstores, and drank rum in steamy, dimly lit bars.

This was early in our time together, and I was still self-conscious about the things I couldn't do. David had to find out what the meaning of my disability would be for him. How it would affect what we did together, and even what he did. Dancing, roller skating, a walk on the beach would be different now. Would I feel envious, would he feel guilty? Would he have to move only in my tracks? No. But neither of us fully understood this at the beginning. For instance, I didn't want to get on the dance floor at the famous Tropicana nightclub in Havana, and so David sat with me. I would probably do it now, or encourage him to dance with someone else.

Over time, we learned the tricks of my tricky body. How we could move together. I was more experienced in some ways. I had lived in this land a while. It was second nature to me. And I also knew the able body. He hadn't known a disabled one, and so he learned on me. I came fully equipped, just powered differently. We grew together. We grew more intimate. He followed my lead to an extent, but he never seemed a foreigner, maybe just a visitor from a neighboring town eager to learn his way around.

Now, many years later, we are a pair of seasoned travelers.

We have our petty irritations and our nagging issues. But, at the end of the day, we just love each other. And we comfort each other. As David well knows, the yearning in my life, the deepest sadness, is for my father. The catch in my throat, the sense of what is lost and can never be regained. Sometimes in my mind I conjure up a story, a made-up story, of David sick, dying, dead. He is gone and I am lost. My father died when I was so young, and then John died, and I am sometimes made sick by my fear that I will lose David too. I must will myself to stop, think of something else, glance over at David sitting on the couch, looking robust, doing the crossword puzzle.

Yet even in that, I have grown more relaxed. Although time is passing, it feels like there is more future, more travel and more stories.

Without a doubt, our favorite story is from our honeymoon. One day, we found ourselves, quite by chance, in the midst of a ceremony being held in the shell of a building near downtown Havana, a building that had been bombed years before by counter-revolutionary forces. We had been walking through a small park when we heard music coming from the street on the edge of the park. Without saying anything, we both started to move quickly toward the music. It was coming from inside a large elegant white building. The facade of the building did not tell us of the devastation inside. There were some steps going up to the entrance, and David ran up to see what was happening. He came right back and said, "Come, quickly," and he urgently pulled my chair up the steps.

We were to learn that the building we entered had been a theater in pre-revolutionary Cuba, but now, with no roof and crumbling ledges where balconies used to be, it was a virtual theater. Below us, on the ground where the stage had once stood, in front of the piles of rubble, a space had been cleared away and swept clean, and a magnificent corps de ballet was performing a dance from *Swan Lake*. With no roof to shield them, the afternoon sun was their stage lighting. Their orchestra was a tinny recording of the Tchaikovsky score, the music bleating through a few small speakers set into crevices in the wall behind their earthen stage.

That was the music that had drawn us to this place. It was the dancers that now captivated us. There was nothing rough or haphazard about their work. It was the finest classical dancing that money can buy. As the music built, their sky blue tutus fluttered around their thighs, their pink satin toe shoes kicked up dust, and they danced a passionate, poignant *Swan Lake.*

Standing around us, in every remaining niche and on every parapet of this once-theater, were Cuban people, many weeping, all leaning toward these young, hopeful women dancing for us. The beauties leapt, they soared, they twirled. Their strong legs carried them, and their arms, their swans' wings, fluttered up and down, up and down. Soon, it was over.

When the applause ended, as if on cue, everyone, including the dancers down below us, turned to look up at the highest ledge, to what had once been the second balcony, where an elegant woman stood, wearing dark glasses and holding in her arms a bouquet of red roses. She was bathed in sunlight. A man standing next to me tapped me on the shoulder, leaned down, and in a reverential whisper said, "Alonzo!"

It was Alicia Alonzo, the legendary Cuban ballerina, and the ceremony, as we later learned, was to honor her fifty-year career. This was the theater where she first appeared in the corps de ballet, where she first danced *Swan Lake,* and the Cubans dance on dirt to remember that history.

She is blind now, and held fast to the two young dancers at her side as she moved forward to the very edge of the landing. To thunderous applause, she plucked a rose from the bouquet and threw it down into the rubble below. She blew kisses to the crowd, and bowed gracefully to the dancers. There was more applause and cheers.

David and I pressed ourselves to the wall to get out of the way as people cautiously descended the crumbling stairs and moved out into the street. The stately Alonzo and her entourage moved silently past us.

When everyone had left the building, David climbed over the ledge of the balcony where we were, making his way down the tall pile of rocks and debris, and plucked Alonzo's rose to bring to me.

11 *Citizens in Good Standing*

I came upon the Society for Disability Studies (SDS) when I needed it most. I had lost track of disability in my professional life. Given it up. I was teaching other things and thought I could get on without it. There was no scholarship about disability that interested me. No one I met in academic circles who wanted to talk about disability with the eagerness and commitment that they were investing in discussions about race and gender. I tried to formulate ideas about the way disability might figure in our study of history, film, anthropology, psychology, or literature, but it was hard to develop a sustained argument or support a proposition. I had to piece together bits of ideas I was picking up here and there. The bits slipped about, and I couldn't hold them together. To keep my job at Hunter College, I did have to publish scholarly articles, and so I drummed up some other projects, got a couple of grants, and did what I was supposed to.

It was May of 1990 when I spotted an announcement for the SDS annual conference and immediately made plans to go to California, though I didn't know what disability studies was, and knew no one in the organization.

This SDS has, not coincidentally, the same initials as the '60s radical activist group, Students for a Democratic Society. While our SDS does count among its members women and men schooled in the earlier political tradition, and does harbor at least one known Weatherman, this organization has disability at its center.

I found coherence there. A train of thought. A stream of consciousness. And, best of all, compatriots. They are the reason I wrote this book.

Before I can even begin to describe SDS, and what goes on there, I'll ask you to place yourself in a few scenarios. These are not actual places and events, but possible ones. They are approximations of the kinds of experience that disabled people, once asked, can recount over and over again. Collectively, the stories reveal a pattern. SDS was the place, as I came to learn, where these hidden histories could be brought to light.

Seat yourself in a medical amphitheater, circa 1952. A young girl of twelve lies on her back on a steel examination table in the center of the large windowless room, dressed only in white cotton underpants and a thin camisole, while four pairs of hands and a hundred pairs of eyes, all belonging to men, examine her polioed body. The girl's mother is sitting in the front row, clutching her white gloves and the handle of her navy blue leather purse. The woman nods her head up and down every once in a while, signaling to the girl that this is OK, let the doctors spread and stretch your legs, turn you over on your side, poke you in your tummy, they are trying to help you get better. Now don't make a fuss, she had told the girl beforehand, if your panties slip down a little, these are doctors, those things don't matter here. Mommy is only allowed to visit once a week, the girl tells herself, it is important to listen to what she says. I need to be good so they don't send me to the Home for Crippled Children.

Fast-forward to the more recent past. Form a human chain with demonstrators blockading a busy intersection in a downtown U.S. city to demand accessible public transportation. It is a brisk November day, and a phalanx of angry cripples has brought rush hour traffic to a standstill. The man to your left has a portable respirator strapped to the back of his wheelchair, and every few seconds he reaches out his lips and takes a long pull on the breathing tube suspended in front of his face. The breaths he draws in come out of his nose in white billows that drift off into the cold morning air. You latch onto the back of his chair to form another link in the chain. The woman who joins the line on your right has no hand to hold and so you wrap your arm around her waist. She then sidles up to the next woman who joins the line and they stick there, shoulder to shoulder. Impenetrable. They will later be your cell mates for a long night in the slammer. The cold pavement of the morning's demonstration is replaced by a clammy cement floor speckled with roaches. Congratulations, you have earned your first stripes as a disability rights activist.

A third story. You are leaving your house on a bright September morning. By your side is your five-year-old daughter. It is her first day of kindergarten. Your neighbor from next door is leaving her house at the same time, and she has her five-year-old in tow. The girls rush to greet each other. They are best friends. All head for your station wagon. You fold your daughter's wheelchair and put it in the back, and off you go. You drive past the entrance to the school, where you all watch the packs of kids racing up the steps to the front door. Your group gets out of the car in the teachers' parking lot at the rear of the building where, as you were instructed to do, you ring the bell and wait for the guard to come and open the metal fire door, and lead you through the kitchen. Once inside, your group divides in two. You and your daughter go down the long hall to a separate wing of the building where her "special" education class is housed. Her cherished playmate, a nondisabled child, turns the other way and enters the kindergarten class next to the principal's office.

Now, follow me down a corridor in a hotel in Washington, D.C., or Oakland, California, and enter the Regency Ballroom or the Claremont Suite on a June day when the Society for Disability Studies conference is in town. There, we are likely to hear a discussion of one of these scenarios. The presentation might include a history of the moment, because these all have a complex history, or the talk might focus on its meaning and consequences. The speaker may be a social scientist studying an event or trend to better understand what happened and why, or she or he might be an activist discussing the strategies used in recent demonstrations for accessible transportation. In one room, a speaker might be analyzing representations of disabled characters in recent feature films (possibly noting that they are all played by nondisabled actors), while down the hall, a fiction writer might be reading a new short story about a young girl coming of age in an institution for "polio victims." After lunch, a scholar from a major university might be presenting a paper on the history of the eugenics movement in the United States and Germany, relating it to contemporary trends in prenatal screening and selective abortion. Simultaneously, a group of education specialists from around the country might be dismantling, at least on paper, the segregated special education system. That evening everyone might come together to watch a performance artist doing a comic turn on the whole idea of "special" education.

This rare blend of academics, activists, administrators, filmmakers, performance artists, policy makers, writers is what you find at the Society for Disability Studies. On the first day I attended an SDS conference, back in 1990, I heard a paper presented by Rosemarie Garland-Thomson, an English professor then on faculty at Howard University, now at Emory University, on the representation of disability in the novels of Toni Morrison. I had never realized that such an approach to the study of disability existed, and the way that she used disability explained something much larger. While I didn't at first understand everything she said, I recognized that underlying the specific interpretations of character she was making, there was a cohesive set of ideas about the way meaning is attached to disability. I listened eagerly.

I had gained a basic understanding before I got to SDS of the ways that policies and social practices structure disabled peoples' lives. My activist background and social science training prepared me to see that, and my everyday experience reinforced it. What Rosemarie's paper opened my eyes to was the glue that keeps it all in place. It wouldn't be possible to set disabled people apart and steal the candy right out of our mouths if people weren't instructed to do it. There is no single primer from which to learn such behaviors, no established decree that sets our place in the social order—it is in our drinking water.

Written into works of fiction, religious texts, newspapers, art, drama, film, the annals of history, and, yes, the academic curriculum are the terms of the contract. Beliefs about disabled people, our worth and potential, are inscribed in these texts. Read the texts, watch the movies, and find the answers. Are we just individual medical "cases" or a political constituency? Are we thought to be a burden or a resource? Expendable or esteemed? Do we have lives of value or suffer a terrible existence, all pleasure eclipsed by the burden of our cruel afflictions? What fictional renderings depict us as productive and creative people? Might there someday be a book where we appear as fully formed people, with energy to spare for such human endeavors?

In the absence of the public voice of real disabled people, the existing texts and images speak for us.

At SDS it is quite different. The disabled people you meet here aren't the fictive versions played in movies by Tom Cruise, Jon

Voight, Audrey Hepburn, Jane Wyman, Raymond Burr, Lon Chaney, Al Pacino, Leonardo DiCaprio, Bette Davis, Charles Laughton, Peter Sellers, Eric Stoltz, or Patty Duke. We play ourselves, speak in our own voices. We are featured players with love lives, careers, children. Opinions. Vigor. On screen, our metaphoric worth outweighs our authentic character; our tragic tones outshine our true colors. We are rarely in charge—of ourselves or the situations we are in. Nondisabled people are.

The nondisabled people you meet at SDS aren't fearsome exploiters, paternalistic social-service types, nor do they appear as long-suffering mates or parents, valiantly shouldering the burden of life with a damaged family member. Do-gooders and stoics would not stand up well under the strong lights at SDS. These nondisabled people are allies and partners. They speak for themselves, not for disabled people.

Personal sufferings aren't discounted by an organization bent on social and intellectual change, but we are adept at sorting the preventable suffering from the inevitable. Our struggles are most conspicuously with the forces that impose hardship and deprivations on disabled people's lives. We each, disabled and nondisabled people, endure the losses and indignities that come along in life. Yet at SDS you are likely to hear disabled people express outrage at our social positioning, rather than despair at the fate of our bodies. Our symptoms may at times be painful, scary, unpleasant, or difficult to manage, and that may never change no matter what policy is implemented or what scholarly paper is written. Yet repeatedly, we report that what pains us the most, and what we rail against, are the strategies used to deprive us of rights, opportunity, and the pursuit of pleasure.

Disabled and nondisabled people cohabit at SDS, not always with perfect ease, but generally with a shared sense of purpose. We are usually in synch and in cahoots. The tensions that have surfaced are mostly over who speaks for disabled people, who sets the agenda, and who gets jobs. These problems have a complicated history. Nondisabled people have spoken for disabled people in most situations, in most cultures and historical periods. Certainly in the United States, institutions and organizations supposedly established to meet our needs are run, for the most part, by nondisabled people. As the disability rights movement has grown and disabled people are more in

the forefront, tensions arise between those who have been tradition-
ally cast in the roles of guardian and benefactor, and those instructed
to gratefully accept their largesse. We all struggle to break free of
those roles, and develop new relationships, but it is a burdensome history. Issues arise not unlike those that arose during the era of the predominantly white board of directors in the early years of the NAACP
or those that occur between men and women struggling to redefine
gender roles, and these conflicts will be worked out just as slowly.

I have attended every SDS conference since my first in 1990, quickly
became active in the organization, and am now on the board. While I
initially came to SDS for the ideas, I stayed for the people.

Corbett and her daughter Meecha both ride power wheelchairs.
One year I remember seeing them, Mom's was teal blue, and
Meecha's purple. They were zooming across the hotel lobby to greet
me, big grins on their round faces.

Corbett is a sturdy New Englander of Irish Catholic stock. Meecha
was born in Japan. They found each other when Meecha was nine
months old and Corbett, as she describes it, "liberated her" from the
institution where she lay, day after day on her back in her crib, her
hands bound to her sides and her body carefully swaddled in soft
cloth. When Meecha arrived in California after the long trip, we all
saw that the back of her head was flattened out from too many
months lying like that. She was a very quiet baby.

When Corbett learned of a disabled baby girl available for adoption, she set out to get her. She was able to find a social worker who
believed in the right of a disabled woman to adopt a baby, and the
woman supported Corbett through all the paperwork and the ardu-
ous adoption process. The financial burden was not as large as in
some adoptions. You see, Meecha was free, whereas nondisabled
babies cost a great deal.

Meecha calls me Aunt Toots, and David is Uncle Toots. Once she
was in second grade, she declared that she had grown much too big
for a ride on Uncle Toot's shoulders, but we all remember how he
could start her giggling by lining up all her windup toys and setting
them off on a race across the living room floor. Meecha is not in the
least bit quiet these days. She has oodles of friends. She goes to an
inclusive school where she is one of a number of disabled kids inte-

grated into the general education system. She takes dance lessons at the Axis Dance Theater, an integrated company of disabled and nondisabled dancers, and swimming classes one day a week.

It is rare for a disabled child to grow up with a parent who is disabled and have access to the disability community. Disability is ordinary to Meecha, and she is often in situations where she is in the majority.

Her mom, my dear Corbett, is lusty and bold, tempestuous and fair. I've heard tell of a time when she could rankle people so badly they would cross the street at the sight of her, rather than share the same sidewalk. It doesn't surprise me that she would ignite that kind of anger, she is no one to cross. Yet I've most often seen her tender side.

There is surety in her voice when she speaks about queer identity and about disability, a clarity that many envy. I wouldn't ever try to interfere with her plans, but I have disagreed with her, and held my ground. One argument went on late into the night. Her position: until nondisabled people have a well-thought-out place in disability studies, only disabled people should be doing work in the field—writing and teaching. I held that both disabled and nondisabled people should work to assure disabled people's leadership in these endeavors, but I wouldn't refuse the contributions of nondisabled people.

It's an argument that we will probably never resolve. There are times I agree with her, times when the political clout of disabled people seems tenuous, and there seem to be so few of us hired in positions of authority. Yet there are other times when nondisabled people working in the field are weighing in on matters that affect us all, and their ideas and commitment are so deeply meaningful that I welcome them. In the same way that men have a valuable perspective on women's history or on the roots of sexist traditions, or white people have a particular take on African American literature and on racism, nondisabled people have a critical perspective that can only enrich the production of knowledge about disability. The dilemma we all face is that sometimes the contributions from members of the dominant group are acknowledged largely because those scholars occupy more privileged positions.

Over the thirteen years I've known Corbett, I've seen many people cross the street, the continent, and the ocean to be *on* her side. She has traveled around the world meeting with disabled women in remote villages in Mexico and Central America, and in cities in Europe and China, helping them to organize and work together to secure employment, education, and basic rights. She raised funds to bring a U.S. group to the United Nations Conference on Women in Beijing in 1995 and made a powerful documentary film about the disabled women she met there and in her other travels.

Corbett and Meecha are quite a pair. They are a tight family unit, and they are part of an extended network of friends living in the Berkeley area who help each other keep going. Because Corbett has a mobility impairment, and because Meecha is getting bigger and bigger, Corbett sometimes needs help lifting her into the bath and getting her ready for bed. Friends, who became Meecha's aunts and uncles, take turns coming over a few days a week at bedtime to smooth the way. In turn, of course, Corbett will watch their children during the day or shop for them. This is the village that is helping raise Meecha and the other children in that circle, many of whom are disabled or have parents who are.

They help each other out too in battles with the schools for appropriate educational placements for their children, or in challenges to the state for support and medical coverage. The people I've met in Corbett's circle have astonishing legal expertise gained in these encounters, and knowledge of the systems that they struggle with for proper attendant care, health care, wheelchairs, and other equipment.

It is a bureaucratically saddled life, and they all live with terrible financial constraints, but there is great gusto in Corbett and company. Picnics, outings to the zoo, potluck suppers. When I think about Corbett from a distance (I'm on the East Coast, she on the West), it seems there is no moment of her life that isn't engaged in changing a system, securing a right, arguing a point. But not when I am with her, in her day-to-day life, loving Meecha, being a wonderful parent. Not when I watch Corbett with a lover or friend, being silly, flirtatious, or even, every once in a while, laid-back. Then I see the balance.

Another of the SDS regulars appears in the hotel lobby. A venerable regular, but younger than your usual sort of venerable.

He swaggers. His arms hang by his side like those of a gunslinger approaching a shootout. Yet be not afraid if you are an honorable man or woman. Moral outrage is the only reason this man would take aim and fire.

And anyway, those of us who know him know those arms aren't fit for real shooting—the polio got to them—but they do swing back and forth as he walks.

He is a central figure in disability studies. I remember him at SDS one year, a participant in a debate that had been set up between British and American disability studies scholars. When he entered the room, already assembled on the dais were the four members of the British team and his three colleagues on the American side, poised to argue the merits of their respective versions of disability studies. We called it the Para Theory Olympics, playing on the name "Para-lympics," given to the event that precedes the *real* Olympics. He walked up to the front, and assumed his position on the dais. Three of his fellow Americans to his left, the Brits to his right.

As we were shuffling our papers and getting ready for the event, he stood up and used his foot to slide his chair back against the wall, a position that would provide needed support for his shoulders and head when he leaned back in his chair. He sat throughout the debate, one or two feet behind us.

Then it was his turn. He held to his position against the wall, and someone from the British team came over to hold the microphone for him. He sat up in his chair, took aim, and fired: "From where I sit," he solemnly said, "it seems to me that the major difference between the American and British schools is . . . hair." The well-tressed American team, the balding members of the British team, and the audience all exploded in laughter.

Dr. Paul Longmore, eminent historian, professor at San Francisco State, author of numerous articles on disability studies and an important biography of George Washington, has spoken, and we remain, even more securely, his devoted followers. He once again has used his unique vantage point for our gain.

On matters of life and death, he is a serious-minded scholar and activist. For instance, he is astute and incisive in his commentary on what is now often called "physician-assisted suicide," but was referred to in an earlier decade by the more direct term "euthanasia." Physicians are often "assisting" the most vulnerable, those not necessarily terminally ill, but economically disadvantaged, institutionalized, and depressed, and Paul speaks out for those at risk.

He knows that he and many disabled people are potential victims if the movement to legalize physician-assisted suicide succeeds. Proponents claim it is a personal right to the control over one's body in the last few months of life. But if the data from the Netherlands, where it has been legal for some years, are any indication, there are many people so "assisted" who are socially and economically vulnerable rather than on the brink of death. Dr. Jack Kevorkian proved his willingness to collude with people who were depressed about the hopelessness of their lives, and help them to a "death with dignity," even though many of his victims were nowhere near death. Kevorkian was stopped, many believe, due to the activism of a group called Not Dead Yet that held vigils outside the courtroom where he was being tried. The group has worked tirelessly to educate the public about the fallacies in Kevorkian's claim of moral righteousness.

Paul doesn't travel much these days. He uses a respirator at night, and has begun to find airline trips too taxing. Yet he keeps a steady stream of critical information moving. I get frequent e-mails from him on everything from the actions of Not Dead Yet to recent threats to the power and reach of the Americans with Disabilities Act. I am on "Paul's List," and while I read every one, I barely manage to do a tenth of what is called for. Many of the messages are forwarded from other groups, but there are those Paul writes himself where he maps out strategies, suggests actions, provides addresses and phone numbers, and drafts letters to be sent to legislators.

Like many polio survivors, Paul struggled to get a decent primary and secondary education. Many of the kids who had polio, probably most, did not return to the classrooms they had been in before their illness. Some went to separate classrooms in their old school. Others were sent to special schools or had home instruction, and still others remained in institutions. I thought of this recently when I read that in the 1999 shootings at Columbine High School, three of the students who were injured now use wheelchairs. All three returned to their classes and appeared to be active participants in the life of their school. Given the nature of the event, and the times we are living in, it would seem punitive and unnecessary to isolate those students in special education. The questions that are so rarely asked include: Why did it not seem wrong when Paul went to school? Why does it still not seem wrong for all the children who continue to be set apart?

Paul steered through the rough waters of the segregated education system; it would be foolish to say he "overcame" it. He was placed in special education classes when he returned to school after contracting polio. His parents and one teacher who came to know him fought the school, and they reluctantly reinstated him in general education for junior high. Largely as a result of getting a general education diploma, he was able to go on to college, where he first majored in political science and pre-law, and then switched to history. He applied to graduate programs in American history, intending to become a college teacher. He told me once: "A graduate school turned me down because of my disability." Throughout his graduate and undergraduate education, advisors and many faculty members told him that no school would ever hire him, and a graduate advisor once said for that reason they would not squander fellowship money on him. "But they did admire my pluck, they said." He was finally accepted at Claremont and went on to earn a Ph.D., even though they turned him down for a departmental fellowship.

He didn't look for a teaching position for years after completing his doctorate because he would have lost health insurance and financial aid that paid for costly disability-related services like his ventilator and personal assistants. Once he was able to get a teaching position, he set out to finish a biography of George Washington he'd been working on, only to find out that if the book was published, the Social Security Administration was going to deny him needed health benefits because of the income from royalties. He published it anyway. He said in a speech he gave in response to this incident: "Without this aid I would have to spend my life in some sort of nursing home. At far greater cost to taxpayers, I might add."

The speech was given in front of the Social Security Administration building in Los Angeles on October 17, 1988. He organized a public event there where he burned a copy of his book, *The Invention of George Washington,* in protest over the SSA policy. While there had been some changes in the regulations at the time, allowing people to earn a modest income, he told the crowd:

Last March I learned that although the reformed rules would allow me to teach college, at least in California, they excluded research fellowships and book royalties. I wrote President Reagan and other top federal officials to describe my situation: Scholarly careers, I explained, are rarely lucrative. If I cannot apply for and accept research fellowships or publish books, I cannot pursue my profession. If I lose the government aid that pays for my in-home assistance and ventilators, I cannot live independently or work.

I had to turn down a research fellowship . . . to support research on my next book on George Washington. I could not, and would not, stop publication of my book. When I receive the modest royalties my book will yield me, the government will punish me by taking away the assistance that pays for my respirator and enables me to live independently.

Clearly, my disability has not prevented me from working and working hard, but it does incur enormous expenses. . . . Because public policy has defined 'disability' as the inability to work productively, it has required dependency, inactivity, and impoverishment.

He closed by saying: "My book is partly about how George Washington came to embody Americans' dreams of self-determination. Self-determination has always meant setting one's own goals, pursuing one's own vision of happiness. Disabled Americans want access to that dream of self-determination. What blocks many of us is not our disabilities, but discriminatory government policies that penalize us for working. . . . We want the chance to work and marry without jeopardizing our lives. . . . We want access to the American dream."

Dr. Paul Longmore is now a full professor in the history department at San Francisco State, and he has also established the Disability Studies Institute there. His scholarship in disability studies and his activism have earned him his place as one of the central figures in disability studies.

Paul has started to use a motorized wheelchair to get around, as walking has become more difficult. When he showed up last year at SDS in a chair, I said, "So, Dr. Longmore, I see you've come down to my level."

Devva of the flowing skirts and wispy syllables. Devva of the West. A creation that could only be fully realized in the Bay Area. I saw her first at an SDS conference several years ago, at the close of a session. They were wrapping up, and the moderator asked if there were any questions. Devva leapt to the microphone to take issue with one of the papers that had been presented.

And "leap" is the best way to describe her locomotion. Her feet come further off the floor than in any movement known as walking. Her arms lift up and out to the side as if she might take off. Lilting steps, light as air, propel her across a room. Yet Devva may stop suddenly, solely for dramatic effect, to strike a campy pose. For a brief moment she is set in stone, perchance in front of a south-facing window. Each of the major limbs and minor digits of the Devva-statue are thus bathed in morning light. Just as suddenly, the pose will melt, and she will flow on.

The dark curls of a Gypsy dancer crown our full-bodied Tinkerbell. Though a star in her own right, our dancer doesn't only play center stage, she brings the audience's attention to the wings and the fly space, as she stretches laterally and vertically to inhabit the untapped regions of a room. The part of the floor without scuff marks, the edges of the carpet where the original color remains, the pillar that everyone assumes is merely decorative—that is where Devva lands. She has the adhesive qualities, though none of the hard, wiry thinness, of Spiderwoman. She is not at all heavy, merely ample. I sometimes imagine her as a drawing by the artist and cartoonist Jules Feiffer.

Once, in the hospitality suite of a Marriott Hotel during a late-night gathering of SDS regulars, as we heard the first notes of a Gloria Gaynor disco rant come out over the trebly speakers, Devva, moved by the beat, mounted a large vertical pillar. It was a full-body mount, as one might straddle a horse and then bend forward to hug its neck. And she stuck there on that pillar for a while, folding her cheek into its fluted surface, riding it up to the sky, as if there was no force pulling her down to earth.

While not absent of erotic flavor, this pillar-humping is a playful act, an expression of the flamboyant child within. As are her hugs. She encases me in a hug that is thick, warm, and liquid. It comes from a body whose bones seem to be made of gummy bears. Such hugs aren't reserved for the initial meeting after a long absence, but are poured over me unexpectedly. Alas, they are not for me alone. The girl does spread her warmth around.

Devva's voice floats too, like her body. Just as the artistry of her dance lends weight to her body's untethered movements, so her ideas are the gravity in her feather-light voice. I sometimes have difficulty understanding her speech, so I watch her lips carefully to catch every move and sometimes ask her to repeat what she has said.

Devva has an impairment that has a long name. It has set her tongue and her limbs free from a set range of motion. Devva hasn't "overcome" this condition, she rides it like an untamed pony. As it has progressed, she has loosened more to go with its flowing movements and its unpredictable course. In the last few years, she has taken up ice skating, a sport usually practiced by those with more intact neurological systems. She glides across the ice with the same buoyancy seen in her walk, but with skates affixed to ice, she relies on her arms even more to keep her afloat. These wings steady her and propel her. Behold her ice-born arabesque!

There is no actress who could play Devva without losing some of her curves and innuendos. No one but the real Dr. Devva Kasnitz could whir like that across a room, her round parts buoying her up as if she were in water. And no one could speak with such conviction and thoroughness about her perspectives on disability studies and anthropology, or on the disability rights movement, the topics of two books she is writing. Dr. K. holds a doctorate in anthropology from the University of Michigan, and is now the academic coordinator of the Ed Roberts Postdoctoral Fellowship at U.C. Berkeley. She served on the board of directors of SDS for many years, and was one of its founding members.

I have always paid close attention when Devva is around. She moves me. I am fascinated by her willingness to make more of herself, to show off the movements that others would closet. I suspect it is not merely for her own satisfaction, but it is for me, and for all of us, who are made lighter and less cautious by her.

My friend Harilyn has a touch of cerebral palsy. Some of the most pronounced symptoms of her impairment are incisive political acumen and expressions of unbounded joy in the presence of paintings by Matisse. Harilyn's ability to recognize contradictions in a political platform and her unwillingness to yield on even a minor point derive from direct experience with the unmet promises of this country to provide equitably for all its citizens.

Her response to a fanciful palette is, of course, an idiosyncratic manifestation of her condition. She has been driven in recent years to reflect such a palette in her personal wardrobe. I recall a particularly bright orange dress, and a necklace she wears even in the gray of winter that is made of buttons of every hue and size.

Due, in part, to difficulty in fully controlling her musculature and because she finds herself helpless in the presence of my wry wit, she cannot keep a straight face around me. My clinical training and long-standing interest in such cases prompt me to evoke these responses whenever we meet. I have observed a strong correlation between Chardonnay and eruptions of uncontrolled facial movements, and the symptom seems particularly acute when our mutual friend and play-mate, Rosemarie, is present. For those occasions, we order a full bottle.

Rosemarie Garland-Thomson is, herself, a very unusual subject of study. She possesses six or seven fingers, distributed between her two arms; I regret I do not at the moment recall how many on each. Her left arm is half as long as the right, and her hugs therefore form a complete circle, without the usual crossover pattern seen in the "normal" hug.

Rosemarie is elegant and smooth, yet exuberant and winning. I don't remember ever seeing her look tired or pale. She has a wonderful smile, and when I am with her I feel embraced and loved. Rosemarie revels in others successes, and works to bring people in to the circles that form around her. She is a distinguished scholar, and is well respected in disability studies circles, as well as in women's studies, American studies, and literature. It was her paper on Toni Morrison that first brought me into disability studies, and her presence in the field continues to keep it vital for me. We have become great friends over these years, and we end each phone conversation with the exchange: "You're the best." "No, you're the best."

Harilyn was the first disabled woman I called friend. We met before I had a sense of why I would want or need a disabled friend, and so I just began to like her. When I was in graduate school, I had a number of speaking engagements every year on sexuality, and learned that Harilyn did as well. We both found these events difficult, as some people would ask us questions that revealed that they did not fully accept the idea that disabled people are sexual beings. Often, too, someone in the audience would ask us a personal question. No matter how professional our presentation, and how much we emphasized that we were there to talk about general experiences of disabled people, and not to speak of our own personal sex lives, we were asked intrusive and sometimes disturbing questions. We decided to team up and would go on these trips together. It made it much easier. In the car going home from a presentation at a college in New Jersey or a medical center in the Bronx, as we decompressed, we learned to lean on each other and trust each other.

Harilyn is a psychotherapist and activist. Her work has focused largely on disabled women and girls. She has written many articles, has several books out, and was the founder and director of the Networking Project for Disabled Women and Girls, an organization that links girls with disabled women who serve as mentors. A few years ago, when the Center for Women Policy Studies awarded Harilyn their annual Wise Women Award, Rosemarie and I met in Washington for the ceremony. We sat side by side in the audience as the actor Danny Glover introduced Harilyn and presented her with the award. When Harilyn spoke she was eloquent and compelling. She said that both disabled and nondisabled women have been taught to disavow part of ourselves, and taught to define ourselves in terms of what we are not, rather than who we are. When she declared, "I want the process of disavowal to stop with this generation," Rosemarie and I, and it seemed most of the audience, started to cry. She received rousing applause and a big bear hug from Danny Glover—I have a photo of that by my desk.

I have been observing Harilyn over a twenty-five-year period, and Rosemarie a mere twelve. It is my reasoned clinical judgment, and I do, after all, hold a doctorate in psychology, that I don't know what I would do without them.

My favorite times at SDS are the nights, after all the papers have been read and all the issues raised and put to bed, when a bunch of us gather in the bar or one of the meeting rooms to talk and, if the moon is right, dance.

Most nights we just talk and drink until we are barely able to stay awake, and then we peel off, one by one, or two by two, to head back to our rooms. Many of us see each other just once a year, and it is hard to say goodnight. The SDS conference is for some of us our only chance to be with other disability-minded people.

But SDS isn't just some safe haven—a refuge from the prejudice and stares of the nondisabled world. It isn't a place to lick our wounds, it is a place of action. Our objective isn't to hide ourselves or mask disability. We have amply demonstrated our ability to grow in the most rugged and inhospitable environments.

We are not delicate hothouse flowers and we are certainly not wallflowers. Ever since my friend Glenn taught me to dance, I've practiced whenever I can. David, my great partner, is always with me at SDS, and we bring music with us. He may go off during the day to sightsee in Washington, Berkeley, or wherever we are, but at night, David returns. On the nights when we get to dance, he dances with most everyone. He has a special place in his heart for Devva ever since they discovered their shared loved of ice skating, and he and Corbett have become legendary on the dance floor. Corbett claims that she is 100 percent queer, except for that time each year when she dances with David. I do feel a twinge of jealousy, but only a twinge, when I see Corbett shimmy up to him and watch David straddle her Big Mama thighs and slide onto her lap. He wraps his legs around the back of her wheelchair and she takes him for a spin around the dance floor. I beg the other dancers to help me break up this duo and save my marriage, but they laugh at me. It is all good clean fun.

The dance is generally a free-for-all, with no distinct lines between the dance floor and the not-dance floor. One year we weren't able to get a large room for the dance, but late on the last night of the conference, many of us were crowded into the hospitality suite. I turned the music up to see if I could get the group going, but most people just gave me a dirty look. Around the room, though, in various spots, I noted people sitting up a bit, starting to move. Some came over to be closer to the boom box on the coffee table in the corner. A couple of people came in from the hall. There weren't many of us that seemed interested, maybe just ten or so, and we were spread out among the clusters of people talking, and those who were packing up boxes of extra materials to ship back to the office.

David and I were in the lead, but then others picked up. Devva was there, of course. In fact, it was the night of her dance with the fluted pillar. She switched partners often though, and I saw her dance with David, a credenza, and at least two other inanimate objects. Sharon Snyder joined in. An English professor at a midwestern university, she is the author of many articles on disability studies, and a co-editor of three important volumes in the field. Sharon is a walkie, appears to be nondisabled, but I never assume to know such things. The music started, and with the fluid motion of the most lithe of her kind, she draped herself crossways over the arms of a plush easy chair, facing up, her head thrown back and her soft red hair hanging down over the arm of the chair. Her invented dance was a flutter kick of her bare legs, holding the rest of her body still. In her horizontal posture, she activated her lower half, as a select group of paralytics, seated upright, activated our top halves.

Petra Kuppers, a performance artist and dancer from England, had left her wheelchair on the other side of the Atlantic, and the cane she was using for walking wouldn't work for dancing. She was disappointed to be without her chair, but then found a perch on the arm of the sofa and joined in. We danced on until each of us, one by one, in the place we were, stopped, and sat back in our wheelchairs, our armchairs, or sank onto the couch, too tired to keep dancing.

Another year, we did get the hotel to put down a dance floor in one of the larger meeting rooms, and we had a good selection of music. It was a more organized event than usual and drew a bigger crowd. With room to move, our wheelchairs bounded across the floor, our crutches twirled in space, like kinetic sculpture set to music. Jonathan Young, who was, at the time, the White House staff person on disability issues in the Clinton administration and a serious dancer with moves none of us had seen before, bounced side to side in his wheelchair, each wheel coming up off the floor and each rock leaving him balanced at about a forty-five-degree angle from the floor. There were a couple of deaf and hard-of-hearing people there, so we put on music with a good strong beat and turned it way up.

There are sometimes children in the crowd. Emma is the daughter of two of the major contributors to disability studies, Sharon Snyder and David Mitchell. She has been coming to SDS conferences since she was born, along with her big brother, Cameron. Emma is a wheelchair user, like her daddy. The first year she came to the dance, when she was about five, as the music started, she slid out of her chair onto the wooden floor and spent the next two hours dancing with the crowd. She crawled around, and wove her way in and around wheels and feet, but mostly perched up on her knees, rocking back and forth and clapping to the beat. When, around midnight, her parents insisted that she had to go to bed, she cried big tears and we all stopped dancing to wave goodbye and blow kisses. Emma has since become an ambassador for dancing; her mom says that now every time she meets someone who uses a wheelchair, she asks, "Do you do wheelchair dancing?"

Neil Marcus, an actor, dancer, and poet who is much admired in our circle, was there that year. He has, I think, the same impairment as Devva. But what has graced her movements with modernistic curves and waves, has bestowed on Neil the taut lines and hyper-extension of a classical ballet dancer. To see Neil rise up from his wheelchair, in a spurt of excitation, and achieve a full-body erection, is a sight to behold. In the midst of our dance, Neil stood up suddenly in full salute and then lingered there, his movement arrested by an unseen force. He balanced on one foot, while the other, engaged in an act of its own, choreographed by a different set of neurons, carved swirls and circles in the air. His left arm caught the more obstreperous right one flung out to the side and reeled it in.

There's mayhem in his arms and deviltry afoot, and a puckishness that courses all through him. Watch his dark eyes dance and his arching fingers twirl. His eyebrows knit and unfurl, knit, unfurl, and knit again as he talks. Syllables shoot out first from the left and then the right side of his mouth. Breathy notes of varying tempos, elongated treble notes alternating with short bass sounds, come from his elasticized pretty pink lips.

I claim a great deal of credit for the dance at SDS. Not for what goes on once we start to dance, but I make sure we dance at every conference, have often been the instigator of the impromptu sessions in the hospitality suites and petitioned for the more organized events in the hotel ballroom, complete with wooden dance floor.

Now "The Dance" is printed in the conference program along with the paper sessions and keynote speaker. I think it should be there, because it is as central to the work of SDS as are our theory-building endeavors or our activism.

It is not only the local and immediate pleasure of these events that excites me, it is that on the dance floor at SDS something is happening that has never happened—at least publicly—before. Beyond being a significant social and political moment—a coming-out dance and celebration of our newfound liberties—it is also a cultural moment. We are creating forms of movement and expression that, once discovered, will be of interest to the dance world and the audiences that enjoy it. In fact, there are integrated dance companies in Israel, England, New York, Cincinnati, and California (and several points in between) that have been attracting a broad audience.

Disabled dancers don't simply serve as a reminder from the margins, that "We're here, too." Our bodies in motion insist that the terms *dance* and *dancer* be redefined. Our bodies on stage challenge every assumption about the shame and displeasure that supposedly shadow disabled people's lives.

Consider how all of the so-called minority groups—for instance, African Americans, gays, Latinos, Asian Americans, and disabled people—have been instructed to be deferent to the dominant group. We learn that we will be accepted and will succeed to the extent that we conform to the style and comportment of the majority culture. Don't act too black, or too gay. Disabled people are expected to mask the behaviors that would disturb the public, and certainly not to exaggerate or call attention to our odd forms or the way our forms function. Well, in part, the art of our dance is to exploit and expand on the quirkiness of our form, and to cultivate the interesting styles such bodies can produce.

If, for instance, Devva or Neil struggled to contain or keep private as much of their impairment as possible, we would lose something wonderful. If disabled dancers merely mimicked or recapitulated standard dance, albeit in alternative ways, we would not have an impact on the art form called dance.

Yet one danger of our public display is that we will be applauded as "inspirations" rather than as interesting or artful dancers. If I thought we served only to "inspire" but not excite, I would have none of this.

I am very interested in promoting cultural events that bring the artfulness I am describing to a broad audience. In fact, the major reason I left my faculty position at Hunter College was to do just that. Yet I think the public is never likely to see anything to rival the SDS dance. The spontaneous, untamed, and untrained (for the most part) dancers, not necessarily mindful of the need for our art to "communicate" to an audience or to make an interesting public statement, are in a class of our own. Our innovations and disportments would never quite "fit" in the confines of a proscenium stage.

Of all the innovations that I have witnessed, participated in, or instigated, none is as profoundly new as the tongue dance. One of our resident quadriplegics, John Kelly, introduced it to SDS, and it has been spreading, by word of mouth of course, all over the country. John Kelly is a brilliant theorist by day, a doctoral candidate in sociology at Brandeis, but at night when the lights are low, he is a dancer. He has never met Glenn, although I would like to introduce them, as each has taught me about dancing.

John has great control and strength in his tongue, and therefore his thrusts and wiggles are nuanced and expressive. Whether performed in large numbers or between two good friends, the tongue dance is overtly sexual, and when Rosemarie first saw it, she went faint with delight, and someone brought a chair to catch her. Now, she is an enthusiastic practitioner, and I have even seen her give demonstrations of her new craft at fancy restaurants, causing onlookers to gawk.

For sheer exuberance, though, there is no one like Joy Weeber. A southern hippie mama, with long curly brown hair and a grand smile, she hugs like nobody's business. Years ago, when I was getting to know Joy, she told me that she had polio when she was a kid. Being in a wheelchair was a terrible fate, she thought, and so she used braces and crutches throughout most of her life. She came to her senses one day, and now she rolls everywhere in a motorized scooter. At an SDS conference a few years ago, Joy and I were rolling down the street, side by side, on our way out to dinner, and she told me about the decision to get a chair. Staying upright had taken an enormous toll on her, physically and psychologically, and since she's used a chair she has more energy than she's ever had and more freedom. "You know," she said, "walking's not all it's cracked up to be!"

I remember her that year at the dance. Joy couldn't stay still. She'd steer her scooter around our little dance floor for a bit, but kept bursting out of the boundaries, through the wide doorway and out into the corridor. Whizzing past clusters of people talking out there, her hair flying out behind her, she picked up speed to head through another doorway back into the dancing room. Steering with one hand and waving the other back and forth over her head, she shouted to us: "Here I come, y'all. Watch out!"

Joy buzzed in and out like that, stopping now and then to dance with us. Then she got a conga line going with the whole crew snaking down the corridor, through the grand ballroom where the waiters were clearing tables from dinner, and back to our own special disco. People with crutches, people on wheels, people on feet, lurching back and forth to the beat.

Emma Goldman, the feminist heroine and anarchist activist, would have loved this scene. After all, isn't it she who said: "If I can't dance, I don't want to be part of your revolution."

12 *Lessons from Children*

David and I returned from our honeymoon in February of 1982, and I set about finishing my Ph.D. I completed a year's internship in an inpatient psychiatric service at a teaching hospital as part of my training to be a therapist, and then wrote a dissertation on sexual satisfaction following spinal cord injury. I had decided, though, along the way that I was more suited to teaching than to a clinical practice, and I had also abandoned the idea of developing a sex education program in a rehab center. I just couldn't bring myself to go back to one of those places, no matter what position I might land.

So, in 1984, as I was putting the finishing touches on my dissertation, I began looking for a teaching position. It was a good thirteen years since the accident. David and I had been married for three of them, I had a fair number of speaking engagements lined up, I was swimming half a mile three times a week, and I was able, when I relaxed and took it all in, to feel quite successful. I received a call one day from the occupational therapy department at a college just outside the city asking if I would teach a course in sexuality for their students. I had reservations about working in a department related to the field of rehabilitation. It seemed that rehabilitation as a field was about helping individuals improve their capacities. I wanted to put my efforts into work that would improve the capacity of the society to accommodate and integrate us.

I went for the interview—I was eager for any opportunity to begin teaching. When I arrived at the college, the head of the department came out to the lobby to meet me. He greeted me warmly, and when we entered his office, he pulled his chair out from behind his desk, brought it around front, and sat catty-corner to me. It seemed at the moment collegial. The interview proceeded. I remember him as cordial and respectful. After a while, he asked if I would teach the course, but I said I would need to think about it and get back to him.

I considered the interview to be over, and was just about to gather my things and leave, when he uncrossed his legs, leaned forward in his chair, and touched first the cushion of my wheelchair and then placed his hand on the outside of my thigh. As he was doing this he began speaking to me in a softer voice than he had used during the interview. He told me that the way I was sitting in my wheelchair, and the angle of the cushion, were putting, as he said, undue pressure on my buttocks. He expressed concern.

I was startled by his touch and by this abrupt shift in tone. I moved my chair back a few inches, trying to get away. He persisted in showing me, by pointing and touching my chair and my leg, how the seat should be set. He spoke confidently and casually, and an outsider looking in might even say kindly, about the seat height of my chair and the position of my legs. He spoke to me as if he were explaining something he knew that I didn't, and he was offering a favor.

I managed the situation with the skills a lifetime being female and a fair amount of time being disabled had taught me. Given the possibility that I might want to teach the course and the peculiarity of the situation, I did not blurt out, "Take your hands off me." Of course, I like to think I would do that now. Instead, I attempted to control his behavior by looking at him directly, changing the subject, and ending the interview.

I called him the next day, thanked him, and declined the position. Although I knew what he had done was wrong, I was unable to summon the words to describe his transgression. The term *sexual harassment* was not widely used at that time, and even if it had been, this incident spoke to a different power relationship, a different set of rules. An authority that gave him license to touch me. I had assumed that he was a prospective employer and I a prospective employee. It would seem, though, that to him, I was also his patient. His gesture would seem to the outside world a generous one, a selfless one, and no one would understand why I felt hurt and violated.

Shortly after that I began teaching at Baruch College and three years later moved to Hunter College. One of my tasks at Hunter was to supervise teacher education students in their first-year field placement. The school that we used is a welcome space on a busy street corner in East Harlem. The students arrive each morning, most led by parents and grandparents walking there from nearby projects and small row houses, while others arrive by bus. Most of the bus riders are disabled children who come from outside the immediate vicinity of the school. They are bussed there rather than to their local school because this is one of the two schools per district that has even modest wheelchair accessibility and programs set in place to accommodate children with a wide range of impairments. It is a school that actively practices mainstreaming. There are a number of disabled children, primarily those with mobility impairments or certain kinds of learning disabilities who are placed in general education classrooms for part or all of the day. Even though the school is more integrated (with respect to disability) than most schools in New York City, it has many separate self-contained special education classes for children identified as having mental retardation, autism, emotional disorders, and other impairments. There is little interaction between the children in those classes and those in general education.

The American school system has changed to a degree as a result of parent activism and the work of the disability rights movement. Yet many of the entrenched social problems still exist. In 1975, the law known as PL 94–142 (since renamed the Individuals with Disabilities Education Act, or IDEA) was passed. It guarantees an education for all children identified as disabled in "the least restrictive environment," meaning, in part, that all disabled children should be integrated into general education whenever possible. The definition of "whenever possible" varies from school to school and district to district. Most districts maintain fixed boundaries between disabled and nondisabled children. They place those with more significant impairments in separate schools. In other schools in the district, like the one in which I worked, there are special education classrooms in which most disabled children in the school spend their day. In such schools, there are some children with simple mobility impairments or learning disabilities in general education classrooms.

There are some schools around the country which practice full inclusion. There, all children attend their neighborhood school together, learning and socializing in the same classrooms. They are placed in classes based on age, rather than on test results, evaluation, diagnosis, or past performance.

Full inclusion is grounded in a broader, more comprehensive philosophical rationale, and there is an increasing body of research demonstrating its benefits. Teachers who were initially resistant have often changed their minds after working in a well-run inclusion program. Even children with the types of impairments that are generally thought to impede social interaction and classroom participation, such as mental retardation or autism, have been incorporated into the life of the classroom with an adequate support system. Teachers trained to create inclusive classrooms have had enormous success using a parallel curriculum that meets the disabled students' needs yet blends in with the topics and materials all the students are using.

The whole institution of special education may have been founded on a desire to assure disabled children access to education, but I believe its continuation rests, in part, on an unconscious wish to contain and control children considered undesirable. There is a certain irony to the choice of the term *special* to describe educational placements that rarely appear desirable. Even in the best special ed classrooms, with the very best teachers, the disabled children are set apart from the rest of the school, with little opportunity to interact with nondisabled children. In this situation, all children miss out on the opportunity to learn and grow together.

I am not claiming that inclusion is a panacea, and there are some who oppose it altogether (the Deaf community has been particularly vehement about this). I do believe, however, that every child should have the opportunity to be in an integrated classroom.

One of the dilemmas of inclusive schools is that because there may be only one or two disabled children in a class, there is little opportunity for them to bond with other disabled children and pick up knowledge and skills from each other. I remember in my early years with disability, I was flying by the seat of my pants, and so many say they did the same. For children who grow up with disability, the process is complicated by the fact that their family and those around them often have little experience in these matters. Parents may be wonderful, and impart strong positive messages, but others, even though well-meaning, may be frightened and confused. There are those, too, who have profoundly negative feelings about disability and about their own disabled children.

In their confusion or shame, the family may insist that the child isn't really disabled—it is just a little problem. They may all collude to deny the extent and significance of the child's impairment. "You could see the chalkboard if you sat closer, and tried a little harder." "You can hear just fine." "If you walk with these braces you'll look more normal than if you use a wheelchair." "You better not hang out with the retards and handicapped kids, because no one will play with you." "You aren't like those other kids in your special ed class, you're not really disabled, you just need a little extra help."

For disabled children, it is, in some respects, similar to the experience of lesbian and gay people, who so often grow up in a culture that is hostile to them, and whose own families may perpetuate the most toxic ideas. Unlike members of other minority groups, young people who are gay or disabled usually do not have access to adults who know the experience, can speak with enthusiasm about their lives, and can teach young people the language and skills they need to find their way.

There are so many stories of disabled kids trying to "pass" throughout their childhood, acting on messages from parents that disclosure of their impairment would bring shame on the family. Of course there are impairments that can't be disguised, and there are stories of kids hidden away in basements or attics, kept at home and out of sight, or institutionalized. There are the other stories, too. Of families who embrace their kids and insist on their membership in the community.

Things have changed over the last twenty-five years, and I think there are more and more families of the latter type. And many have been instrumental in the fight against isolated, restrictive classrooms that deny their children the benefits of a well-rounded, integrated school experience.

The students I had over the years at Hunter were generally diligent and engaged, but many were saddled with enormous family and financial burdens. I was often in despair, and angry at the way that the New York City school system had not adequately prepared them for college work. Among my group, I often saw students who were smart, and terrific with children, but there were too many who had a limited knowledge of the world beyond their own. Some had never been given essential tools, and struggled to write coherent, accurate sentences. In my early years working at Baruch College and then at Hunter I always sent such students for remedial help, and I would see improvement and a new optimism in those who had received tutoring and ongoing support with writing. Over the years, though, college support services and remedial education were drastically cut back, and students were put on a long list of those waiting for help. I helped where I could, but my own class sizes increased, I was overtaxed, and I was not trained to teach the kinds of skills the students needed.

And in the elementary school where we worked, a school that was well run, and staffed by a committed group of women and men, I too often saw smart teachers impart inaccurate information, weak teachers with weak skills, strident teachers making learning too hard, and the good teachers doing the best job they could in overcrowded classrooms, with few supplies and few supports.

In the face of all this, I and others are demanding that attention be paid to the ways we are specifically failing disabled children. We argue that in addition to efforts to redress inequities based on class, race, and gender we must attend to those based on disability. I think that special education is not a solution to the "problem" of disability; it *is* the problem, or at least one of the major impediments to the full integration of disabled people in society.

There is no way to put any of these issues on a scale and measure them. In the school where I worked, with almost entirely African American and Hispanic students, there were few resources and limited funds, and we all knew that a mile away was another public school that had a much higher percentage of white students, a much better teacher-student ratio, classes in music and art, more supplies, and more space. How could I demand of this and other beleaguered schools a restructuring of the system to integrate the classrooms, the retraining of teachers so that they can work in teams in integrated classes, the development of innovative curricula that would meet the needs of heterogeneously grouped students, as well as all the other shifts of practice and procedure that such integration would entail?

It is not only because I care about what happens to disabled children, but because I am convinced it would benefit everyone. I think we should do away with all tracking of children, those decisions about educational placement usually made when children are four or five that predetermine what they are capable of learning. Let's train all teachers to utilize a flexible repertoire of approaches to reach a broad range of learners. Let's reduce class size, use team-teaching methods, and well-trained assistant teachers. Let's erase the line between disabled and nondisabled children, drawn at a very early age, imprinting each group with indelible ink. Let's identify the supports and accommodations that every child needs, rather than catalog the "special" kids' deficits and incapacities.

Whenever I faltered in my belief, ridiculed myself for being a pie-in-the-sky, liberal optimist, I thought of the children I saw at the elementary school. Particularly the disabled children. It wasn't that they said anything directly to me about school and how they felt. It came from watching them, identifying with them, concerned that even here, in a school that was doing a better job than many, these children were not getting what they needed to move out into the world and be part of it.

I spent quite a bit of time at the school over the eleven years that I taught at Hunter. There are a number of other field-placement sites that Hunter uses, but it was the only school that had even modest wheelchair accessibility, and so I was always assigned to that school, as were the two physically disabled students from Hunter whom I taught over the years who also needed an accessible site. As of my last visit in 1998, I saw a school with minimal material resources, classes that had to share textbooks, and crowded rooms. The gym was only available to students in special education and for them only once a week, only a few of the classrooms had even one computer, and there were no paper towels or hot water in most of the bathrooms. But the place was clean and well cared for, and filled with a dedicated staff that did, and I'm sure still does, an enormous job in the face of these and other less tangible constraints.

I usually liked being there and gained enormous respect for many of the teachers and the staff. Although there were things I saw that I wished I hadn't, practices that seemed to defeat the very purpose we were there for, there were frequent reminders of the professionalism and commitment of the staff.

I remember one day I was sitting in on a sixth-grade class when the Dean of Students came in to tell them that a boy that they all knew, a boy who had just gone on to junior high the year before, had been shot in a neighborhood drug incident. Many of the children already knew what had happened, and this announcement confirmed that the boy had died that morning. The man sat on a desk in the middle of the front row and reached out to touch the boys and girls who were crying all around him. He seemed somehow with his voice and his gestures to hug all the students at once. One boy was sitting in the back holding the big white rabbit that was the class pet. I learned later that he was a close friend of the boy who had been killed, and he sat there stone faced, stroking the rabbit, holding on for dear life.

That wasn't the only day that I cried at the school. There were other times, like the day I saw the shame a ten-year-old boy felt when he couldn't read out loud, or when a teacher who should have known better berated a child over and over for some minor failure and I stood on the side not knowing what to do to help. I also cried, although at the same moment had a big grin on my face, while sitting in the back of the auditorium watching a group of exuberant second-graders dancing in the Puerto Rican Day festival. Among the children was a boy who uses a wheelchair, and he twirled and clapped along with his classmates, and they all do-si-doed together. He grabbed his partner's hand and pulled himself toward her, then grabbed the rim of his wheel and pulled himself back. She curtsied, he bowed at the waist.

Another day I welled up in tears as a group of seven- and eight-year-olds in a bilingual special education class presented me with a Spanish lesson they had prepared for me when I told them I was going to Puerto Rico and needed to learn some words to use there. Their teacher told me that they had thought up the words themselves, translated them, and, with her help, written *pollo* / chicken, *buenos dias* / good morning, *casa* / house, and other essentials on a big piece of poster board to give me. These were all children labeled mentally retarded who were being taught by a woman with extraordinary talent and insight.

As good as this class was, I could find no reason to justify the children being sequestered, set apart from their peers. All disabled children, not just those who can be more readily assimilated in mainstream society, should be learning together.

Every day that I went to the school, something moved me. The crossing guard in her yellow slicker shepherding the kids across the street, or the sight of a group of assistant teachers and some of the maintenance staff sitting on the floor in the cafeteria intently working on a mural to brighten the front hall. There was the welcome I received each morning from the slickered crossing guard who stopped traffic to let me cross. She always said, "Good morning, professor," and gave me a hug when I got to the other side.

Most heartening were the optimism and goodwill of my students, who gave so much of themselves, often staying overtime to work with the children. Hunter is part of the City University of New York, a public university. So many of the students were talented and smart, many of them had children of their own, almost all were working while going to school, and they were all struggling to support themselves.

One semester I had a Chinese woman in my class who had raised five sons, all of whom were married with children of their own. She had been born in China, had moved here when she was a young woman, had never gone to college, and had decided to go back to school to become a teacher. For her field placement, I paired her with a nineteen-year-old African American student, and over the semester they bonded and helped each other tremendously. When I would look in on these two women working together in a fourth-grade class, I would think, "This is what is best about America."

Another term I had a student who uses a wheelchair. I placed her in a first-grade class that was a mainstreamed general education class. As I watched her work with the children, two of whom also used wheelchairs, I marveled at this historic moment. It is unlikely that this scenario would have occurred ten or twenty years before, and rare for it to be seen even today. My student, who had also been mainstreamed in her own elementary and secondary school, in another era would likely have been placed in special education and therefore would have had a much harder time gaining access to college. The two children who use wheelchairs would probably not have been in a general education class. There was a high likelihood that I might not have been there, any number of obstacles could have stopped me along the way: I might have been unable to find a college or graduate school that was accessible; my graduate school might have rejected me; or I might have been denied the teaching job at Hunter based on disability and found myself without legal recourse, because the Americans with Disabilities Act had not yet been written. Even if I passed through all those hoops, I might not have been able to find an accessible elementary school to supervise students in.

What if my accident had occurred at sixteen, rather than at twenty-three? I would not have been able to return to my high school, a place with many steps and no accessible bathrooms. My private school would have been under no obligation to serve me, and back in the early '60s my public school options would have been very limited. I might have wound up, like some of those women I interviewed when I was a student at Columbia, in a special education classroom, or on home instruction for my last two or three years of high school, all of which would have made it a lot harder for me to have ever been admitted to Columbia.

Even today, private schools are under no legal obligation to admit disabled students. I thought of this the other day while going to meet a friend for coffee on one of the elegant side streets of New York's Upper East Side. On a street of town houses and small apartment buildings, I rolled past a private school at about three o'clock in the afternoon, a school that looked very much like the one I had gone to. The sidewalk was crowded with boys, all wearing navy blue blazers and gray trousers. They were in various states of end-of-day tousled-ness. Shirts out, ties loose, the parts in their straight brown or blond hair zigzagging across their little heads. One could project into the future and see them all as Wall Street tycoons after a heavy squash game.

There was not a black or brown boy in sight, although there was a smattering of Asians. And there were no visibly disabled boys. I noted a flight of steps at each of the entrances to the building. I'm sure the school has no written policy saying "No black and brown boys admitted" and no sign saying "Disabled children not allowed," but the unwritten codes—formalized in tests, admissions procedures, tuition, recruiting activity, and architectural decisions—effect the same outcome.

The privilege that a private school education confers, on predominantly white, economically well-off children, and the relationships formed in those institutions serve people all their lives. Children admitted on scholarship accrue some, but certainly not all, these benefits, and many such institutions have made efforts to diversify their student body along racial and class lines, although the number of students admitted is usually very low.

Over the years, I have read many analyses of the stratification of the education system along racial and class lines, critiques I generally agree with. Yet I have read nothing in the press—either in major newspapers or in other periodicals—about the privileging of nondisabled children in the school systems, both private and public. This is particularly important at a time when a voucher system is increasingly likely in many cities across the United States.

If parents are offered the chance to apply tax money toward private education, many of those parents with sufficient knowledge to work the system and sufficient economic resources to supplement the voucher money to cover full tuition will aim for parochial or non-parochial private schools. Yet the parents of disabled children will have little recourse as few private schools will accept and provide accommodations to their children.

The disabled children will remain in schools like the one I worked at in East Harlem, along with the children whose families do not want to use or are not able to negotiate the voucher system. I fear we will have an increasingly demoralized, underfunded, and segregated public school system.

In my comings and goings in other parts of New York, children often look at me, some just plain curious, others, I'm sure, startled at the sight of an adult in an oversized stroller propelling herself down the street, and still others frightened by disability, or my particular brand of disability. In this building, though, disability is commonplace, and most children at the school barely noticed as I came in and out of their classrooms observing my students at work. The disabled kids, though, particularly those who use wheelchairs, watched me. There were a number of kids who were always checking me out, and I stopped and talked with them, or we slapped high fives as we passed in the hall.

I caught myself many times feeling a sense of protectiveness, an inordinate concern for the disabled children. I could see that they were cared for and that the teachers, for the most part, paid attention to them, but I didn't know where they would learn the things I had learned about how to handle this life. Where would they get the lore and the language, where would they learn to value the bodies they have, and their ways of seeing, hearing, and thinking, how would they learn that they could be what they wanted to be, what kinds of lessons would they learn about their civil rights as disabled citizens, how would they learn to combat discrimination? Their parents may have been adept at teaching them about the discrimination they were bound to face as African Americans and Hispanics, but what about the particulars of disability oppression, including that which might come from their own communities?

Even more fundamental, how could they imagine life as an adult? Of all the adults who worked at the school, there was only one woman with a visible disability, and the children didn't have much contact with her. How about in their family or neighborhood? Probably limited. Disabled children often grow up without much contact with disabled adults. Many people who grew up with a disability have told me about fears they had growing up that they might die or disappear or be locked up somewhere, because they never saw adults that were like them. These days there are, at least, a couple of disabled children on shows like *Sesame Street* who are active and speak for themselves, but there are rarely adults in those or other shows the children watch.

I recall seeing a child one day whose aide was pushing his chair. The boy was sitting very still, listless, not looking in the direction he was headed, just along for the ride. I quickened my pace to catch up to them. As I wheeled by, he saw me out of the corner of his eye, and sat up straight, moved his hands from his lap where they had been folded, and started to push his own chair, working hard to catch up with me.

I was at the school several times on the day when class pictures were taken. It is a fun day to be there, at least as an observer. As most of the kids wear fancy clothes and are too excited to pay attention to much of anything, I'm sure it isn't always a treat for the teachers. I noticed that it is the custom for all the children who use wheelchairs to be removed from their chairs and carried up a few steps to the auditorium stage and placed on folding chairs. I spoke with people at the school who said they have thought about raising money to build a ramp to the stage, but in the meantime this was the solution. I asked, of course, why they have to take pictures on the stage when it is inaccessible. People generally said that was where they had always taken the school pictures, the photographer was already set up there, and that, it seemed, was that. No one else seemed bothered by this. The families of these children or the school personnel might even persist with this plan, believing that these actions have a positive effect on children, demonstrating that the disabled child is "just like everybody else." But it is a fiction. The message I read in this action is: You are like everyone else, but only as long as you hide or minimize your disability.

Jose and Denise (not their real names) were two kids whom I paid particular attention to and watched grow over the years. Jose appeared to be a fearless, buoyant kid. He was about eleven or twelve the last time I saw him, really cute, with an earring in one ear, a great smile that he displayed often, and a snappy wheelchair that he decorated with colored beads that slid noisily up and down the spokes of his wheels as he moved. He could wheel faster and harder than I could, even in my prime. He was mainstreamed in a general education class for the full day. He was active in class and seemed to have quite a few friends. Jose always had an aide, probably because all physically disabled children are assigned an aide full-time, rather than because he needed one. Most of the aides basically left Jose to his own devices. In some cases this was because the aides recognized that Jose did fine without help, in others because Jose was adept at keeping them at bay.

He was often assigned a female aide, as the majority of aides in the school are women. When he went to the bathroom, the aide would go with him. And on a few different occasions here is what I saw: Jose and his female aide went together into the girls' bathroom. He pushed his chair past giggling nine-year-olds running in and out of the stalls and preening adolescents vamping in the mirror, and down to the end stall. I was in the bathroom a couple of times when Jose and the aide went past. The girls ignored him. They just kept chattering. He was not a threat to the girls' private space. Ordinarily, they would yell at any boy who came within three feet of the door to the bathroom and make a big deal about shooing him away, but not Jose.

Am I wrong to think this would be painful and confusing for him?

That it will have an impact on his development, his understanding of himself and his place in the social world he inhabits, a world so profoundly marked by gender? I thought he looked embarrassed when I saw him in there, but maybe I am imagining that is how I would feel. Some may even say that Jose stands a chance of being liberated from the rigid gender roles that his nondisabled peers are forced into. But we can't liberate all of us from rigid sex roles by forcing only disabled boys into girls' bathrooms.

I spoke with the coordinator about this, a thoughtful and concerned woman, and we tried to come up with alternatives, but as of the last time I checked on it, no other solution had been found. I know that problems are piled up on the principal's desk, but I am concerned that this isn't even recognized as a problem. That this child's social and sexual future is already so compromised in people's minds that these practices are not thought to have long-term negative consequences. But the cost isn't just in the long term, and the loss is not just Jose's. Jose appeared to be so resilient and so winning that I remain optimistic about him. I also saw that the school did a great deal for him. The year he graduated from sixth grade he participated in the Big Brother/Big Sister program. He was assigned to help out in a first-grade class one period a day. Whenever I came in the room and saw Jose moving among the students' little desks, helping them write their ABCs, or helping the teacher get the students in line for lunch, I felt a surge of hope. He was one of the kids who had always watched me, and when he saw me come in the room, he would sit up tall and take on an air of great earnestness. I would try to get over and observe him, the way I observed my students. That way, when I saw him later I could compliment him on his technique, give him some tips.

My other favorite kid to watch was Denise. At the time of this story she was in the fourth grade. She had a round face, dark brown skin, soft brown eyes, and many braids fastened with brightly colored barrettes circling her head. She uses a wheelchair which at the time she was just starting to push herself. I would see her going about the school, either her aide pushing her chair or occasionally Denise, sitting somewhat slumped over, slowly weaving her way down the hall, pushing first with one hand, then the other. I watched her many times, and I couldn't tell why she moved so haphazardly. I don't know if she was not fully committed to the act of mobilizing herself, whether her aide pushed her chair too often and didn't give her the chance to learn, or maybe she was trying hard, but didn't have the physical skill to propel herself any faster. I couldn't tell if she might be better off in a motorized wheelchair, and wondered whether her family could afford one. She often had a faraway kind of look and seemed lethargic. But sometimes in class she sat up tall in her chair and thrust her hand up toward the teacher, eager to answer a question.

One afternoon, I came into her classroom, and the only people there were Denise, sitting at her desk writing in a notebook, Denise's aide, sitting near her, and my two students. Even though she was mainstreamed, meaning she was placed in a general education class, she often spent time alone with adults. There were times like this when the rest of the class was somewhere deemed inappropriate for her and she stayed behind in the classroom. Each morning all the children identified as "special" got free breakfast, and while the cafeteria was noisy with the sounds of the children in the special education classes who were sitting together, because Denise was mainstreamed she sat alone with her aide. While she was having breakfast, the children in her class were in the playground, and they were there after school too, while she waited at the front door with her aide for the school bus to take her home, a street some distance from the school.

So the day I came into her class, I made the fourth adult in there with her. I was taking notes and observing my students working on the bulletin board in the back of the room when Denise looked up from her work, and in slow, stretched-out movements turned to look at me, then rolled her head to the left to watch my students, and back again to me. But then, not slowly, but pointedly, jutting her chin out and staring straight at me, she demanded: "You a teacher?"

I, back to her, with mock toughness, "Yeah, I'm a teacher."

She shook her head. She wasn't buying this.

I called my students over to verify the information.

"I sure am," I said, "and these are my students. They're college students who are working here in your class to learn to be teachers."

She gave us that look that says, "All adults are basically ignorant, but we have to humor them."

What in Denise's experience would lead her to think that I could be a teacher? She would, I'm sure, be equally incredulous to hear that I am married, that I love someone and he loves me. That we kiss and hug and all that other stuff. How could she possibly believe that?

My students rushed to corroborate my story using some pretty convincing evidence. I have a classroom back at their college where I write on the board just like Denise's teacher. I give tests too, and they are very hard. They told her that they call me "Professor Linton" because "professor" is the title for teachers in college.

She stared at us all for a few seconds, and then fixed her eyes on me.

"But," she said with conviction, "you can't be a teacher, you in a wheelchair."

My heart stopped. What could I say to change her mind right now? I couldn't think of anything.

I had thought that thought many times. I had talked myself out of and then into becoming a teacher, worried that I would be unacceptable as a college professor, a spectacle, a low-to-the-ground inferior version of a lofty academic. I wonder now, looking back, if I persevered because I grew up nondisabled, grew up white, or grew up privileged? Or maybe it was because I have a big mouth and love to talk. One thing I do know is that I hadn't even thought about becoming a professor, or a professional anything, in those years before the accident. I had become more purposeful, more ready to do something important since.

Denise turned away from us, back to her desk. She picked up her pencil and hunkered down, slowly bending her head till she was just a couple of inches over her workbook. She was through with us.

13 *Rufus*

It may be hard at first glance to notice how I've changed since hooking up with Rufus. With Rufus I am swifter and cleaner, although a bit noisier. More spontaneous. I stay out late, and have a couple of drinks at dinner, knowing that I won't be the one driving home. I can carry more weight, do more errands.

I've become a more outdoorsy type. We've gotten to know Central Park, top to bottom. We've been to the pinetum, the zoo, and the gardens at the north end of the park. Fed the ducks. Gathered branches of autumn leaves knocked down after a rainstorm.

I didn't know that I was missing something like this in my life. I had been going along at a steady pace. I had my way of doing things.

Yet I had begun to limp. A wheelchair kind of limp. A less forceful push, a harder time on hills. I lost momentum on uneven sidewalks, particularly when my right arm was called upon to do the extra work of keeping us on track. My shoulders had borne the weight of my body for all these years, and they were shouting for mercy. Rufus came to the rescue.

Rufus is a cherry red, full-steam-ahead, motorized wheelchair. I named it the first week I got it. I had been using a wheelchair for nearly thirty years—a manual chair, or, as we call it, a push chair. Although I had several over the course of those years, from the clunky institutional style to the sleek sportser I now use, I never named them. They were allies, but generally silent partners in the business of getting me around.

Rufus is not silent. It signals my arrival with a high-pitched whir before I have the chance to open my mouth.

The first couple of days riding Rufus, I moved cautiously. I went around the block a few times, then ventured up to Broadway to buy a newspaper. Each day I went further. I had David go with me the first time I tried taking the bus. I quickly learned how the wheelchair lift works, and I did it solo the next day. I began to learn the distance the chair could go, we could go. I plug Rufus in at night, and in the morning the battery is fully charged. Miles to go before we sleep.

I named Rufus after those scruffy dogs, the ones always waiting in the hall by the front door wagging their tails, urging you to take them out. Aren't those dogs all called Rufus?

I deliberated for a long time before buying a power wheelchair. I feared a reaction like the one Bob Dylan got at the Newport Folk Festival in 1965, when he first appeared on stage with an electric guitar. Dylan, the hero of the folk purists, was heckled and accused of selling out . . . just for plugging in. Would my fans think I had taken the easy way out? Was I capitulating to the demons of technology?

When I pictured a power chair in my mind, it looked big and complicated. It seemed to me that to cross that bridge would mean a change in the way I did everything. The lightweight, collapsible manual chair I had used for many years would be replaced by a large, unwieldy machine that wouldn't fit in our car, wouldn't fit in the house, wouldn't fit anywhere. Would we need to buy a van with a lift? Would we be able to travel with this thing? And outsiders would see me differently. As more impaired. Would I go there willingly when I didn't have to?

Then one day I was talking to Corbett and she told me she had gotten one and how great it is. She doesn't use it all the time, she said, just for excursions when she wants to go long distances. She likes it because she can push Meecha's chair with one hand, and steer her chair with the other. They can go to the park or out shopping and carry bags on the back with a picnic or groceries.

I had seen it as an all-or-nothing proposition. A momentous decision, changing how I did everything and how people would see me. Corbett made it sound easy and fun. I decided to rent one and try it out. It only took a day and I was hooked. While I didn't go very far at first, I went easily and quickly. While I started off steering into walls, and banging into David's shins, I found after a while I could maneuver in tight spaces, turn on a dime, and back onto the lift on the crosstown bus in ten seconds flat. As for others and how they would see me? It's never been quite right with those generalized "others," no matter what vehicle I ride. There are so many who project their beliefs about disability on me. And it has gotten better in recent years. The times have changed, and, more and more, people seem to be incorporating me in their vision of the natural order of things. Disabled people have become less of an event. Pedestrian, if you will. Or, at least, some of us, some of the time, in some places.

Once I had my own power chair, I began to use it often. To the supermarket, the gym, the theater, to work. Other times, either just around the house or when I need to take a taxi or get on an airplane, or go places I cannot get to or don't want to go with Rufus, I use the manual chair. I have become adept at code-switching, shifting from manual to power chair modalities, the way people who are fully bilingual can easily switch back and forth between their two languages.

I have entered this new phase of disability with a deliberateness and a consciousness I missed the first time around. When I first became disabled, I couldn't study my situation or reflect on it too actively—I was too taken up in each moment, and too frightened. I'm now able to think, and even write about it. I go back and forth between the two chairs and make comparisons, in a way I couldn't, when I first became disabled, compare walking and riding.

There are the familiar manual chair moves: With shoulders even, chest jutting out a bit, elbows bent and pointing back, palms facing in, and thumbs forward, I grab hold of the rubber rim on the outside of my wheels and push. The motion starts with my hands at high noon on the top of the wheels; I push forward for a split-second and then down, quickly straightening out my arms. I let go of the rims at nine o'clock (for the right wheel, I guess it is three). To continue moving, I bring my hands back up, catch hold of the rim as it goes round, and push down again. To turn to the left, I push solely with my right arm, keeping a loose hold on the left rim to adjust for the curve as I move into the turn. Right turns, backwards, stopping on a hill, or slalom courses of traffic cones or soda bottles that kids set up along the roadway in the park for skating—each has its own maneuvers.

These moves are all so natural that a number of times when I've been in a canoe that started to drift too close to shore, instead of picking up my paddle, I reached down and grabbed for wheels on the side of the canoe. I've done that in a taxi whose driver ran a red light, and once in Los Angeles when I was awakened by a minor earthquake I reached down to grab the side of the bed as if I could stop it from moving.

Imagine, then, my body's surprise when I first tried a power wheelchair which moves with a flick of the wrist on the joystick. With little more than a nod of my thumb and forefinger, I'm off like a shot down the street and stop by merely letting go. The first few times I went down the street, though, I didn't know what to do with my left hand, an extra, and found myself smoothing my hair back multiple times in the course of a block. I felt an unaccustomed, passive feeling. It was strange. I can go faster than I ever could in a manual chair (except on steep downward slopes), yet I am sitting stock-still. It is a sensation that I don't always like.

I find I keep moving in Rufus and have to tell myself to slow down or stop to just look at things. The most invigorating part of using a power chair is being able to cover new territory, and that pushes me forward. Simultaneously, I think I am also compelled to move in reaction to my inert physical state.

The pleasure of Rufus, the ease of it and the endurance, came with twinges of loss. The brawny moves I was used to in a chair I pushed myself. The firm grip on the rims of my tires, and the satisfaction of handling a manual chair well. The fun of a downhill slope—just letting go and coasting. The smoothness and quiet of the ride in a lightweight chair. Rufus is heavy and takes bumps hard. It whirs. I can hear me coming.

And with a sad blue pain that startled me, I was caught one day thinking: I am not walking or running, merely whirring. I so rarely think about how I might move, how I did move. I was not expecting to feel this when, for the first time in many years, I was out alone gliding easily up and down the paths that cut through the park. The feeling sideswiped me just when I was taking pleasure in this new freedom. And I let it come, out there in the middle of Central Park on a blustery day with no one around. The gains, it seems, had resurrected the loss.

I'm tender now too, I think, because I am getting older. I'm in my mid-fifties now—the most peculiar feeling of all. I'll have to do a good job with this like I did with crippledom, I tell myself. Keep kickin'. Don't put away those outrageous clothes or your red lipstick. But this time, kvetch more, be cantankerous, it's OK, you've earned it. And get a sidekick.

Despite the palpitations, or maybe because of them, it has been great having Rufus. It is a moving experience, and the emotions that have come with it woke me up, unfurled my flags.

The smallest differences seem the most profound. I always went to major destinations—Tokyo, Paris, Radio City Music Hall, Greenwich Village—but I was out of touch with my own neighborhood. Now, if I open the fridge and find we're out of milk, I head to the den where Rufus is parked, unplug the battery charger, swing my body over onto the cushion, pick up my legs, one by one, and place each on its own foot pedal, flip Rufus's switch, and we're on our way out the door. Whiz up to the corner, the next corner, into the grocery store, wave to the cashier, give her the thumbs-up on her new haircut, purchase the milk and some wheat biscuits while I'm at it, ask her to put them in the bag on the back of my chair, and then back home in minutes.

I always did errands before, long lists of them, but they were planned in advance, and calculated around an easy parking space for my car and the number of packages that needed to be carried. Now, even for the small things, like a quart of milk, the effort doesn't outweigh the reward, and so I do it. The act itself is its own reward—being part of the place where I live. Even if I have many things to do—pick up a video, drop off the dry cleaning, buy a newspaper, the ingredients for dinner, and a new bracket for the shelf in the kitchen—I can forge ahead, knowing that even all those packages won't slow Rufus down.

In addition to my neighborhood ventures, I've become fond of the bus. It took federal legislation to begin to integrate the public transportation system I use. For many years, that system, unswayed by the argument that many potential riders were out there just waiting to drop their fare in the box, resisted conversion to the more accommodating bus service now in use.

The ADA pushed them to overcome their resistance. Mass-transit authorities across the country had insisted that separate "special" transportation would serve people with mobility impairments better. Not only is that plan restrictive in that it limits the number of rides a person can take, the disability community argued, but it is an isolating and inconvenient means of transportation. While it is a necessary component of the transportation system, important for people who cannot use the available public transportation, it is inadequate. A separate van system requires users to book rides well in advance, anywhere from hours ahead to a couple of weeks depending on the city. Also, the vans are notoriously unreliable in terms of time, particularly during rush hour, and riders inevitably have to go out of their way, as drivers pick up and drop off other passengers. Further, some of the services are very expensive, you often can't travel with a friend or partner, although an attendant can accompany you, and you can only go to a single destination and then back home.

Representatives of municipal systems also argued that there were few people who would benefit from lift-equipped buses. The ADA pushed them to overcome their resistance. Now that virtually the entire fleet of the New York City public bus system is equipped with lifts, there has been a dramatic change in use. Figures for 1998 indicate that there were anywhere from 33,629 to 52,643 passengers per month who utilized the wheelchair lifts, and this was an increase of, on average, about 25 percent from the previous year. Figures for 2002 indicate the numbers had climbed to nearly 64,000 times per month. I account for about forty of them.

These changes took years of struggle. National organizations like American Disabled for Accessible Public Transportation (ADAPT), a group known for its in-the-streets activism, began to stage demonstrations in the early '80s aimed at getting lifts on all city buses throughout the United States. There have been hundreds of arrests. ADAPT members have chained their wheelchairs to the gates outside public buildings, they have linked arms and blocked traffic on major highways, they have occupied offices, and they have been carted off to jail, their wheelchairs, canes, and crutches thrown in the van behind them. In New York City, the Eastern Paralyzed Veterans Association and Disabled in Action led the efforts to bring the MTA in compliance with the law.

I ride the bus in New York City several times a week. I used to take my car everywhere, or occasionally hail a taxi, but once Rufus and I got into the routine, I began using buses regularly. I "went public" around 1998 when almost the entire fleet of New York buses had been outfitted with wheelchair lifts. I had tried taking the bus at various times since the late '80s, when the MTA first started installing lifts on the buses, but it was much more difficult than it is today. The lifts were not available on many of the buses, and even when a bus showed up that had one, there were times that the driver couldn't find the key or didn't know how to operate the lift. Other passengers would turn and stare at me and look at their watches. While that still happens, these days passengers are more familiar with the procedure because the equipment is used so often, and the drivers are now well trained and the equipment in better shape.

It took federal legislation to do it, but I have become part of the commuting and communing world. The bus drivers are efficient and professional, and most often quite friendly, and I meet people—neighbors, former students, and strangers—on the bus. It is a pleasure to be among them.

A typical ride on the bus goes something like this: When the driver sees me at the bus stop, he or she steers the bus in tight to the curb. The driver then gets up, comes to the back of the bus, opens the door, and, using a key, activates the lift. The lift descends to the street, I back onto it, a small lip rises up in front of my toes to keep me in place, and then I am raised up off the street and into the bus. As this is happening, anyone sitting in the seat opposite the door needs to get up so that the driver can fold that seat against the wall and I can back into that space. When I board, I tell the driver where I will get off, and when my stop arrives, we go through the procedure in reverse.

When it all goes smoothly, as it does most of the time, the whole routine takes about two or three minutes. When the bus is crowded, the control that releases the door doesn't work, or the lift jams, it takes longer. An extra minute, maybe two or three.

The people inside, and those outside at the bus stop, must wait. It can delay their trip, and sometimes I see irritation in their faces. I understand that feeling. New Yorkers don't take inconveniences without protest. We don't mask it, we usually register our disgruntlement. Something can always be done, and we are quick to say what it is, and how to do it.

Yet here, everyone is silent. There is nothing "wrong," per se, nothing to be fixed. And people know that if they were to voice their annoyance, they would appear selfish and unliberal. This is all new, and we are making up the rules and social protocols as we go. The shift in bus behavior is one of the most obvious examples of the adjustments Americans have had to make as a result of the entry of disabled people into the mainstream. When we were hidden, and shuttled about in our Invalid Coaches, we did not delay anyone.

As I write this, about six years have passed since I have been privy to the pleasures of public transportation, and I am thrilled to be in the midst of the clutter of New Yorkers that you find on the bus. While I don't often ride at rush hour, when people can be less sociable and helpful, the sights I do see convince me that the bus does bring out the best in people.

People bond on the bus. Particular circumstances unite us. A back door doesn't close properly, and the driver needs someone to pull it shut after each rush of passengers exits. The driver calls out "Please shut the door," and the request is relayed back through the crowded bus. Another time, everyone gets into the act, wagging fingers and shouting out the back door, as the bus driver scolds a taxi driver who has blocked the bus stop and won't budge. On a rainy day, a woman stumbles while boarding the bus, and two people in the front leap to help her; others vacate their seats and move back to give her room. The driver turns to make sure she is settled in before starting up again, and everyone waits.

Sometimes there are fights and tension. Some days, everyone looks sullen and alienated.

I notice the good times, though, the times when all of us riders seem of one purpose. The woman in a tailored business suit and a man in slouchy pants, standing together, commiserating about the traffic. Old and young, by chance sitting side by side, start laughing at a curbside altercation between a spandex-clad Rollerblader and a delivery man on a rusty bicycle. A young white man sitting in the front jumps up to give his seat to an elderly black woman. It seems so natural, like something that always was and always will be, anywhere, anytime.

And I and other disabled passengers, alongside the nondisabled, going to work, to shop, to the movies, to the doctor's, or to a friend's house. So natural. It would seem that once the transit authority had the technology to put in those lifts, they willfully and enthusiastically supplied them. That they, on their own steam, invested resources in their development. As if those ADAPT demonstrators didn't have to link arms across an expressway in the rain and cold just for a few little wheelchair lifts, for a TTY or relay phone number for deaf people wanting information, and for bus and subway maps, and schedules, in alternative formats for passengers who are blind.

As much as I am pleased by the use of this technology that gives me access to the bus, whenever the driver comes through the crowded aisle to the back door to operate the lift, I am troubled by the way the device sets me apart from the other riders. Because the lift is specific and conspicuous, it seems only to be for those who use wheelchairs, and it creates an unfortunate forced choice option for passengers. We must declare ourselves users of steps or users of lifts. I see people struggling up the steps, who, because of age, impairment, baby carriages, and so forth have enormous difficulty. The design of lift-equipped buses singles me out and makes my needs seem extraordinary and still falls short of creating truly "public" transportation.

Once, a woman on the street stopped to watch as I backed onto the lift. She was leaning on a walker and supported on one side by a woman who was probably her aide. She was silent, but attentive. I caught her eye. "You can use this," I said to her, and her face widened in a grin. The bus driver leaned over my shoulder to add: "Just ask the driver anytime." The woman said, "Really?" and stayed to watch the entire operation, the return of the lift to its resting position, my backing into the space by the window, and the bus driving away.

Now that I am a regular bus rider, I am particularly attuned to the drivers. They so often do their jobs with grace and good humor. One rainy day, I recall, the president was in town, sirens were wailing, and Manhattan had become one big parking lot; yet the driver of the M104 shepherded us down Broadway, paused to give clear directions to a befuddled tourist, and smiled encouragement at a child trying his hand at putting a MetroCard in the slot.

I've even gotten to know some of the drivers. One driver on the crosstown route always wears on his uniform jacket an array of red and gold apple pins, awards for exemplary service to the city. I nominated him for one a couple of years ago. There is an annual ceremony for drivers who have been recognized by disabled people for excellent service. Drivers bring their families, and there are speeches and a big breakfast spread. My nominee gave me a hug when I arrived at the ceremony, and now when he sees me at the bus stop, he says, "Hey girl, you riding with me today?"

One summer night a while back, I met a driver I know only as Maria. When our bus pulled into my stop, she came to the rear door to activate the lift, but it jammed. After a few tries, she ushered the other passengers onto the next bus to arrive. Then Maria and I sat in the back of the darkened bus, with the doors open to let the warm night air in, and waited for the maintenance truck. We talked about her children and about her bus route, the M5. I told her how growing up in New York, my mother and I often took that bus to go on shopping excursions to Macy's. Once I started using a wheelchair in my mid-twenties, I could no longer get on the bus and began to drive everywhere, folding my chair and pulling it into the back seat of my lumbering Oldsmobile. I am finally back on the bus, and it has been wonderful, I told her, largely because of the drivers.

It seems, and I may be projecting a wish here, that most of the drivers take pleasure in helping disabled passengers ride the bus—assuring that the full public is served. I fear, though, that the driver's action is sometimes perceived as a benevolent gesture. One day as I was boarding the bus, a woman stopped to watch. As the lift ascended, she looked up at me and said: "Now, isn't it nice that they put these lifts on the bus so you can go places?"

"Nice? It's because of federal anti-discrimination law," I called after her, but she was already walking down the street. I wanted her to understand how big this is. While there are people at the MTA who have been instrumental in bringing about accessible buses, the changes are largely in response to the passage of the Americans with Disabilities Act in 1990.

In an article in the *New Yorker* about riding the bus, the author groused about how a "guy in a wheelchair held things up for three minutes." He said that "law and propriety dictate" that buses pick up, as he called us, the "wheelchair-bound." While he allowed that the lift is a "civic mitzvah"—the city's good deed, I suppose he meant—he said that the municipal employee had been "reduced, or raised, to a valet."

I would be embarrassed if I felt the drivers saw their role as personal valet or good Samaritan. They are public employees acting in fulfillment of federal law. They provide a critical service, one that enhances the comfort and safety of all New Yorkers.

So I will nominate a driver this year for a Big Apple Award. It is my personal thanks to the women and men who have given new meaning to the term *public transportation.*

Yet the system will not succeed without a cooperative public. I have been impressed by the steady learning curve of my fellow riders. Increasingly familiar with the routine, they move quickly to accommodate wheelchair users. One rainy night, a truly collective effort was necessary to get me off the bus. When the lift descended to the street, the front lip on the platform would not go down. The driver jiggled the key, but it would not budge. I offered a solution—a trick I learned from another driver. I said that if everyone sitting on the right side of the bus moved to the left side, the plate would go down. Reluctantly, he and I asked the passengers if they would move their tired bodies.

It worked, and I rolled off toward home. The driver laughed at this very human solution, and he and the passengers standing behind him waved and bid me goodnight.

Leaving my building one day riding the Rufus, a neighbor said to me, "Oh, look, you've got an electric chair." She added: "You'll be so much more independent now." That word *independent* gets bandied about so much in descriptions of disabled people.

Have I been dependent, and if so on whom or what? What is the nature of that dependency? Is it a bad thing? I disagree with the woman. Not out loud. It took me some time to think this through.

Rufus does help me move out into the world with greater ease, and I do have more flexibility. I can go this way and that on the street, not worried that I will get so far from the car that it will be an ordeal to get back. I can put heavy bags on the back of the chair, Rufus just takes the extra weight in stride, so I can take care of chores more efficiently and David doesn't have to do all the heavy grocery shopping. Yes, I can go some places on my own that I hadn't before, places with steep hills and long distances to cover. But none of this would be possible if the environment were not accessible.

When I use a manual chair and encounter a street corner with no curb cut or a step getting into a restaurant, I can ask someone to give me a boost. In Rufus, I can't mount that step except with a team of three or four very strong and competent people.

I can make more adjustments to inaccessible environments, albeit with the help of others, in a manual chair. If David and I go somewhere that has a few steps, he can usually pull me up the steps or ask a passerby to give him a hand. Once inside, we might register a complaint about the entrance, but the proprietor sees us already in there and will be more complacent about building a ramp. It is a kind of "passing"—taking on the burden of keeping up with the majority, without making demands for change. People who use power wheelchairs or who have other impairments not easily accommodated in the environment as it is currently structured know all too well that some disabled people make the adjustments themselves, masking the need to make the environment accessible for all. We "passers" fool the public into thinking that disability is an individual thing, a matter of personal fortitude and courage. It fuels the myth of "overcoming," and it compromises others' rights.

With Rufus I learned firsthand what I had known and written about in more abstract ways all along: that changes to the communications, social, and built environment are necessary ingredients for equity and justice. It is not simply shiny new technology that will improve people's lives. For instance, before the ADA went into effect there were rarely curb cuts on city streets. There were none, as I recall, within a twenty-block radius of my house. The curb cut requires no advanced technology; it probably could have existed from the minute curbs were invented in the first place. Without them, though, Rufus would be just a hunk of metal, all charged up with nowhere to go. Rufus didn't liberate me, any more than the birth control pill or the washing machine liberated women. These are useful tools, but the tools only work for us when broader, more systemic change occurs.

So, am I more independent? I think not. I think my dependency is more public, and I am reliant on a broader range of people.

I don't feel the need to thank the federal, state, or municipal governments as abstract entities for the accommodations provided to me and other disabled people, as I believe they are our due, but I do feel the need to acknowledge the bus drivers, shopkeepers, bathroom renovators, Braille sign makers, curb cutters, door wideners, TTY installers, lawmakers, policy setters, and all the other human actors

who make these systems work. I think in the case of public employees, such as bus drivers, it is even more important. They are agents of
the civic good, and as I now reap the rewards of greater "good," I
want to recognize those who make it happen. I am dependent on
them, and it is a dependency that feels very fine to me.

It is not only riding the bus or zipping to the store for a quart of milk
that are the pleasures in this age of Rufus. There are other new habits
barely visible to an outsider to my life. They would be unlikely to
notice, or maybe not count as important, the shifts in my wardrobe. I
have taken to wearing nice gloves, those that would get messy and
wear out quickly pushing a manual chair. My hands, well above the
chubby little Rufus wheels, now sport gloves of pearl gray, bright
orange, and bottle green, purchased at my favorite New York spot—
the Columbus Avenue Flea Market. I can wear clothes with big
sleeves and in light colors, things that would be more likely to get
dirty in a manual chair. As only my right hand is needed for steering,
I've gone out for the evening carrying one of the small silk purses that
my mother used to wear to the opera. I now can use an umbrella.

It took me a while to figure out all the potential benefits of having
a free hand while moving. One day, some weeks after Rufus arrived,
I went downtown to spend the afternoon with my friend Harilyn at
the Museum of Modern Art. When we were leaving, I spied an ice
cream vendor, and something clicked in my mind. I said, "Harilyn, I
am going to do something I haven't done in twenty-seven years." We
both got gooey caramel crunch ice cream bars and strolled down Fifth
Avenue eating our treats.

It was the opportunity to wear elegant gloves and a beige tailored
jacket that convinced me to take Rufus to a fancy luncheon that I was
invited to, a benefit for a New York museum. My friend Sylvia had
taken a table and asked me to join her. These kinds of events happen
in New York every day, but I had never been to a luncheon like this
and thought it would be fun. I asked Sylvia to check with the hotel to
make sure it was accessible, including the bathroom. "Yes," she said,
"they told me everything is fine, they have recently renovated the
hotel."

The bus let me off on Fifth Avenue, and I made my way through the
streets to what is reputed to be the most expensive hotel in Manhat-

tan. The doorman tipped his hat, and I asked where the elevators are. He opened the side door, to the left of the glass revolving door, and directed me to go straight ahead. From the bright sharp sunny day I entered the dimly lit velvet quiet of the lobby. The gold-framed mirrors sparkled, the brass was polished, the silk upholstery shimmered. I moved down the wide corridor and saw a set of carpeted steps up to the elevators. There was a plywood ramp on the right, but it was steep and narrow, it had no sides, it was unadorned, and, seemingly, attached to the steps as an afterthought. Though the long corridor stretched out in front of the steps, the ramp was short to take up as little space as possible; it was too steep for me to mount, and it was ugly. The attempt to make it as unobtrusive as possible had rendered it useless and an eyesore. I felt like they put it there to comply with the law, while they hope the law is rescinded so this nuisance can be banished to the basement.

Realizing it would be dangerous to try to go up by myself, I went back to the front to find the doorman to help me up the ramp. He was outside escorting people through the revolving door and didn't see me, so I had to pull open the heavy side door myself in order to get to him. He was cordial and followed me back down the hall. I moved to position myself at the base of the ramp and showed him how to push from behind as I accelerated. And Rufus, the little engine that could, with the extra push from the big burly doorman, got us up that steep, steep ramp. When I landed at the top, there was a flutter of activity as four elevator operators, startled by my sudden appearance, rushed toward me just to make sure that I got into the elevator safely. They were well-intentioned, but were blocking my path. Once they heeded my request to back away, I entered the elevator.

I arrived on the second floor. The guests were moving toward a short, steep set of stairs that led down to a vestibule where people were signing the registration book. There, they were greeted and given table assignments and a program, and then they proceeded back up another set of stairs, of equal height, to the reception. They wound up, a few yards away, at the same level, across a chasm that I could not bridge. I looked around for another route, but I saw none, nor anyone who could help. After a while, a waiter went by, and I asked if there was another way in to the luncheon. Some minutes later he came back to say they couldn't find the ramp. They had intended, I surmised, to put down a ramp for me to descend the stairs; there, I would receive a card with my table number, and the waiters would then pick up the ramp and set it on the next set of stairs and push me back up. I was relieved. The ramp would have been even steeper than the one downstairs.

The waiter said that he would take me through the kitchen. He barked commands at his colleagues, and they cleared the way for me. We got through the kitchen, and arrived in a large foyer where people were milling around. I asked him where the ladies' room was. He pointed to the back of the huge ballroom, crowded with tables, to a raised platform up three steps and said, "Yes, lady, it is right back there." He rushed off. I would have to curtail my liquid intake.

After the luncheon, I left the ballroom, searching for the door to the kitchen that I had come through. I saw a group of men in dark suits milling about, each with a walkie-talkie at the ready. I assumed they were with the hotel, and asked one man to show me which door to use. It turned out they were Secret Service agents, preparing the hotel for the arrival of Vice President Gore. They jumped to their charge. The leader deployed six of the Men in Black to escort me through the kitchen. The two frontmen pushed open the pair of swinging doors to the kitchen. My guardians looked first to the right and then to the left before allowing me to enter. They signaled for me to proceed, and the others quickly moved in close behind me. Orders were given, and waiters flattened themselves against the wall, their arms to their sides. With this flotilla I would be safe from stray canapés and baked Alaskas. I steered Rufus through the waiter gauntlet. We moved swiftly, stealthily. This was serious business. I could steal no food, nor make any jokes. I looked around for Will Smith, but alas, I'd been assigned a duller lot.

My Secret Service detail left me at the elevator, and backed away. I rang the bell and asked the elevator operator if there was a wheelchair-accessible bathroom I could get to. She thought for a minute and said, "Ah, yes, we have a special bathroom for you on the third floor." We arrived. "Straight ahead and on your right, ma'am," she told me. I soon found it. The door was locked, the corridor deserted. I went back and rang for the elevator. This new operator left his elevator to try the door. "Yes, ma'am, it is locked. I'll get security." In time, a man in uniform appeared. He, too, tried to turn the knob.

"Yes, ma'am, it is locked." He tried various keys on his big ring, but didn't have the right one, and so he left. I was by then desperate to use the toilet, just on the other side of the locked door.

In another few minutes, an assistant manager arrived with the key and he opened the door. By then, four people had been witness to my urinations, and it took fifteen minutes just to get in the door of a huge, elegantly appointed, fully accessible, marble bathroom. I contemplated spending the night, but I remembered that the assistant manager had, despite my protestations, insisted on posting himself on the other side of the door, "Just to make sure you are all right."

The peculiar combination of oversolicitousness and flagrant disregard for the well-being of disabled people had never been more apparent to me than it was that day. People fall all over themselves (and you) to help, but when disabled people state what we need to lead our lives, to live with dignity and comfort, to have a place at the table, we are ignored. The impulse to protect is strong, but not to accommodate. The hotel management in its multimillion-dollar renovation provided what it determined we need, and the authorities who are supposed to monitor compliance with federal and local laws signed off on it. While the project may have met some of the codes, though clearly not others, it failed me and all the people the laws were designed to protect.

I didn't write a letter to the hotel as I should have.

Rufus and I just won't go back there again.

But we do go often to the Guggenheim Museum, just a mile north.

No stringent access codes were in place when Frank Lloyd Wright designed the Guggenheim, and I tend to doubt that he conceptualized the grand spiral ramp as a wheelchair-access feature. While it has not always been a totally wheelchair-accessible building (though recent renovations have moved it forward), it is a wheelchair-pleasing building.

The wheelchair user, as most visitors do, takes the elevator to the top floor. It is the last stop, but it is not the top of the building. As you leave the elevator, the spiral continues up to the right at a steep angle, and, on our first visit together, I was delighted to see how Rufus flowed right up, with nary a lurch or waver. When I had visited the museum in a manual chair, I would ask someone to give me a push up to the top, but that day, with a full head of steam, we went up, up, up to that tip of the spiral, then down to the next landing, and, just because I could, up and then down again.

What a sensation. I loved that building like I'd never loved it before, and I had always been enraptured by it. Even when I watched it being built, in 1959, I remember thinking it was something new, something I and the whole world had never seen before, and we must pay attention to it. I would always ask my mother to drive down Fifth Avenue so that we could see it. My mother pronounced it "amusing," and my Aunt Selma cast her eyes up to the sky and shook her head when she saw it, but in my twelve-year-old wonderment, I felt reverence and awe. And in all the years in between, it has been my Magic Kingdom.

The visceral excitement that I feel when I descend the spiral has, if anything, only increased with time. I have visited the museum in a manual wheelchair as well as a motorized one, and the experiences are quite different. I enjoy the building itself more in a manual chair; I am more attentive to the art when I am aboard Rufus. In the manual chair, I tend to move more quickly, as there is a continual pull downward and it takes effort to slow down and brake. The slope doesn't have any effect on Rufus's movement; the chair moves much like it would on a flat surface. It takes equal effort to go slow or fast; stopping is easy. When I am moving quickly I notice the play of light on the walls, I am attentive to the overall theme of the exhibit, or the progression of a single artist's work over time. At a slower pace I focus more on individual pieces.

At a quick pace, usually in the manual chair, I am less attentive to realistic paintings, particularly ones that have rich detail and setting, and require full frontal viewing to absorb the atmosphere and pick up any story the artist is telling us. Divining hidden meanings and interpreting symbolic elements are nearly impossible at warp speed. What does happen, though, when I coast down the spiral at a fair clip, is that my eye captures, for a brief moment, swooshes of color and fragments of form that resemble fireworks exploding and then fading in the night air.

While spiraling down, I am reminded of the most dynamic Impressionist paintings. Impressionists employ color and visible brushwork to show the dissolution of form in light and atmosphere. It is said that with the advent of train travel, painters in increasing numbers were leaving Paris to go to the South of France to paint. As the trains moved (more quickly than horse-drawn carriages) and light caught images and fractured those images, painters began to visualize form in more component parts than the more static views of earlier painters.

A painter on a train going to the South of France, and me spinning down the ramp at the Guggenheim, are different creatures, and we each have used our velocity for different ends. Yet in our new vehicles, we both have been catapulted into a new way to see art.

One cloudy but pleasant spring day, Ruf and I went off to the Gugg to see the exhibition "The Worlds of Nam June Paik." We decided not to take the bus, instead taking a long stroll through Central Park, with a stop for ice cream along the way. I was feeling jaunty and unfettered.

I had been looking forward to this. Paik is a video artist, and I had been promised this show was wonderful and gave the building even more drama and verve. I arrived and entered the vast rotunda. For this exhibit, the skylight was shrouded in black to show off the colored lights that zig-zagged across a sheet of water cascading down from the ceiling, several stories above us. The semi-darkness sharpened the lines of the flashing images projected onto the face of the inner spiraling wall. In a circle, dozens of monitors, each with a different video, were planted in the center of the ground floor, facing the ceiling.

I took a deep breath, I knew I would be there for hours. I stopped many times, there was much to ponder. Fish tanks, swimming with small iridescent fish, sat in front of video screens. The fish darted about; the images flickered behind the fish. Remarkably, the installation was at a height that allowed me to get a full view of many of the objects straight on. Most of the time in museums, I must crane my neck and look up to see the art and I lose so much. Here, as I took in everything around me, I wondered if the material lent itself to a lower placement, but there was nothing obvious that indicated that. Some months later I saw a picture of Paik in a magazine, and he was sitting in a wheelchair. I wondered if that influenced how the material was displayed, as well as the addition of a new ramp to one of the formerly inaccessible galleries. I made a note to myself to write to the museum to thank them for the new ramp, and to ask if it would be there permanently. Recent visits have confirmed my suspicion that the ramp was only there for Paik. I still haven't written the letter.

Rufus and I were moving at a fast clip through one of the cozy side galleries, eager to get back to the main exhibit. A young boy espied me darting among the sculptures. I saw him tracking my moves. Artfully, I wove in and around the Giacomettis and the Brancusis.

When I am in a power chair, kids seem to pay more attention to me than when I am in a manual chair. Maybe it is the high-pitched whir—David says I sound like a pencil sharpener—but it is probably also the speed, the cherry red base of the chair, and the joy stick. They often ask me: "How do you make it go?"

Later, as I was gliding down the last lap of the spiral ramp, there the boy was again, and, while his mom studied a flickering candle set inside a tinny, emptied-out television monitor, he attached to her finger and pivoted a full 180 to watch me whiz by. My chiffon scarf of mauve and silvery gray fluttered behind me. His eyes widened; his jaw slackened.

I wondered: Does he know who Isadora Duncan was? Does he make the association? Does he fear I might die a macabre and extravagant death just for the sake of a little art on a spring afternoon?

Enough about art, it's time to get back on the bus.

One day I left my house and headed up to the bus stop, on my way to a meeting for a new project I was working on. I was dressed in my classiest best. A dark green linen suit, a long stretch of flea-market fabric, probably the remnants of someone's dining room curtains, draped across my shoulders. I had taken some trouble with the accessories: my Grace Kelly orange sunglasses, amber beads, and even lipstick, in a bold brownish tint.

When I got there, the bus was ready to pull out, and the dispatcher asked if I would mind waiting for the next bus. "Not at all," I said. "I'm not in a big hurry." The next bus pulled in, and I moved to wait at the back door where the lift is. He entered the bus to lower the lift, fidgeted with the key, and then said, apologetically, "Now you'll be angry with me for keeping you waiting, this lift isn't working."

Just then, a woman came around the corner riding a clunky institutional manual wheelchair. Her gray hair was flying in all directions in the wind, her blouse was misbuttoned, and all her other clothes were similarly lopsided. The fat-toed sneakers that were sitting up on the footrests of her chair did not seem to be a matched pair. Her socks hung about her ankles, and they were gray-dirty. Her face was a ruddy color, dotted with marks of wear and tear. Her shoulders sloped forward, and she grunted as she pushed her chair. I felt the impulse to ward her off. To move away.

She approached me, though, and asked if I had been waiting long.

"No, but this lift isn't working, we'll have to wait for the next bus."

"Oh," she said and rolled her eyes. It was a commiserating eyeroll, one that said to me—you and I, we know the lift-isn't-working story all too well.

"Someone," I reported to her, "has put chewing gum in the keyhole."

"Oh my. Can you believe the utter stupidity of some people," she exclaimed in crisp syllables, with a faint accent of cerebral palsy.

The dispatcher descended the back steps of the bus and shrugged his shoulders. The woman greeted him by name, "Hi Fred," she said, and he waved. He apologized to us both, and said, "I guess you'll have to wait for the next one."

When the bus arrived, the dispatcher again mounted the back steps to help speed up the process, and to make sure that we got on. I went in first, and positioned my chair facing front. The woman came up next and with some maneuvering in the tight space, pulled into the slot in front of me. The window next to her was open slightly, and as the bus began to move I was hit by a strong smell of stale urine. I couldn't tell if it was her, or whether it was on the floor under me. It was a sickening smell, and I looked behind me to see if I could move my chair back, get away from it. There was nowhere to move. Would people think it was me? Would the stuff get on the wheels of my chair and stick with me all day?

The woman had opened the window further, and stuck her face out into the breeze. She was smiling. What pleased her, this breeze, discomfited me, as it sent more of the harsh smell my way. She turned to tell me that when she was a child she liked to put her head out the window on the school bus. I imagined her young and clean, riding to school. I wondered whether she'd been in an institution, as many disabled children have been through the years. Did her family abandon her to the state, or did she live with them? If she lived at home, was she loved and cared for, or did her parents force their shame on her and keep her out of sight? How did she wind up, dirty and poor, here on this bus?

I was struck by her casual manner and her trust in me. She recognized our bond and I, untrue to my words, had forgotten it. It is *we* that have to wait for the bus with the working lift, it is *we* who needed federal legislation to be able to ride a bus, any bus. We are together in that. I felt ashamed of my wish for her to go away. My urge to have others not see us as one. Not smell us as one. I found myself thinking how peculiar it was that she seemed so optimistic, and then scolded myself for questioning the value of her life and the pleasures to be had in it—just as others might question mine.

I can't discard her. I must see myself in her and her in me.

I started talking to her, without consciously setting out to do so.

"Not much traffic today. Yesterday," I said, "Clinton was in New York and it took me forty-five minutes to get across town."

"Oh yeah, I remember, and it was raining too, wasn't it?"

"Yeah, it was a mess."

I couldn't see her too well. Her chair was facing front, and she could only swivel a bit to talk to me sideways. I leaned forward, toward her. "I'm getting off at the next stop," I said.

"Well, I hope the driver remembers. If he doesn't, we'll shout so loud he'll never forget again," she said and laughed out loud.

The driver did remember, and came to the back door to let me off.

"Well, have a good day," I called out to her as I got onto the lift.

"Yeah, you too."

A couple of weeks later, I saw her sitting in the middle of the sidewalk on Broadway with a cup in her hand, asking for spare change. I stopped and fished in my pocketbook for a dollar. I smiled, unsure if she would remember me, and unsure about how she would feel if I gave her the money. A number of times when I've passed disabled men and women on the street who are asking for money, they startle when they see me reach to put something in their cup. "No, no, not from you." "Oh, no, I couldn't take money from you." I don't know sometimes whether to just leave, their embarrassment seems so great, or to use my standard line: "No, it's OK, if I was there, and you here," I say, indicating we are interchangeable cripples, in all respects but my steady income, "you'd give me something." That seems to make it easier.

So I was hesitant as I approached her. But she greeted me and said "Thank you," as I reached over to put my dollar in her cup. She was at home here. This was her job. Her smile revealed missing teeth, but it was a true smile and it lingered. I smiled back. "How ya' doin'?" I asked my neighbor. We were face to face, chair to chair, our toes nearly touching. I on one side clutching my fat wallet, she on the other with her McDonald's offering basket. We sat there, while all the passersby, head and shoulders above us, eddied around our wheelchair island.

I commented: "Look at all these shops with steps getting in." We turned and noted three stores in a row, their goods and services off-limits to us. She opined: "It's illegal, but they just get away with it." I concurred.

Of all the outward trappings of my privilege, I feel most guilty about Rufus. Why shouldn't she have a lightweight manual chair, or a power chair if she can use it? I know that pushing the old, rusty chair she uses now must be a terrible strain. It is too large for her, and she has to stretch her arms around the high metal side pieces to reach the tire rims. I can't figure out what I can do, what I should do, and I do nothing.

She was looking past me now, and had turned somewhat to catch the attention of the people going by. I backed up a bit to turn and leave. While I called out a casual "See you around," I felt tight inside.

She said, "See you later," and I went off toward home, melding into the crowd of spenders and buyers, the hunters of yellow grapefruits, whole-grain bread, and exotic condiments, and left the gatherer, the spare-change artist, to ply her trade on our neighborhood street.

Rufus has brought me face to face with many such dilemmas, and many such pleasures. It is not only that Rufus transports me to places where I have these encounters, but using a power chair has upped the ante of my disability. I am not talking about changes in the physical properties of my condition, but the change in my interface with the environment. Power chair users require greater levels of accommodation, and at each level we test the principles of equity and justice. I require more of the United States than I ever have before, but no more than is my due.

14 *Odyssey of a*
Sure-footed Man

Homer Avila blew into my life, and I was excited by his "artsiness" as well as the artistry I eventually witnessed. He had dark soulful eyes, and a worldliness about him that was unsullied by snobbishness.

I first met Homer in March of 2002 at a conference on disability and film. I was in the rear of the auditorium, behind the last row of seats, and someone slipped up behind me, slightly to my right. He was using lightweight metal crutches. He slid them under the seat in front of him and then quickly vaulted over the back row and landed smoothly and quietly in an empty seat. I glanced over to take a better look at him, and guessed he was the dancer with one leg that Jennifer Dunning, a dance critic for the *New York Times,* had written about.

I watched him throughout the day, and wondered what he thought of that gathering. Late in the afternoon I asked him if we could get together sometime to talk. He didn't seem to need a reason, and quickly wrote down his number and said to please call.

In the two years that I knew him, we were not together in the same place more than fourteen or fifteen times, yet we talked on the phone usually once or twice a week. Homer took dance classes often when he was in New York, had a rigorous schedule of rehearsals and planning meetings for performances, had various doctor's appointments, and had many friends that he checked in on regularly. In addition, he traveled a great deal. He'd call to say he was going to Germany to dance with the Frankfurt Ballet or that he was on his way to Washington to dance at a celebration at the Kennedy Center for the reopening of their Opera House. I called his cell phone one afternoon, and he was in the Miami airport heading to a dance festival. The airline had lost his luggage, and he had no dance clothes for a performance he was scheduled for that evening. I stayed on the phone with him, sometimes talking, sometimes just holding on as he alternately pleaded with and cajoled people into tracing his bags. We laughed when he told me that he had to slip me (his phone, really) into his pocket, as he moved about. He couldn't wield his crutches and hold the phone at the same time. We extolled the virtues of shirts with pockets so that you can keep your hands free for pushing wheelchairs and holding crutches.

We didn't speak for a few weeks after that, and I learned that in that time he had been to California to work on a new piece with Victoria Marks, a choreographer I knew of, and then to New Orleans to visit with his mother and nephew, and then back to California to work with the Axis Dance Company, a company that integrates disabled and nondisabled dancers.

Because in the circles that I travel in, disability is ordinary, a man with one leg, who is a dancer, who travels around the world to perform, may be of interest, but he would be only one of a number of people we know of with significant impairments who are actors, dancers, or performance artists.

Homer's name started to crop up in conversations I'd have with friends and colleagues. I would say that I had met him, and we were getting to be friends, but I hadn't yet seen him dance.

I was on the road a lot myself, and many of our phone conversations were between me in L.A. and Homer in Vermont, or Homer in San Francisco and me in St. Louis. It took some months until I actually saw a performance. I had not asked much about his dancing—neither about his technique, nor how he moved on the stage. He had said that he didn't use his crutches when he danced. Though he had for a while considered using a prosthetic leg, he so enjoyed the liberty that his light body gave him that he lost interest in that. He eventually got a prosthesis, but I never saw him with it, on stage or off. And dancing with crutches didn't appeal to him. There is a dancer and performance artist Homer and I went to see at the Public Theater—Bill Shannon, a.k.a. Crutchmaster—who dances with crutches as if partnering with them. We were both excited by his performance, and Homer said he'd leave dancing with crutches to Bill.

The first time that Homer and I got together to talk, it was in a Starbucks in my neighborhood. He walked in, came right over to where I was sitting, leaned down, and kissed my cheek. We were, he was telling me, already connected. He went to get some coffee, and carried it over with two fingers around the cup and the other three wrapped around the handle of his crutch. In precise, fluid movements he placed his cup on the table, unhitched his backpack and placed it under his seat, removed his denim jacket and slipped it over the back of his chair, laid his crutches on the floor under the table and out of the way, and sat down. Nothing that mundane had ever been so elegantly done.

He had come uptown for an appointment with a massage therapist. We talked about bodies, our bodies, and the struggle to keep them in alignment.

He began right away talking about "the work," almost as if it existed outside of him. His schedule for the next few months: where he would be dancing, with whom, and the music he had in mind. I found it hard to keep straight the many projects he talked about, and the bits about his life that he wove into this accounting. He briefly traced his lengthy career as a dancer, and the many companies he had danced with prior to the amputation of his leg. I pieced together that he had been disabled less than a year, and that he had begun taking dance classes again about two months after his surgery. In a quick and efficient sentence, he told me that he had cancer, they had removed his right leg and hip, and, he added, he was now fine and feeling good. During the months prior to the surgery, though he had been dancing, he had a great deal of discomfort, and the surgery relieved him of this and made him more agile.

In some later conversation he quipped that he had lost two legs and gained one. "Ah," I said, "you mean you lost two-leggedness." "Yes," he said, "exactly." We talked about getting some famous designer to create skirts or sarong-type outfits for him—not to mask the missing limb; indeed, the draping he desired would reveal the space. "That would be great," I said. "Pants have such a presumption of the two, a pair." I also heard him tell an audience in Atlanta, in a post-performance discussion, that he "had lost one leg and gained wings."

There was never a tone of fatalistic resignation, nor a sense of some cosmic purpose to what had happened to him. He didn't feel he was being tested, though he certainly felt challenged, artistically, to make something of this body he had, and to share "the work" with as large an audience as he could find.

What I recognized in Homer was something I knew well from my own experience: that the blow dealt your body was manageable to the extent that what you did in that body was worthwhile. It took me much longer than the two months it took Homer to get out of bed and start dancing. In part, my injuries were more extensive, and recuperation and rehabilitation took much longer, but also I had to gird myself just to go out in public in that first year, and endure the stares of people at the novelty that I was. In 1972 there was rarely anyone else in a wheelchair on the streets, in museums, at theaters, and none at the college I enrolled in when I got out of the hospital. As for dancing, though I was not a performer, it would be several years until I found my way back onto a dance floor again at Glenn's party, when the rock and roll and the pot and David, the fine partner I had found, catapulted me back into pleasures I had forsaken. My shame and my awkwardness as the paraplegic wheelchair dancer have all but disappeared, but it took years, not months.

How had Homer managed to do it so quickly? He showed up in a dance class less than two months after his surgery, stood at the barre alongside lithe ballet dancers. He figured out how to dance on one leg in front of the mirrors that covered the long wall of the dance studio, reflecting two-legged dancers doing what came naturally to them, and had been natural to him, just weeks before. They watched too, I'm sure, and witnessed the slow emergence of Homer's one-legged artistry.

About two months after that first class, he got on a plane, traveled to California, and took an intensive ballet seminar with choreographer Alonzo King. On September 9, 2001, five months after the surgery, he gave his first public performance in Vermont. He began dancing again and never stopped.

I found myself in awe of Homer: for restarting his life, for creating extraordinary dance with his new body, for his seeming clearheadedness about living in the body he now had, and for making a significant impact on the cultural landscape—one that raises questions about the nature of dance itself.

I would sometimes find myself saying—quietly, just to myself— "He is inspiring" or "He is brave." These are terms I reject vociferously when I hear them applied to me and other disabled people I know. The words seem mawkish. Are we inspiring just for existing? Are we brave for merely going to the supermarket and carrying out our daily chores?

People I knew who had met Homer talked about how his dancing had caused them to reconsider their reticence to play music after an illness that had affected voluntary control of their muscles, speak in front of an audience with a voice that quivers and is sometimes hard to hear, dance again after many years off stage and a weight gain of twenty or thirty pounds.

The musician is Alice Sheppard, an English professor at Penn State who works in disability studies. She said that even when her impairment began to affect her ability to hold her flute, and to regulate her breathing, she tried to continue to play. Eventually, she gave up. Alice wrote to me recently, saying, "I tried, believe me I tried. But my flabby spazzing body no longer played with any accuracy and it was painful both physically to do and emotionally to hear."

She saw Homer dance, and had an important conversation with him. She said: "Homer showed me how to hear the flaws and flubs differently. They were no longer fuckups, but feelers of a new music. Homer showed me that technical brilliance could be relocated. Homer showed me how to hear a new music and dared me to play it again."

All of this makes me think of altering my perspective on bravery and inspiration. Maybe it would be legitimate for me to say that Homer, or Corbett or Devva or any of the lot of us, *is* brave for defying expectations and struggling to make this life possible. That when our actions are purposeful, our art exciting, or our words meaningful, we *do* inspire.

What thrilled me about Homer included his dance, his ideas, his belief in the dance he was creating. All those took enormous will. Sweat and tears, though he hid the latter from me. He would be angry sometimes, and resentful when producers didn't give him an opportunity to show his work. He stuck to it, and he produced, in the three years he danced post-surgery, a repertoire of dances choreographed for him and performances that captured the attention of critics and a public unaccustomed to viewing such an extraordinary body in the spotlight. A review in the *New York Times* said of one of these that the work "burrowed into dance in a way that communicated the pleasure of the movement that is its heart."

Homer got under my skin, and through learning about his life, I have revisited my own.

One of the ways I got to know Homer was by watching a videotape of a talk he gave, a conversation really, at Juilliard, with a group of senior dance students. The tape shows Homer in front of a class of twenty or so students, sometimes standing, sometimes sitting on the edge of a desk, talking with them about his life as a dancer and his experience with impairment. Interwoven in the hour-and-a-half talk about everything from his early discovery of dance when he was in college, where, he told the students, he was a competitive gymnast and ran track, to a recent performance at the Kennedy Center, he revealed his anguish in those early days after the surgery.

"There was a moment between 3:15 and 3:30," he told the students, "on a Tuesday in the hospital. I felt that whatever was keeping me alive was so small I could hold it in the palm of my hand. I just felt that I couldn't stop the process of shutting down. Found myself leaving life. Then there was something wondrous—I was still there, in spite of myself. During those fifteen minutes—an intimacy I developed within those fifteen minutes. I stared at the essence of my life. Something strong and clear helped me to coming back to my life."

In listening to Homer, I remembered my own turnaround, or more accurately the series of turns-around that brought me back. There was some day a few weeks after the accident when I awoke from the nightmares and I started to look forward, toward what I would do when I left that place.

In admiring Homer's resolve, I could admire my own. He helped me take credit for what I had done some thirty years ago, and he reminded me that even in the bleak early months of my confrontation with the injury to my body, I was interested in things outside of me— I could be amused, distracted, and, more important, excited.

I listened to Homer tell the students: "I was like a baby—couldn't move. Found myself incarcerated in this body, confronting fears. How could this happen? What would I do? I didn't think there was anything left to do. But," he said, "there was a small voice inside me—go forward."

One day, shortly after his surgery, he said, Juilliard dance students were giving a performance in the rec room at Mount Sinai Hospital. "Of course," he said, "I went. I was in my wheelchair. It felt like angels coming to receive me."

As I watched Homer on the video I began to cry, for Homer and, also, for me, for all I had been through. Homer was sitting on the edge of a desk, and he leaned in toward the young dancers: "To see people bring their passion and clarity to this place—the hospital environment is so sterile, devoid of life—and to see people's eyes light up." Homer was telling the students about the power of their art.

I recalled my first official outing from the rehab center, where I was to spend six months after having already spent four in the hospital. We were to go to the Apollo Theater in Harlem, to see a Senegalese dance company. I was the first to sign up for the trip, though I remember spending the next few days worried about how the world would perceive me in my debilitated state. I dressed in whatever clothes I could find that made me look like my old self. I weighed about ninety pounds, and my waist-length hair had been chopped off in the emergency room some five months before, and was still kind of ratty and lopsided, but I put on a hippie shirt with big pouffy sleeves. I managed, with the help of a caring nurse, to get a pair of jeans on over the metal back brace I had to wear in those days.

They loaded all of us "wheelchairs," as they called us, onto a bus, strapped us down, and we proceeded uptown to the theater. The bus pulled up in front of the famous Apollo, and the lift on the bus carried each of us down to the sidewalk. I rolled off the platform and managed to push my chair across the rough pavement on my own steam. I had not yet pushed my chair myself outside the confines of the rehab center. It took more effort than gliding down those linoleum corridors, yet I wanted to be able to control my pace and direction.

I felt excitement just entering the lobby. People milling about in fancy clothes, with expectation and laughter in their voices. I pushed on to the doorway to the theater—saying multiple "excuse me's," and negotiating around people clustered in the back waiting to take their seats. I couldn't know then how many times I would do that in my life—at that point I didn't know if I would ever do it again—and I never imagined how at ease I would be, how natural it would become for me.

All of us "wheelchairs" were lined up behind the last row in the orchestra, much further back than I would have liked, but I caught the excitement of the dance and sat up tall in my chair, and applauded with enthusiasm.

What the night gave me, and it was just what the recreation therapist who organized the trip must have wanted, was the recognition that there was a world outside the hospital that I could take part in. I might have arrived there in a wheelchair, but I could derive pleasure from the dancers' movements, feel the thump of the drums in my bones, and I could carry home with me images of swirling bright colors and rhythmic steps that I conjured up late that night back in my hospital bed, where I was, once again, a patient.

What I also thought of that night were the other patrons. Some smiled and welcomed us, saying things like "It's so good that they brought you here," or "So glad you could be here," somehow signaling that we were not like other audience members. Others looked away. I felt lost in that sea of walking people, and I didn't like being stuck in the back of the theater, but these were the only places we were allowed to sit. It was my first taste of the kind of awkward spaces I would be forced to inhabit, particularly in the first years of my experience with disability.

I worried that all my pleasures would be compromised. Initially, they were. The sense of being out of place, of not belonging. The stares. The peculiar way that some people responded to me. The steps that were everywhere, and the inaccessible bathrooms that forced me to abstain from drinking liquids on the days I would be going to the theater, the movies, or even out to dinner. Over time, I have become accustomed to it or, more accurately, resigned to it, but also things have changed enormously. More places that I go are accessible, although really only a fraction of the restaurants, theaters, and such really offer decent access. The public has changed, in response to the greater numbers and heightened visibility of disabled people. Mercifully, we have become more ordinary.

I understood Homer when he told the Juilliard students about that first performance he saw in the hospital and his thrill at the dancers' potency. What he remembered, or chose to report to them, was his and the audience's pleasure. He didn't say if there was also pain watching them do what he feared he would no longer be able to do.

It seemed, though, from what he said to the students, and what I sensed from Homer, that moments like those helped him see that his life held promise.

He paused after telling the students about the performance and his feelings, and it seemed he didn't know what he would say next. He looked out at the young women and men, and he asked them what their greatest fears were. Homer listened intently as a few of the students told of their fear of damage to their bodies, and what it would mean to their future. A couple of them cried as they spoke to him, and they seemed to be confused about what would be appropriate to say to this man. Homer stood there and listened and nodded his head in encouragement. He didn't say much, but somehow conveyed that it was all right for them to say what was on their mind. After a while, he said, seemingly out of the blue, "I enjoy walking down the street."

The tone shifted, and he talked with them about his world travels, endless rehearsals, the joy of choreography, and the thrill of performance.

As he talked to the students, he became increasingly physical, gesturing with his hands, standing up, leaning on the desk, moving his crutches off to the side. He was animated as he described the choreographers he had worked with, names that registered with this group of senior dance students. He jumped up on the desk and sat cross-legged (in this case, it was his one leg crossed in front of his body), with his back arched and his elegant neck stretched out. He described the duet that Alonzo King had created for him, and the solo by Victoria Marks, and his own choreography. He said, "I can't have people contain my life."

On one of Homer's trips to Germany, in February of 2003, he met Patricia, an artist from Holland. He let me know, slowly, over the course of two or three phone conversations, that there was someone in Europe he wanted to get back there to see.

A few months later, Patricia came to New York, and Homer brought her to our house for dinner. Homer was in love, and David and I enjoyed watching them care for each other and laugh together.

Patricia would eventually say to me, as we got to know each other: "My friends didn't understand my relationship with Homer. But I told them, 'It isn't just any one-legged dancer, with terminal cancer, who lives thousands of miles away and is twenty years older than me. It is Homer!' "

In December of 2003, Homer checked himself into Sloan-Kettering, the cancer hospital, for radiation treatment. I called his cell phone one day, not realizing he was in the hospital, and when I tried to pin him down for a date for coffee, he was vague and elusive. Finally he said: "I'm not too mobile right now."

"What do you mean?"

"Well, I'm in the hospital for a few days."

"Where? I'll be right over."

It was then that he told me what he had known for about a year: that his cancer had spread to his heart and his lungs. He had at that point already outlived his doctor's prediction for his life. He had been admitted for radiation to stop the bleeding in his lung, so that he could get on an airplane and visit his mother for Christmas. He had not told her that his cancer had returned, and he wanted to go to New Orleans and tell her and his nephew.

Very few people knew, and I promised him I would not reveal this news. I kept my promise even as we planned for a performance at a conference in Atlanta that I had been urging him to perform at, and urging the organizers to sponsor.

In early March of 2004, about six weeks before he died, Homer came to Atlanta to dance at the conference, "Disability and the University," sponsored by the Modern Language Association (MLA) and Emory University. The focus of the meeting was on the field of disability studies and its impact on the academy. The MLA had put enormous effort and resources into creating a landmark conference. My friend Rosemarie, who was also a friend of Homer's, raised additional funds for the performance and, together with the planning committee, arranged to have Homer dance on the closing night.

When he arrived at the conference center in Atlanta, Homer was immediately immersed in a nest of disabled people. I introduced him to everyone I knew. He was gracious and friendly, but subdued. He looked tired, and it worried me, and I urged him to try out the swimming pool and the sauna. He disappeared for a few hours, and when he appeared at dinner, he looked refreshed and eager. Later that night, I found him sitting alone at the bar, downing a very large glass of beer. He said that the beer, combined with the sauna, would assure him a good night's sleep.

The next night he was on stage. It was a small makeshift stage in a conference-center auditorium, but Homer made it work for him.

He danced with passion and verve. He swung his arms in the air, he threw himself on the floor, he swerved . . . he pulsed with life. I watched his every move, I knew I would not see him dance again, but I held my breath for much of the performance. What if he should fall? What if he had trouble breathing? What should I do? Rosemarie was the only other person there who knew of his condition. We had arranged this performance before we learned about the recurrence of his cancer, and before we knew how compromised his health was. Homer wanted to go ahead. He wanted to dance more than anything in the world, and it would be unthinkable to stop him. This was a conference on ideas about disability, and whatever state Homer was in, if he determined that he wanted to go on stage, this audience would find great meaning in his movements.

He was scheduled to do three solos. Two at the beginning of the evening, followed by the Flying Words project, a performance group with Deaf poet Peter Cook and his hearing collaborator, Kenny Lerner, who use a combination of American Sign Language, mime, movement, and spoken word to tell elaborate and fanciful stories. Then Homer would do a third solo.

My favorite piece of the evening was one I'd seen him do a few times before, choreographed by Victoria Marks, to music by Miguel Frasconi. It has segments with loud, pounding music, and then switches, abruptly, to lyrical, almost wistful music. Homer moves through the piece as if pulled by ropes, up, down, to the side. First fast, and then for a spell in slow arching movements that convey pain and longing, and then, as if whipped about by a sudden thunderstorm, the music shifts and he begins to move in quick staccato beats. At the end of the piece, during a passage of music with slow, drawn-out notes, Homer stands on his leg, facing the audience, his arms out, palms up, and shouts, "I am Homer David Avila, I am Homer David Avila." His voice rips right through you. The stage fades to black.

I recalled as I watched him that night something Homer had said once in an interview: "When life is fierce, one gets ferocious."

In another solo, he recited a poem. His breathing was heavy, but he uttered words in a beautiful cadence that matched his steps. I remember the words: *thunder, light, winds of,* and *body.* The poem was followed by a long pause, Homer lying stretched out on the ground. Suddenly he extended his leg, and started sliding across the stage. He jumped up, and then leaned over, balancing on his hands and moving, animal-like, on all threes, across the stage.

After the performance, a large crowd gathered in the bar. Many people wanted to buy the artists, Peter, Kenny, and Homer, rounds of drinks. We sat in the lounge area where couches and upholstered chairs held many of us, some of us had our own wheelchairs, and others sat on the floor. I was part of a circle at the far end of the room, with Homer in the middle, sitting cross-legged on a large rectangular coffee table.

Though Homer, somehow, even in his early months with disability, seemed to know what he needed to know, he was in our book a novice. Those of us in the group who had logged ten, twenty years or a lifetime of being disabled, and who studied and wrote about it constantly, probably all felt that Homer might stand to gain from our experience.

We were clearly eager to learn from his. The kind of creative use of the disability experience that we had translated into words, Homer was writing with his body.

A topic that kept coming up that night was the growing ranks of disabled artists and the exciting cultural moment we were part of, and that many of us had helped stimulate. Particularly, we noted a significant number of dancers who present these ideas and this work to the public. Of course, Homer did have an impact on those already in the field, and, as he would be the first to say, they had an impact on him.

He seemed then, and throughout the time I knew him, to want to work with dance companies that included disabled people. He was as interested in those troupes as he was, for instance, in the Frankfurt Ballet, a company he toured with in 2003.

He wanted to create dances and he wanted to dance, and he was appalled at the roadblocks and rejections he and others encountered. I believe that if he had lived, he would have become a strong voice for disabled artists. Not only those, like Homer, who incur injuries mid-career, but young people coming up who are discouraged from and often denied careers in the arts.

In a 2002 interview he said about the collection of dances choreographed just for him, a grouping that he called *(Body of) Work in Progress:* "I have a limitation, but the work does not." Homer had exacting standards for performance, but not for the bodies who perform. He wanted to explore what people have and how they move.

For those of us hanging out at the bar that night, there was much to celebrate. The conference, so far, had been a success. This event was a testimony to the way the field of disability studies was receiving broad attention after years of struggle for recognition. And Homer and the Flying Words Project had given us more reason to be proud for paving the way for the legitimization of disabled people's artistry.

Homer held court, sitting on his coffee table, but he was not an aloof artiste, rather a fellow traveler wanting to hear everyone's story, and think through important ideas together. I labeled him polymorphously curious.

Recently, Patricia sent me a copy of a letter she had written to some American friends shortly after meeting Homer, telling how she'd met him, and about the start of their relationship. She had promised to send it to me, as we never got around to talking about that in the times we spent together.

Patricia wrote that a few months before meeting Homer, she had begun an art/writing project on the relationship between the body and the mind. A number of questions drove the project: If the body changes, does that change someone's mind? How are body and identity related, how do they influence each other? Is someone who is chronically ill in danger of *becoming* the condition?

Patricia is a conceptual artist, who uses every medium imaginable in her work. She had no idea what form this project would take, but was motivated to explore these ideas in whatever way made sense to her. She began exploring the Internet for the first time in her life, and came across a site about . . . "Homer Avila, a New York dancer and choreographer who was continuing his professional career after having lost his right leg and hip (after twenty-five years dancing on two limbs) to a rare form of cancer." She clicked a button, and was able to watch a segment of a recent performance of Homer's. She was, she wrote, "stunned."

After some more searching, Patricia learned he was to appear with the Frankfurt Ballet, and through a series of coincidences found Homer's e-mail and wrote asking to interview him when he arrived in Frankfurt, an easy train ride from her home in the south of Holland.

So they met. She spilled her beer all over herself and Homer on their first meeting, and a glass of wine on the second.

They laughed at that, and other things. They talked, and they both cried together within hours of meeting. She wrote to her friends: "His sensitivity and sweetness blew me away. I was so deeply touched by him, how on earth could a being that had been through so much pain in his life (unimaginably more than the loss of his leg, if that wasn't enough) be so gentle and sweet? And be so young, so much more a naughty boy than an old man?"

She wrote more, and toward the end she said: "Our relationship continues like that. Except that besides miracles, the gods drop bombs as well." She promised to elaborate when they could talk in person. She was referring, I suppose, to the news that Homer's cancer had returned, and his life expectancy was then only a few months, or maybe a year.

It was a year, even with some heavy doses of chemo toward the end to stave off the disease, and so they only had fifteen months together.

The questions that led Patricia to Homer are among the questions that fuel my work. I am prone to ask about political meanings as well, and the social and cultural climate. What, for instance, made it possible for Homer to give the public performances he did? I think, and he once agreed with me on this, that the disability rights movement and our work in disability studies have fostered a new climate of acceptance, and interest in disabled people's experience and ideas.

There were not enough chairs to contain all of Homer's friends, so people stood along the sides of the room and latecomers filled up the hallway. Many of them were dancers with long necks and slim, taut bodies, wearing soft, flowing clothes in fanciful colors. There were others in attendance, women and men, in business suits, and a woman in a formal hat and tailored black dress.

In the front of the long narrow room, next to the wreaths and bouquets, and the small table with a book in which to write your name and a message to the bereaved, was a wooden podium.

Without being summoned, individuals rose and went to the

podium. They carefully stepped over their neighbors' knees, and slipped sideways through the thicket of people standing along the wall. The movements were graceful and quiet. No one said, "Excuse me."

Each speaker took a deep breath, and began haltingly to speak of Homer. Though each one stood tall, the voices were subdued and most were choked with emotion. Homer had died on Sunday, and now it was Thursday afternoon, April 29, 2004.

I was in the back, in front of the archway leading to the reception hall, and I couldn't hear every word. Yet I heard most of the stories. There were chance encounters that led to long friendships. Others told of Homer helping younger dancers to hold their resolve, and not succumb to the strain and defeat ever present in the dancer's life. Almost everyone mentioned his smile, and the fact that he seemed to be everywhere they went—at every dance performance, every concert, every foreign city.

Everyone marked Homer's life by his surgery and stated whether they had known him before or, in a few cases, only since the amputation of his right leg, in April of 2001. Whenever it was that they met him, what struck people about Homer, pre- or post-surgery, were his generosity and quiet resolve.

One of the dancers recalled going to see him at the hospital just three or four days after the surgery. She said that Homer was sitting up in bed, talking on the phone. Papers were scattered across the covers.

"What are all these papers?" she asked.

"I've got work to do."

He was already planning, choreographing in his mind, strategizing whom he would speak with, who could set a place for him in the dance world. I don't think he knew what he would do—maybe choreograph, maybe teach; it had not yet occurred to him that he might dance.

The woman said that while she was overcome by emotion at seeing him, and fearful of her reaction to the devastation that he had experienced, Homer swept up the papers into a pile, patted the bed, and invited her to sit down. "There's plenty of room," he told her. "There's only one leg in there."

After she spoke, a woman rose and came to the front, a tall woman, with a halo of hair framing her brown face. She began to speak, but only began, and, instead, arched her back, raised her arms in the air, and swooped and turned, rose and fell, in a plaintive dance, a paean to Homer. After her silent dance, she sat down. It was Edisa Weeks, Homer's partner for many years in Avila/Weeks Dance.

Sometimes after a person spoke, there was a long pause till another came forward. I thought I might say something, but I didn't know what it might be. Others said they had only known him a short time, and yet felt close to him. I could say how hungry he was for ideas, for people, for food. He ate with relish, but very slowly. He was appreciative, but not effusive. He directed his attention to you with a quiet concentration that gave you a chance to say whatever you wanted or could.

At the end of Homer's funeral, following a long silent space after his brother John spoke, Patricia told us that she would like to play a song that Homer had requested be played at his funeral. It was by a singer I'd never heard of, Eva Cassidy, from her album *Songbird*. I held my breath, I knew this would be hard. I had been crying for two hours. As each person spoke, there was one more reason to miss Homer, and mourn the loss of all the parts of Homer revealed here— the man I would never get to know fully.

The song was not what I expected. Homer had esoteric taste in music, and I didn't think it would be a familiar song, and certainly not a sentimental one. He would have liked to have known that it is the same song that was played at the end of Ray Charles's funeral, about a month after Homer's.

It was a choice that made us sob, many out loud, but as was Homer's way, it comforted us as well. Not because it was an easy salve for the pain of missing him, but because it reminded us of the whimsical and optimistic Homer:

"Somewhere, over the rainbow . . ."

A few days after the funeral, Patricia and one of Homer's closest friends, Ann Greene, came to our house for dinner. David and I met them at the door where we all hugged and cried a little more.

Patricia was wearing Homer's gray corduroy pants and soft denim shirt, the clothes he had worn to the hospital on Saturday night, the night before he died. A nurse had given her those in a blue plastic bag when she arrived from the airport. Patricia was taller than Homer by about five inches, and the pants barely reached her ankles. She wrapped her arms around her body to show us how she could touch him, in there with her. She had on a pair of clunky white sneakers, nothing like the exotic platform shoes she usually wears, and we all laughed that she had managed to find a complete *pair* of shoes in Homer's closet, usually filled with single left shoes.

I could see his face in my mind: penetrating dark eyes, a craggy face, full, sculpted lips, high forehead, and soft, tight brown curls that went this way and that across his head.

Patricia is tall and willowy. Her complexion is fair, and she has striking red hair that reaches below her knees. She often wears it parted down the middle and swept up into two pointed cone-shaped buns on either side of her head—like rabbit ears.

That night we talked about all the personal papers and boxes of videotapes in Homer's apartment. Patricia was going to stay on in New York to sort through them, and see if a selection could be organized for the New York Public Library's Dance Department Archives. We learned of the many companies Homer had danced with pre-surgery: Bill T. Jones, Twyla Tharp, Mark Morris, Momix, Ralph Lemon, and then the company Avila/Weeks Dance, which he formed with Edisa. The significance of his career was the arc of it, not only what he had accomplished in recent years.

Patricia wound up staying in New York over a month, and in subsequent visits we watched some of the tapes of Homer's performances and interviews with him. From those tapes, and in conversations with Ann and Patricia, I learned more about the Homer I hadn't been able to find in the short time I knew him.

While I had the impression that Homer had attended that first dance class with a determination to restart his career, Patricia said that he had gone there as the only way he knew to work on developing his body and learning balance. The physical therapy offered to him in the hospital was, as he said in one of the videotaped interviews, "so gross, prehistoric." He needed to learn how to move about in the world, and he turned to the training he respected the most—ballet.

Once he began taking class regularly, he discovered not only the strength and capability of his transformed body, or his "reconfigured" body, as he called it, but that this new instrument had attributes and creative potential he had not foreseen. It was a body that aroused his curiosity, and he pursued an almost formal inquiry into its qualities.

He found something in his body that I saw when I first met him, that it was an interesting-looking body and one that moved well. Not moved well "despite" its limitations, but a body that had something to say.

What were the obstacles Homer faced? He remarked once to Patricia that every time he walked down the street, people would turn to stare—double, triple takes were common—but he could not get a certain group of dance impresarios to take just one look, particularly in the New York dance world. He had traveled and had successes in Europe and across the U.S., had been on the cover of *Dance Magazine,* with a six-page spread inside, but he was frustrated by the many roadblocks.

There were probably many reasons for this, ones we'll never know, but among them surely is the idea that a dancer with one leg, or any dancer with a significant impairment, is a gimmick, not legitimate. Their moves are thought to be compensatory ones, recapitulations of the movements of more fully endowed dancers, with a reduction in artistry and excitement.

Yet what do we lose by defining dancers' bodies in so narrow a way?

Homer once wrote that his prior dance training had been "predicated on recognizing my physical liabilities and working to reduce them to nonfactors." That direction no longer made sense to him.

I said in my paper in Atlanta, in talking about the unexplored potential of disabled artists, not only dancers, but artists of all forms: "The way that our bodies are configured, and the ways that our sensory systems function, all affect how we move through space and perceive the world.

"Art is created by bodies," I noted. "Bodies emitting sounds, wielding brushes, bodies spinning themselves through space, bodies typing words."

Yet which bodies get to perform these acts and how? For instance, if a painter's hand is unsteady or has other uncontrolled movement, what is gained and what is lost in trying to stabilize her hand? Might her brushstrokes, unmediated, render something on the canvas worth viewing? Not only because the resulting painting comments, in color and form, on the way her body functions, but because her work might display rhythm and pattern that are exciting.

Near the end of the presentation, I said: "What I am concerned with are the things that constrain our bodies—I want to give disabled people's bodies every opportunity to imprint on the page, on the canvas, on the stage, on mounds of clay. Our bodies and senses as they are—making marks."

15 *The Cripple Girl and the Blind Boy Go to the Museum*

I once, on a whim, typed the word *blind* into my computer's the-saurus. The terms *ignorant, imperceptive, insensitive, irrational, oblivious, obtuse, random, rash, stagger, unaware, unconscious, uncontrolled, unknowing, unplanned,* and *violent* came up on my screen. My *Roget's Thesaurus* also provided *inattentive* and *purpose-less.* These meanings lurk under the surface when the word *blind* is used, whether on its own or in pairings, in such phrases as *blind pas-sion, blind rage, blind justice, blind drunk,* and *blind faith.*

How can the culture get away with attaching such an absurd pro-liferation of meanings to a condition that affects, simply, visual acu-ity? Of all the impairments, blindness seems to call up the most fan-tastical of responses. These are used, uncritically and without apparent irony, by many and often.

Yet maybe I am, just like everybody else, *blind* to the real conse-quences of blindness. Is it possible that these are not arbitrary mean-ings attributed to blindness or metaphors run amok, but the true characteristics of the blind? The next time my friend Gene comes to visit me in New York, I thought, I must do some research on this.

Gene is tall and lean, blond and blue-eyed. Blind. Gay. Lives in the Midwest. Looks corn-fed. He arrived at my doorstep with his guide dog, Gen, short for General, a full-figured German shepherd.

I had cleared my calendar for a couple of days in anticipation.

The first night we went to the theater. It was a long, wordy play,

213

and we both fell asleep in the second act. Thus I did get to witness Gene being, as the thesaurus says, *unconscious* and *unaware*. The fact that I was as well did not occur to me.

The play was a disappointment. There was not even one of those stock disabled characters seen so often in theater. We had no one we could deconstruct on the ride home. The pitiful, solitary neighbor. The sweet innocent. The bitter cripple. As much as we hate those renderings, we always have wicked fun rewriting them. In our post-theater musings, we re-issue them as the characters who take charge of the town, do something naughty, win over the audience, or finally have a love life.

But we had fun, and afterward we met David at a midtown bar for a nightcap. Had we been in Germany, I told them, we might have gone to this new nightspot I'd heard about on the radio. It seems that a German installation artist, named Axel Rudolph, has opened a restaurant in Cologne where diners eat in total darkness. The lack of light in the restaurant, called the Invisible Bar, presents no problem for the waiters, who are all blind. Sighted patrons, it seems, are flocking to the place. It is reported that they fumble around in the dark and need to be led to their tables and to the restrooms on the arm of their waiter.

Gene was amused by the idea, but said he had no interest in being an instructor that evening, and ordered another mojito, a syrupy rum concoction with fresh mint that always makes it feel like summer, no matter what season you drink it in. I did notice that both David and Gene seemed to *stagger* a bit when they got up to go to the bathroom. When they left, I wrote the verb down in my notebook.

The mojito is Gene's favorite drink, and he got me hooked on it when I went to Minneapolis some time ago to speak at the University of Minnesota, where Gene used to work. He was then the assistant director of disability services at the university, and is now the director of those services at San Francisco State.

When I first heard about the Invisible Bar, I was intrigued by the idea that blind people suddenly had this cultural cachet, but I was quickly suspicious of the motives and the outcome. I checked in with a blind authority. I asked my friend Cathy Kudlick what she thought of such a place. Cathy is a historian who researches and writes about blind people in obscure times and places.

She sent me a long e-mail rant that said, in part: "This is just my opinion, but I think these restaurants where sighted people go to play at blindness are superficial and insulting—when I read about them (and there have been a number, mostly in Europe), I get the same sense of mild nausea that I do when I read about Marie Antoinette going to live in her little peasant house outside of Versailles for a few days in the years before the French Revolution. The experience is not genuine, nor can it ever be, because the visitor always knows that it's nothing but a visit. In fact, such restaurants can actually be counterproductive because people live blindness without any of the skills and experience that make functioning easier, so they invariably come out shaken and fully convinced that blindness must be either a free-for-all or an impossible horror. I've noted that the reports make the Germans and Swiss Germans seem more orderly than the French, where things apparently degenerated rather quickly. Once again, such experiments say much more about the able-bodied world than they do about disability."

Cathy's response did not seem in any way *rash* or *irrational*.

We all slept in the next morning, and then Gene, General, and I went for a long walk in Central Park. This was a few months before Rufus came into my life, and it was great to have Gene push my chair up the big hills so I could show him some of my favorite spots. I slid out of my chair onto a park bench, and we sat side by side in the sun eating New York hot dogs. I was feeling pretty *oblivious* and worried that maybe some of his blindness was wearing off on me.

I told Gene I almost stopped talking to him when he cut his hair. He used to have a long mane that stretched down his back almost to his waist. And then I saw him one day with a buzz cut up the back, and the only remnant of his bold hairdo was a blond forelock that dipped raffishly over one eye.

"It was a great disappointment," I said.

"Ah, Simster," said Gene, using his favorite nickname for me, "don't worry, I'm still the same wild and crazy guy."

We went back home and while we were waiting for David, I played a CD from a show I had seen the year before—something I wished Gene had been there for—called *Gospel at Colonus*. It was a rendition of Sophocles' *Oedipus at Colonus* that merged traditional Greek theater and the black gospel tradition. It was a perfect pairing.

Sophocles' story was transformed into a sermon, and the call-and-response of the chorus could easily be imagined as taking place either in Ancient Greece or at a church down the street from the theater where we were in Brooklyn. The preacher was played by Morgan Freeman, and his sermon recounted the story of when Oedipus, as an old blind man, came to Colonus looking for a resting place.

The Greek "chorus" was in fact the gospel chorus the Institutional Radio Choir, and they, along with the J. D. Steele Singers and J. J. Farley and the Original Soul Stirrers, sang many of the rousing songs, written by Bob Telson. I told Gene that I had seen the play four times, one time traveling to Philadelphia where it was on tour.

"Why?" he asked.

Apart from the sheer genius of the piece, the music, and the excitement of watching Morgan Freeman preach was an idea that the play put forth—something not evident in any theater or piece of literature I know of. It was the *idea* of blindness—how it is perceived and how it is understood in the popular imagination. In the productions that I saw, Oedipus was played not by one actor, but by the Five Blind Boys of Alabama—a famous gospel group. When they first appeared, they entered stage left in procession, all wearing white suits. Each man had a hand on the shoulder of the blind man in front of him.

The play didn't contribute to the metaphorizing of blindness; instead it commented on, pointed out, the cultural uses of blindness which occur all the time. With *five* men occupying the space formerly allocated to one actor, and five *blind* men enacting a role almost universally played by a sighted man, it rendered blindness simultaneously both more metaphoric and more concrete.

This rendition of the Oedipus story reminds me of the production of *Othello* a few years ago at the Arena Stage in Washington. A white actor, Patrick Stewart, was cast as Othello, and all of the rest of the cast was black. The casting brought to the surface the racial tensions in the play and made them more substantial, and less ephemeral, and yet rendered race as theme and idea more thoroughly than other productions ever have. Similarly, casting the Five Blind Boys brought to the surface the very idea of blindness and forced the audience to look at blindness more directly.

Gospel at Colonus is occasionally performed in regional theaters, and Gene and I have vowed to see it together one day.

The last day of Gene's visit, we went to the Museum of Modern Art. This was some years ago, before the major renovation of 2004. By arrangement, we got the special blind people's tour, the feeling people's tour. I tagged along, Gen and I hanging back while Gene donned thin plastic gloves that protect the sculpture from the acid in skin oils. He got a touch of the Matisses on the second floor. Lingered over the well-muscled John the Baptist positioned just outside the sculpture gallery. We went on to a few of the hard-edged metal sculptures of the mid–twentieth century. Gene and the guide got to talking about the mass and weight of different pieces, the degrees of abstractness and varying moods of the four versions of the busts of Matisse's wife. Gene compared them to a set of Picasso busts at the Smithsonian Sculpture Garden in Washington. I had never thought about how you can feel abstractness.

Helen Keller did. In an essay called "The World I Live In," Keller, the uber–blind woman, wrote: "Ideas make the world we live in, and impressions furnish ideas." She instructs the sighted on how she gains access to such large and complex ideas as beauty, incongruity, and power with her hands. "Remember," she says, "that you, dependent on your sight, do not realize how many things are tangible."

Our museum expedition proceeded to the outdoor exhibits. We stepped, wheeled, and pawed out into the hot August day. The sculpture garden is a generous space in midtown New York. It is a long rectangle with two reflecting pools, birch trees that sway easily in the wind, and an assortment of primarily twentieth-century metal sculpture. The space is surrounded by buildings on three sides, and in the old MOMA, on the fourth side, a brick wall separated the garden from Fifty-fourth Street. The wall had a number of openings with gates, so passersby could look in.

It felt like the place was ours, despite an array of tourists and locals sitting around on benches and at tables on the terrace outside the café. At every sculpture, we circled round, moved in close. The guide gave me a pair of gloves too, and Gene guided my hand and urged me to stroke the dips and waves of the metal, and prod the crevices and corners. We rubbed and grazed. Then, on my own, I shut my eyes and tried putting the pieces of the puzzle together in my mind. I had watched Gene all along, and noted how he reads a sculpture. A quick overview, scanning line by line, top to bottom, and then back to certain locations for a longer visit, accumulating details, making decisions.

With license and abandon, we did the forbidden. I'd copped a feel before in a museum, a furtive fondle when the guard wasn't looking. But here I was in full view with authority to touch and to linger. This was my invitation into a world where, as Helen Keller put it, "the hand is supreme."

Gene's favorite piece was the Picasso goat. I get his point, it is hysterically funny. Down-turned mouth. Erratic details—it is not so much made of found objects, as it looks like a found goat, wandered off some hippie farm in Vermont. Slightly high, listing a bit.

My favorite that day was a giant bronze by Gaston Lachaise. A nude woman of enormous proportions, nine or ten feet tall, pinched-in waist, big hips thrust out at the crowd below her, and round breasts with erect nipples. She dominated the west end of the garden. There were a number of obstacles in the way, so I couldn't get near enough to feel her, and even if I could, she sits up on a pedestal; I would have just been able to reach her feet. But Gene clambered up the pedestal and latched on. He thrust his hand up the inside of her copious thighs, rubbed her belly, stroked her breasts. I was deeply envious. He was touching, I was gazing. He was no more circumspect in his touch of her breasts than of her feet. She was his for the taking.

I thought of my own self-consciousness when I look at a nude statue or a painting, afraid I might appear to others as hungry, desperate, wanting more intimate gratification. This started when I was an adolescent, visiting the marble statuary at the Metropolitan Museum of Art, lingering in the rooms with the Greek gods. I would stare longingly at their pelvises, melting inside yet determined to appear cool and sophisticated, a disinterested observer. Not Gene. He appeared unencumbered by such conflicts. Although I know that women's bodies don't hold the same appeal for Gene as men's do for me, his actions broke social rules bigger and broader than personal desires. Whatever your tastes in matters sexual, you just don't slide your palms across someone's erect nipples in public, even if they are bronze.

Maybe, though, blind people are forcing the rest of us to reconsider the social conventions and rules that govern breast touching, bronze and otherwise.

Recently, a friend sent me an article from a British newspaper. It seems that a lap-dancing club, the Pussycats Club in Hove, East Sussex, applied for a variance to its license to allow blind patrons to touch performers. The director of the club took up this issue with the town council after two blind men visited Pussycats with a stag party of sighted friends. The men had asked to touch the women so that they could get a better idea of what the dancers looked like, but the club's license forbids any physical contact between dancers and guests except the touch that occurs when customers slip money in the dancers' garters.

The owner of the club, a Mr. McGrath, said: "Both men said they very much enjoyed the dances and sensed highly the proximity of the dancers and, in particular, enjoyed the smell of their perfume. Given their disability, they felt controlled touching ought to be permitted for registered blind persons only and with the dancer's consent."

Mr. McGrath said that eleven of the fifteen dancers had said they would not object to being touched. "They said that touching should be voluntary and restricted to the breasts and only when the dancer is wearing a bra and not topless. The dancer would retain full control, taking one hand of the blind customer and placing it on her breasts while dancing for an agreed time."

It did not appear to me that the council was considering something usually called "special" treatment, but rather breast-touching was being conceptualized as an accommodation—like providing a Braille copy of a college exam—to provide more equitable access to the experience. Similarly, for years in Scandinavian countries they have provided live models for blind children in sex education classes, so they can feel body parts that others have access to with sight. These actions come, it seems to me, from a sense of fairness, not out of a benevolent impulse.

Touching sculpture, lap dancers' breasts, and models' bodies in sex education classes are not equivalent acts, and each will arouse controversy in its own way.

For instance, I've spoken with a number of people about the practice of guided touch tours of museums. Some educational and curatorial staff at museums have approached this with enthusiasm, conducted staff training and outreach to blind people to urge them to come to their museum. I've spoken with other curators who seem cautious and anxious about the whole thing, and say it should only be done in very controlled and limited ways. Many museums ignore the topic, and therefore ignore all blind people who might visit.

Most museum people are adamant about the use of plastic gloves as a protective measure. They say that even sculpture that is kept outside and exposed to harsh weather will not sustain the damage to the finish that skin oils produce. Yet I've spoken with one sculptor and one curator who say that plastic-glove use is a bogus issue, that the minimal residue of skin oils on most pieces would have no impact. Another perspective comes from a colleague who works on access issues in British museums, who says that part of the controversy is that wearing gloves may be more damaging as they can be abrasive. A question then is whether to select less fragile pieces or create reproductions specifically for tactile tours.

When I told my friend George, who is a sculptor, about my visit to the museum with Gene, he was at first appalled at the thought of any members of the public touching "great" sculpture. He conceded that it might be OK to touch certain sculpture, but not precious and valuable works, because the skin oils would damage them. He took a few more bites of the fabulous meal I had prepared, and then, proving why George is my friend, abruptly canceled his previous proclamation, and said, "Maybe there will be a time when the worth of sculpture will be determined by how much it is touched, how worn away by enthusiastic touchers."

Preservationists, sculptors, dancers, and models must have a say in how these acts are carried out. Indeed, in my deliberations about the lap-dancing club, it was the role the dancers were reported to have played in setting the terms of the accommodations that was of interest to me, and even moved me beyond my usually protective feelings toward women who work in those settings.

I venture to bet that the blind visitors to the Pussycats Club would prefer to touch the dancers' breasts without their bras on, and museum-goers would probably prefer to touch sculpture without plastic gloves mediating that experience. That is a negotiation that needs to take place between blind people and other interested parties—like the dancers and the preservationists. And, while these players are at the bargaining table, I would add Chippendale dancers (male) and the potential blind patrons of those clubs as well—it is only fair! In museums and universities, research needs to be conducted on the impact of touch on various kinds of sculpture, and the best types of glove—for both the sensory pleasure of the toucher and the protection of the sculpture. Another set of studies might evaluate the best methods of conducting tactile tours of museums.

The impact could be far bigger than specific accommodations for blind people in various venues. For example, my friend George's idea of the reconsideration of the worth of sculpture based on frequency of touches, though seemingly far-fetched, is an example of the type of radical thinking I hope these dialogues engender. Certainly the whole issue of touch has been at the center of the kinds of "hands-on" exhibits currently in vogue in many kinds of museums. Educational and curatorial staff have been convinced that a certain type of engagement, namely a physical engagement, with art or other museum presentations results in enhanced learning.

All this is to say that the active participation of disabled people in the cultural and social mix of a country forces us to reconsider many conventions and rules. The confluence of these events and ideas caused me to think about the sanctity of the breast and of art in our culture. I certainly think such reflections and actions are potentially to everyone's benefit, but for the times it specifically benefits disabled people, I'm all for it!

As an example, if blind people alter the conventions of touching behavior in a club or a museum—but alter it just for them—putting "opportunity," so to speak, in their hands, then disability, at least for this moment and place, is the advantaged position. Certainly, I thought Gene had a certain degree of advantage in the sculpture garden. We both did.

When our guide was called away for a phone call, we stayed on and continued to feel our way around the sculpture garden. The guards were not paying attention to us, figuring we were still under her supervision. So we just went around and felt everyone up. We were having a great time and acting like we owned the place, or at least owned the right to enjoy it. That was the moment when Gene was able to climb up for his encounter with the grand Lachaise nude. Gene's guide dog, Gen, was oblivious to our cavorting. He was lying nearby, head on crossed paws, panting in the August heat. The crowd, I suspect, was not oblivious. Playing against type, we were giggly and audacious.

It is a sense of entitlement I most often feel when I am with other disabled people. Two, five, twelve, or more of us heading out to dinner after an all-day meeting. A phalanx of cripples going down the street, at our best, our most natural. Our quirks and tics, exposed to fresh air, blossom. We wheeze and snortle, thrust and parry. We move through space, assisted or solo, using scooters, or wheelchairs, canes, crutches, guide dogs, ASL interpreters, personal assistants, or voice synthesizers. On down the street and into a restaurant, and waves of people part to let this "special" party roll through.

This day, it was just me and Gene. A party of two. But we carried with us the experience of those many times sitting at big tables, eating and talking the night away.

I looked up to catch Gene begin his descent from his intimate, yet quite public, rendezvous with this buxom bronze beauty. There he stood, cheek to breast with his blind date, and I swelled with appreciation for the wonderful time I was having with him. In his company, I had become *purposeless* and, in a very lovely way, *uncontrolled*.

Gene turned toward me, sly grin on his face, full facial nudity (no dark glasses for this blind boy). His t-shirt with its big pink triangle proclaimed to the crowd: "Silence = Death." He was, it seemed, quite purposefully revealing both his eyes and his desires.

16 *Our Body Politics*

On January 8, 1997, some twenty-six years after I stood with John and Carol, hitchhiking to the anti-war demonstration, I boarded the Delta Shuttle from La Guardia, again bound for Washington.

I would get to this demonstration, my first in all those years. I took a taxi from the airport. When I arrived at the Supreme Court building, where I was told the demonstrators would be assembling, I began to cry. It was a cold January morning, and I cried for me, for John, and for Carol. I missed them that day and felt so sad that I could not remember them as clearly as they deserve to be remembered. When I returned home late that night I set about looking for pictures of them. They weren't hard to find, but they were in a drawer I rarely open. There was Carol, in a leather jacket, taking a big bite out of a bright red candy apple, her long silky hair billowing out behind her, and John sitting in the big chair in our living room in Cambridge, laughing hard, his eyes crinkled, and his dark mustache curled up over his sweet mouth.

"I wrote a book," I told the pictures. "I'm a professor. I want you to hear me, I want you to be alive, see this life I have and have your own."

I sat with them for a long while and then I heard myself whisper: "I'm sorry."

A memory of John came flooding back to me, something I hadn't really ever thought about. When I was eighteen, just a few months into our relationship, I became pregnant. It was 1966, we had no money, and I borrowed $150 from a friend and found an abortionist. John supported me through the ordeal. He showed in every way that he took equal responsibility for the pregnancy and expressed guilt that I had to endure the horrible procedure. I lay on a kitchen table as the woman, a nurse, or so she said, threaded a wire coat hanger through a red rubber tube and inserted it into my vagina and up into my cervix. The pain was excruciating. Over the next days as I suffered cramps and bled profusely, John was tender and caring. I shouldn't ever forget that.

John and Carol were with me that whole day in 1997, even before I found those photos. Running through my mind was my personal story of the day's significance, in the midst of the public event I was participating in.

What would they make of the scene I witnessed at the base of the grand steps leading to the United States Supreme Court? It was just before noon. People were arriving from many directions. Chartered buses and vans from local independent living centers and group homes were unloading their passengers down the hill. The front doors opened and people walked off; the rear doors opened and lifts descended with wheelchair-riding citizens, many seasoned demonstrators, placards at the ready.

I went over to meet the contingent from Disabled in Action, a New York–based coalition of activists, which included several friends of mine. They had rented a bus with a wheelchair lift to bring them all down to Washington. They had boarded the bus at 5:00 that morning, and gotten to Washington just an hour before me. There hadn't been much heat on the bus, and they looked tired. I felt guilty for my shuttle ride from La Guardia, with the snack and hot coffee served by a flight attendant.

Across the street, I saw Gene walking toward us with General, and called out to him. Gene had used up all his frequent flyer miles so that he and his great friend Joy could come from Minneapolis. I was delighted to meet Joy, an actress with a muscular little body and a great smile. She is a wheelchair rider like me, with strong arms and a forceful push. Gene and Joy had traveled in Europe the summer before, and that is where Gene perfected his technique of pushing a wheelchair up a steep hill, which he had used with me in Central Park.

Passersby looked, and looked away. Groups of schoolchildren, on field trips to the nation's capital, watched us intently. A few of us took it upon ourselves to approach the kids and ask if they wanted to know why we were there. Once having offered, I realized how hard it would be to explain this to them.

For the younger adolescents we spoke in broad terms, telling them that the Supreme Court was in session inside that building, there were important men and women who were about to make a decision on something that would have a major impact on the lives of disabled people. That is why we were here today; we were here to speak up about matters that affect us. Some of our group, I told them, are inside, providing testimony.

The older high school students got a fuller story. The justices were inside deliberating about something called physician-assisted suicide. I asked if anyone had heard of Dr. Jack Kevorkian. Many of them had. Some people, I said, pointing to the well-mannered rows of people from the Hemlock Society standing to the right of the steps, believe that Dr. Kevorkian and other doctors should have the right to help people who say they want to die if they are very sick. Others, I said, pointing to my rowdy compatriots, parading back and forth across the broad sidewalk, believe that a physician's job is to help people live as comfortably as possible, even when life is very hard and you are very sick.

Some of the students were looking the other way, wanting a quick out from this peculiar lesson they were getting, but the rest of the group, invited to look head-on at people they'd always been told not to stare at, were paying close attention. More of the demonstrators came over to give the students flyers and to talk with them. The kids really liked the name of the group, Not Dead Yet, that had organized the rally, and some chanted along as we shouted, "We're Not Dead Yet, We're Not Dead Yet!" One of the marchers was lying face down on a stretcher-like conveyance, propped up slightly so he could look around. As he went by, he gave the students a nod and a wink, and several of the kids smiled back and tentatively waved at him.

The signs the demonstrators carried conveyed our messages: "Our homes, not nursing homes," "The people united will never be defeated," and "We want the: Right to Live." A group of people all wearing identical red t-shirts from a local independent living center carried a banner that said: "If disability isn't a crime, why are we always locked up?" A boy of eight or nine, riding on the back of his mother's wheelchair, wore a black t-shirt with pink neon letters that said: "Piss on pity."

I watched the kids watching my colleagues—this ragtag army, militant, unflinching, and deeply compassionate. I knew that some of them were one social security disability check away from a nursing home or institution. They were out here fighting for their rights and the rights of others as they sucked on their breathing tubes to get the hit of oxygen they needed to propel their voices above the din. These are the people who shout the loudest, because they know they could find themselves in the hands of a seemingly benevolent physician who would collude with them were they to say at a weak moment, "I am helpless, my life isn't worth living."

The kids all laughed when a woman in an electric blue wheelchair whizzed by, with a bumper sticker on the back that said: "I'm too sexy for a nursing home." I laughed too.

The class reassembled and lined up for their visit to the Air and Space Museum. Their teacher thanked us, and we thanked them for their interest.

I wanted to tell the students more. That the shouters were saying, in effect, my life *is* worth living. That incontinence, respirator dependency, twenty-four-hour attendant care, pain, paralysis, blindness, and other conditions often depicted as tragic and intolerable don't determine a wish to die. It is, more often, institutionalization, guilt about being a burden to others, fear of being alone and debilitated, poverty, inadequate medical coverage—all these things that lead to depression and a sense of hopelessness. I wanted the students to know that our government could help people be more comfortable, and more comforted, and provide support for people to live in our own homes, rather than nursing homes, if it was willing to do that. While the assisted-suicide debate may seem to be about assistance in dying for people with terminal illness, people who have been told they have just a few months left to live, we were there in Washington because we know that in practice people with non-terminal illnesses have been "assisted." For instance, Not Dead Yet has exposed Kevorkian's participation in the death of a number of people who were not terminally ill, people with conditions similar to those of the people demonstrating here today.

The Supreme Court rendered its decision several months later, in

June of 1997. They did decide that physician-assisted suicide was not a constitutional right, but Chief Justice William Rehnquist encouraged the states to take up this issue in their own legislatures. In other words, we won a victory, but only a temporary stay. Oregon has already legalized physician-assisted suicide, and other states are deliberating. Nat Hentoff, in a series of articles for the *Village Voice* and the *Washington Post,* has attacked this issue forcefully. Where other papers have compared the Right to Die movement to the pro-choice agenda, Hentoff evokes the Nazi euthanasia program in his analysis. He has examined practices in the Netherlands where, for over ten years, Dutch doctors, as he says, "have been empowered to help patients kill themselves, and increasingly, physicians there have been directly killing patients, sometimes without being asked to" (*Village Voice,* February 18, 1997). He cites a 1995 study conducted in the Netherlands in which 23 percent of doctors interviewed said that they had "euthanized" a patient without a specific request by the patient to do so. "Patients" can be of any age. Hentoff writes about a three-year-old with spina bifida, but otherwise in "fair general condition," who was administered a lethal dose of drugs at the parents' request. A physician interviewed for the article indicated that this is not a rare event.

Diane Coleman, president of Not Dead Yet, has said: "The wish for an easy and certain method of suicide under extreme circumstances is understandable. But that wish must be weighed against the increasingly routine, socially and medically acceptable killing of older and disabled people" (*New Mobility,* August 2002).

I have weighed the two options and believe it is unacceptable and too dangerous to allow physician-assisted suicide. I may regret that choice one day if I am terminally ill and in great pain, but I hope it still seems like the right decision.

I've attended a number of demonstrations since then. One was the Court's hearing of the *Olmstead* case, in May of 1999. Two women with mental retardation living in a state institution in Georgia petitioned a state court to be allowed to live in the community. Their doctors agreed that institutionalization was unnecessary, they could live on their own with proper supports. They won in the appeals court, but then Tommy Olmstead, Georgia's commissioner of human services, challenged the ruling, and it was brought to the Supreme Court. Their lawyers argued that the state could transfer the money it was spending to keep the women locked up to pay for rent, attendant care, and other expenses, which would probably save the state money. The case challenged one of the fundamental tenets of the ADA—the "integration mandate." The plaintiffs prevailed in that decision, and the two women are now living in the community.

The March for Justice, held in Washington, D.C., in October of 2000, was in support of the *Garrett* case. Jesse Jackson, Dick Gregory, Martin Luther King III, and two Kennedys spoke at the rally, and Jackson and Patricia Ireland, president of the National Organization for Women, weighed in at the press conference the morning of the rally. I hoped that meant that the broader civil rights community had finally begun to embrace the issues of the disability rights movement, recognizing that the issues we argue for share common cause with other rights-based agendas. I have not seen most of these high-profile folks at other demonstrations.

This case, *University of Alabama v. Garrett,* challenged Title II of the ADA, which bans discrimination by state and other public entities on the basis of a physical or mental disability. The court eventually decided against Garrett, saying that an individual cannot sue the state for damages under the ADA. It was a terrible blow; the decision eviscerated a major portion of the ADA. This was effectively a decision that affirmed states' rights, which was in large part the reason that so many in the civil rights community had become involved. As Jesse Jackson said at the press conference, discussing what was at stake in this decision: "I thought the Civil War settled that."

Each demonstration, we hoped, would get national news coverage. But time after time, despite advance notice, and press releases spread to all the networks and news services, there was no, or only minimal, coverage. I would go home at the end of the day, expecting to see something about the event, but there was rarely a peep, nor much comment in the morning's papers. After one of these events, I do recall that a major network commented that "there was a carnival outside the Supreme Court today," complete with a long shot of the crowd.

The demonstrations I've attended have been loud and forceful, but, at least in the parts I have been present at, involved no civil disobedience and no arrests. I know people, members of ADAPT, the central disability rights activist organization, who have arrest records as long as your arm. They have blocked traffic on highways and chained themselves to buildings to earn their lockups. I know there have been demonstrations where the police came in and herded demonstrators into police cars and vans; I know of people thrown out of their wheelchairs, hit with night sticks, left alone in cells with no accessible toilets. In the actions I've taken part in, the police were more like clucking school crossing guards than menacing riot controllers.

In a perverse way, I am disappointed that I haven't been arrested. It is, in part, a wish to test my mettle and prove that I am more than a check-writing, fly-to-demonstrations-on-the-Delta-shuttle kind of liberal. But it would also help to assuage one of my most deep-seated fears. I have always worried that if I were to write to the FBI under the Freedom of Information Act to obtain my file, I would learn that they haven't kept one on me. What? Am I not deemed a threat to national security? After all, I attended my first demonstration at thirteen. Two years later, I was planning to sneak out of the house to go the March on Washington in 1963, but I got the measles and had to stay home in bed in cotton pajamas. That same year, there was the anti-anti-bussing rally outside of Gracie Mansion (the mayor's residence), which my best friend Nina and I actually instigated, with a few pieces of cardboard and some magic markers. A few years after that, there was the 1967 demonstration at the UN against the war in Vietnam. And the current ones.

I wonder what John and Carol would think of my present commitments and activities. Would they think that my life had become more particular—more focused on concerns about my personal condition than about the broad political issues that we were going to Washington to fight for? I remember a conversation we had before leaving for Washington. One of the reasons we were moved to go to that demonstration, as opposed to earlier anti-war demonstrations in Washington, was because it was spearheaded by returning vets. Angry at U.S. policy and disillusioned by the realities of the hopeless situation they had seen, the Vietnam Veterans against the War wanted United States citizens to know that their prior zeal had waned, and that they no longer believed it was a just war. Their opposition to the war was a response not only to what they deemed to be illegal foreign policy, a wrongful incursion into another country, but to the economic and racial inequities at home that determined who would go to war and who would be on the front lines. All were angry at the poor treatment they had received back at home. We wanted to show them our support.

I remember watching television stories about disabled vets returning to their hometowns. You would see such soldiers in full dress uniform, wheeled down Main Street in Memorial Day or Veterans Day parades. It seemed that they were displayed as symbols of heroism and of the kind of sacrifice that a true patriot is willing to make. Their uniform and their solemn salute of the flag signaled that they still supported the war that had ravaged their bodies.

The angry disabled vet, like the Jon Voight character, Luke, in the film *Coming Home,* was not given such a welcome. It must have been hard for any vet to oppose the war, but I am attentive to the way that disabled vets took a particular risk in coming out against the Vietnam War. To acknowledge one's own doubts about the war, and to accept others' doubts, was to risk being read as a tragic figure. Looking back, I don't think I had the imagination or experience to see these men as something other than tragic or ruined figures. Once I became disabled I began to think differently, and when I saw *Coming Home,* in 1978, I hoped that the film convinced everyone in the audience, as it convinced me, that disabled people could be bold, forthright, sexy, and interesting.

The disabled and nondisabled vets who did oppose the war swelled the ranks of the anti-war movement. Had I arrived in Washington on April 22, 1971, and participated in the demonstration, I might have encountered some of the disabled veterans. I've looked at photos of the action, and there are often men in fatigues sitting in wheelchairs in the crowd. Those vets could look to important sections of the American public for support. Many of the people who believed we were doing the wrong thing in Vietnam supported good treatment of those who suffered for our mistakes. But, once the war was over, the liberals who had been concerned for their welfare turned their attention elsewhere. The fact is that in the 1980s those disabled vets, along with other disabled people, had to chain themselves together and block major highways to gain the right to ride on public transportation, they had to get out of their wheelchairs and cast aside their crutches and pull themselves up the steps of the Capitol to bring attention to discrimination against disabled people in America, and, after all that, in recent rulings, they have now lost the right to sue the state for discrimination based on disability. These facts have not yet garnered active support from the individuals and organizations usually concerned with issues of social justice and integration.

For now it does seem we are alone in this. Despite occasional guest appearances at our demonstrations by celebrity politicos and the attention to disability issues by a few senators, notably Tom Harkin and Ted Kennedy, it is largely disabled people and a tight circle of allies that fight our fights. You may want to tell the FBI that I am very angry about this.

A year after the 1997 demonstration at the Supreme Court, I left my job at Hunter College. While there was much about the job I liked, I wanted to spend all of my time on disability matters, and it wasn't going to happen there.

Further, my experience at that demonstration and others I attended made me want to work outside the university on social change and also cultural change, to bring attention to our issues and our ideas.

My first book came out at that time, *Claiming Disability: Knowledge and Identity*, a book about disability studies as an area of inquiry. I wrote about the way the traditional curriculum sequesters the study of disability in fields related to medicine or education. I argued that in doing this, the curriculum not only mimics but contributes to the marginalization of disabled people in society. By placing most of the study about disability in fields designed to help individuals cope, or to repair their bodies, we explain disability as a medical condition, rather than organizing information in a way to examine disability's social, cultural, and political properties. Adding disability studies to the academic curriculum would provide a place to learn about the external conditions that shape our lives. Disability studies functions, in some ways, as women's studies does to examine social roles, social stratification, representations in fiction, theater, film, etc. Yet while women's studies has had an impact, albeit inadequate, on the way women are depicted in film and are written about in newspapers, and on hiring practices, disability studies' impact has not reached as far into the popular imagination. This is what I wanted to work on.

How to do it? I was politically motivated, but not a politician or legislator. I am a writer, but not a journalist. The route I chose was the arts. How, I wondered, might I influence artistic institutions or individual artists to take on the subject of disability? What did I know or have that they could use? How could I make what I find so interesting, meaningful to them?

Taking disability public has become my work. I formed an entity called Disability/Arts, which is a consulting service, and I have been involved in projects with museums, state and regional arts councils, and independent filmmakers. The projects have been exciting, but there is an ongoing struggle to get cultural institutions to take on this subject. While the body of work disabled artists are producing is ripe for plucking, the resistance to it is great.

There is an emerging cadre of dancers, actors, writers, performance artists, and painters who identify as disabled and who actively use the idea of disability in their work. I have been most excited by art that explores what disability *provides* the artist rather than what feats someone can perform *despite* disability. The new genre of disability art exploits the unique configuration of body and voice that results from impairment and from the disability experience.

In addition to that consulting work, for the last two years I have been on a lecture tour with a documentary film that was made in Israel about a disabled woman who was a Holocaust survivor. The film, called *Liebe Perla,* is about Perla Ovitz, a woman of short stature who is a Holocaust survivor. During the Nazi regime, Dr. Josef Mengele kept Perla and her brothers and sisters, all people of short stature, captive in Auschwitz and used them in his medical "experiments." The film traces that history and Perla's friendship with Hannelore Witkofski, a researcher who has studied the fate of disabled people during the war. Hannelore is also a woman of short stature, but born in post-war Germany. It is an astounding, intimate film, and I chose it because it says as much about the present moment as it does about the fate of disabled people in Nazi Germany.

I've been to colleges and universities in the U.S., Canada, and England with the film. Although each presentation is different, there have generally been big crowds and rousing discussions after the film. With these activities I am able to keep one foot in academic environments and the other in cultural institutions.

I feel at home in theaters and museums. When I was a child and young adolescent I wanted to be a dancer and actress. I began dance classes when I was four, and took classes in ballet and then jazz until I was eighteen. I took art classes and also studied at the American Academy of Dramatic Arts for two years when I was a teenager. Around eighteen, before I left for college, I dropped all those classes, deciding that theater was a confined life—the young actors I met seemed to only think and talk about theater. When I began college, right after high school, I declared art history as my major. Of course, I only lasted three months at that try at college, and spent the next few years drifting, not sure what I was going to do. Looking back on it, I think I spent a fair amount of time working to *not* think about my future life.

After the accident, while I was still in the hospital and deciding about going back to college, I imprinted on the only professional people in my domain. There were medical personnel and psychologists/counselors. My world was so constricted that I thought only about one or the other, because I couldn't imagine my disabled self working in any other setting. Also, I was dependent on funding from the state's Office of Vocational Rehabilitation. I knew that for my undergraduate work I could choose any major, but was told if I was planning to go to grad school I would receive funding only if I pursued a master's degree in rehabilitation counseling. So, to get a doctorate in psychology, which is what I had decided to do, I had to press on my family to help with tuition. That ruling, though, reinforced for me the idea that people with disabilities were welcome only in restricted fields of endeavor. That would be the only place I would fit in.

So I pursued my degree in psychology, and for the most part found it interesting. There was always a part of me that leaned toward the arts and the humanities, and so I studied those on my own. In my readings in psychology I never could find the kinds of explanations of disability I was seeking. I was more interested in the broader cultural meanings imposed on disability than the individual psychological response to a particular condition. Both in my personal experience and in my professional life, I found psychology's presentation of ideas about disability insufficient and distorted.

In leaving teaching, and leaving the field of psychology, I was trying to find ways to broaden both my understanding and the public conversation about disability. I was interested in getting cultural institutions to ask the questions: "Who gets to make art?" "Whose art gets shown?" and a significant parallel question: "Who gets to participate in cultural events?" Not just be present in a museum or a theater, but have a voice, share in the bounty.

These questions have been primarily asked with regard to race, gender, and class in recent years. There is some recognition that there is an ideology that informs institutions—hidden and overt agendas that determine what gets shown, how, who decides, who participates in all of the decisions that get made, and who attends and the nature of their participation.

These are disruptive questions. The kind that once asked publicly make it more difficult to keep the process of exclusion invisible.

On March 22, 2003, a few days after the United States started dropping bombs on Iraq, David and I were visiting friends in upstate New York. We decided to participate in an anti-war demonstration that we heard would be going on nearby. Approaching the center of town, we saw that all four corners of the intersection were filled with people. Local police and state troopers were posted at each corner, and yellow tape cordoned off each of the clusters. It was a big crowd for a small town.

We parked behind the supermarket, and headed for the main street. What we did not know was that there would also be a pro-war rally at the same time.

At first it was hard to tell who was who, which side of the street to go to. It seemed all four corners were the pro-Bush faction. Then we saw a smaller group in front of the gas station, holding signs that read: "Books Not Bombs," "Support Our Troops—Bring Them Home," "No War." So of the four corners, three and a half were pro, with our contingent taking up just one-half of one corner. We made our way toward them.

There were curb cuts on all four corners, and the crowd with the signs that said "We support President Bush" and "Get Saddam" quickly parted to let me through. The policeman held up the yellow tape, and David and I ducked underneath. They didn't know which side we were going to, or where our allegiance lay.

When we joined our interest group, someone offered us signs to carry. I took mine and went through the crowd and pushed to the edge of the sidewalk. I was at the yellow plastic ribbon that had been placed there to keep us from straying out into the street. I went to the front to be visible to the passersby. I know people look at me, and I wanted to use that to gain attention for my team.

Yet I wondered what people might think of me out there. Would anyone looking on view me as a reminder of one of the sad consequences of war? I was uncomfortable at that thought. It made me feel like a symbol of something bad, rather than a protestor with an opinion. Was I willing to frighten people into being against the war? Was I willing to proffer myself for this cause? Would my body say: this could happen to your son or daughter, so oppose President Bush? That's not how I want to win anybody's heart or mind. Of course, I had no way to control their interpretations, and so I stayed at the front to broadcast my borrowed message. The small, hand-painted sign bleated the plaintive cry: "Peace, Not War."

Our corner was the juncture of the pro- and anti-war factions, neighbor standing across from neighbor on the ideological divide. Each group in turn chanted its slogans and tried to get the eyes and ears of the people in cars passing through town.

After about two hours, the crowds on both sides were thinning out, and we decided to leave. We said goodbye to our group, and headed back toward the car. The place where I had to cross the street was still packed with Bush supporters. I steered Rufus through the crowd, and people moved to get out of my way. Right in front of the curb cut was a lanky guy in tight jeans. I said, "Excuse me, coming through." He pivoted around, looked me up and down, and said, "I'm not moving. Go around me." I was startled, but only for a second. I felt my hand move toward the joy stick to move Rufus forward. I could have plowed right into him and knocked him off balance. I stopped myself. Instead, with both hands, I reached out and grabbed the man by his belt loops and pulled him to the side and out of my way. He was caught off guard and lost his footing for a second.

He blurted out: "Hey, that's not nice."

"Yeah? Well, get over it," I yelled back.

This was the playground version of war.

Very quickly, protestors from both teams were admonishing the guy. "How could you do that to a woman in a wheelchair?" "That was really insensitive." "I can't believe you did that."

I went on my way and left him to defend himself. I was kind of rooting for the guy, though. I have an ideology and he has one, and I am as hostile to his as he is to mine. He deemed my beliefs a threat and saw it as his patriotic duty to block my path. I respected him for that.

A demonstration I missed—but only by a couple of hours—was at the Supreme Court, and it was about affirmative action. It was on April 1, 2003. I arrived in Washington to attend a conference entitled "Genetics, Disability and Deafness," and when I came out of Union Station, I saw hundreds of young people with placards that urged us to support affirmative action. Students, mostly African Americans and Hispanics, had come on buses from around the country to participate.

Had I known about the demonstration, I would have caught an earlier train and joined them. There was a huge crowd streaming down the hill from the Court building, and this activism, coming as it did just two weeks after the war in Iraq had started, filled me with a needed sense of hope about this country.

I met my friend Anne at Union Station for a drink before we headed out to the conference. We chatted excitedly. We always have a lot to talk about.

Anne Finger is the president of SDS, a fabulous writer, and a good friend. She has a deep soft voice that soothes, even as it edifies. The first time I heard her speak at SDS, a number of years ago, she read a short story about an imagined meeting between Frida Kahlo and Helen Keller. It is a delirious story, filled with exotic and lusty imagery. Frida learns to finger-spell so she can communicate with Helen. When Frida realizes that to make the letters *z* and *j*, she must stroke her finger across the length of Helen's outstretched palm, Frida comes up with convoluted sentences just to work words with those letters into their conversation. I remember that as Anne read sentences that contained the words *jackal, Zanzibar, jungle, zoo, Zurich, zebra, jaguar, Japan, zinfandel, zither,* the audience exploded in laughter.

I told Anne about an upcoming conference on universal design that

I thought we should attend. Rosemarie and I want to go, I said, and present papers.

The conference was originally planned for Havana, and that was part of what was motivating us to go. When I learned that the Bush administration was no longer granting licenses for such travel to Cuba, I made some calls and found out the conference had been rescheduled and was now going to be in Brazil. We expressed our disappointment and outrage. We railed at the State Department for their duplicitous policies about repressive governments they like, versus the ones they don't.

It was not just that I wanted to visit Cuba, and revisit the site of my honeymoon; it was that the conference *belonged* there. Universal design is a multi-disciplinary approach to the environment. A premise of the philosophy is that the built and communications environments should be more viable for all users. I thought each of us could speak about the contribution of disability studies perspectives to these endeavors—to provide a historical foundation, a sociological, aesthetic, or political analysis, and more. How perfect it would have been, though, to have that conversation in Cuba, in a place where the ideas of universality and community are interwoven in the ideology of the country.

Anne and I waited outside Union Station for the shuttle bus that would take us to Gallaudet University, the site of the conference. I had never been to Gallaudet, the national university of the Deaf, and I was looking forward to it. The van driver got out of the bus to lower the lift in the back for us (Anne is a wheelchair user, too). He greeted us warmly, by raising both his arms up on either side of his head, and pivoting his wrists back and forth two or three times. I was holding my suitcase, so I could not return the gesture, but said, "Hello." He heard me, smiled, and said, "Hello."

In the next few days there were many moments when I wouldn't know whether to use my crude gesturing techniques (I, unfortunately, don't know American Sign Language) or whether to speak. At the conference, there were interpreters everywhere, and it was easy to find someone to bridge the divide. When I would leave the conference center to explore the campus, it was, in many ways, like traveling in a country whose language I don't know. I watched clusters of students going by on their way to class, and they walked along almost in semicircles so they could easily see each other sign. All across the campus, there was a buzz of activity, but a quiet buzz.

There was a range of people at the conference. Faculty from Gallaudet and elsewhere representing many disciplines, genetic counselors, scientists who work in genetic research, and graduate students also from various fields. Topics ranged from scientific research on genetics to bioethical dilemmas raised by genetic research.

After the first morning's round of papers, Anne and I went outside into the early spring warmth. Gallaudet has beautiful grounds with many nineteenth- and early twentieth-century brick buildings, and we sat together under a flowering apple tree, side by side in our similarly equipped power wheelchairs. Anne said that she had a thought about the upcoming universal design conference. Though we were disappointed about it not being in Cuba, she reminded me that the Brazilian president, Lula da Silva, is a populist elected in a landslide victory. I agreed that says something positive about the country we were going to. Further, she had read that President Lula has four fingers on one hand—he lost his pinky in an accident when he was a factory worker. President Lula's four-fingered hand has been touted as evidence of his true working-class roots.

"Well," I said, "Rosemarie has four fingers on one of her hands so she'll fit right in, and your name is Finger, and so you will be topical."

In my head, I started to put together ideas for what I would say at the conference. I might begin, I thought, with the story of how when King Ferdinand was in power in Spain, people began speaking with a lisp, because the king had one. Strong remnants of that convention are still found in Castilian Spanish. I'd use this story as a way to discuss how a characteristic, usually disparaged, may be elevated in status by its association with an elevated character. I would say that I doubt Brazilian people would cut off a finger as a gesture of solidarity with their new leader, but that I did think this gives us ample opportunity to examine how when personal power gets attached to physical or psychological characteristics, it alters the meaning of those traits. This proves once again that disability is socially constructed. The various conditions any of us have have little meaning outside a doctor's office (and even there the social meanings cluster around it). The social significance, the political significance of a particular condition is the dominant meaning. What disability yields you in the social arena is what makes the difference in your life, not what works or what doesn't.

That idea is very much in evidence in the film *Liebe Perla,* which I presented on the second day of the conference. Perla, the central figure in the film, and her brothers and sisters, were, prior to their capture by the Nazis, a well-known traveling theater group, the Lilliput Troupe. Perla says in the film, and in interviews I've read, that her family received excellent training in music and theater arts. I do not know whether the troupe was considered a "novelty" act because of the actors' height, but it is clear they were very popular and toured all over Europe.

Height, then, may have been a reason for the group's appeal, or conversely, the audience may have been indifferent to the actors' size, and solely enamored of their talent. In either case, my point remains. A characteristic acquires meaning only in context, and as historical and cultural contexts shift, meanings change.

The Nazi era was invoked many times in the course of the conference. The idea that there could be, as Hitler proposed, a "life unworthy of life." Mengele's charge was to eliminate such "unworthy" life. Perla was held by Mengele at Auschwitz, along with her brothers and sisters, and he kept them alive because of their scientific significance to him. He was particularly interested in people of short stature—it is thought because he wanted to unlock the formula for height in order to promote selective breeding of tall, pure Aryans. Following the so-called experiments, most of the short people were then murdered.

One of the things I discussed when I introduced the film was that despite the progress we've witnessed in the last fifty years in the lives of disabled people, a very large majority of us remain unemployed (some put the figure as high as 70 percent), and many are locked up in institutions or spend a great deal of time in segregated settings such as sheltered workshops. It was, in part, the isolation and alienation of disabled people from the community that made it so easy for disabled people to become the first of Hitler's victims.

In our time, the poor conditions—unhealthy conditions—in which many disabled people live can result in death, or poor health, depression, unnecessary dependency, isolation, etc. It is too easy for policy makers, educators, and general citizens to ignore the problems of people who are unknown to them. Removal of disabled people from the community hurts the people who are isolated, denying them the pleasures of independent living, but their removal from the community also makes it easier for the rest of us to forget about them and devalue them.

There are significant differences between the Nazi agenda and the current agenda of the United States and other countries attempting to discover and utilize genetic information to "better" the population. There are similarities, though, that we too easily ignore.

The film *Gattaca* was also discussed by a few speakers. The 1997 film depicts an imagined era sometime in the future, when the genetic makeup of individuals wholly determines their future. Genetic engineering is used to manipulate characteristics in utero, and then assessment of individuals' genes is the admissions test for school, job placement, and the selection of mates. In the film, the genetically disadvantaged are called "invalids"—as in "not valid."

From the perspective of someone who has been called an "invalid," albeit with a different pronunciation, I find that imagined future not as far-fetched as it might seem. A goal of genetic testers is to limit anomalous characteristics in the population. As the reach and hold that genetic science has over the process of reproduction and the repairing of bodies grow, I am concerned that those with such characteristics will be increasingly disparaged and underprivileged. They might be called "invalids," as the film *Gattaca* predicted, or maybe the new term will be "preventables," applied to those children born to parents who had the hubris to have an unmediated pregnancy.

Certainly, in the present moment we are witnessing a growing belief, and a profitable industry which bolsters that belief, that imperfection is preventable or at least remediable. Plastic surgery, cochlear implants, prosthetic devices of all sorts may seem to serve only individual users, but to the extent that they mask impairment, the public profile of disability shifts, and these methods increase the perceived need to cover up imperfections or to hide yourself away.

The nineteenth- and twentieth-century impulse to contain and control disabled people utilized mechanisms such as institutions, tranquilizing medications, special schools, and sheltered workshops. The twenty-first century's techniques might not employ bricks and mortar, or syringes, but petri dishes and microscopes. It may not require padlocks, national policy, or standardized testing. Instead, amniotic fluid, ultrasound images, and hair follicles may be more instrumental in decisions made about a person. The undergirding policy might be written by insurance companies rather than by the government.

The ideas that are my stock in trade—about four-fingered presidents and social construction of disability—will not be sufficient to fight against these forces. The activism against governmental entities that has been the major focus of the disability rights movement may miss necessary targets as discrimination may increasingly function in privatized and covert transactions. The artistic endeavors that I promote will have to be creative and profound to catch the attention of an unwary public and radicalize their thinking.

I sat there in the audience listening, and sometimes participating in, the conversation about genetics and the implications for the twenty-first century. It occurred to me that one hundred years ago, in 1903, W. E. B. DuBois said, "The problem of the twentieth century is the problem of the color-line,—the relation of the darker to the lighter races" (*The Souls of Black Folk*, 1903).

Might the disability-line finally be more widely recognized in the coming decades as another underlying fault line that stratifies the society?

I am aching for a demonstration these days. Something to give focus to the rage I am feeling about the war in Iraq. As I write, we are midway through 2005, George W. Bush has been reelected, and corruption and deceit mark every move of this government.

And their biggest move, the invasion of Iraq, has had unbearable consequences. The death toll of American soldiers is nearly two thousand, about forty-five of them women. Thousands of Iraqis have died.

The number of wounded survivors is over ten thousand. Many of them are left with devastating impairments. I see photos of their flayed bodies, or I read a story of a mother sitting vigil by a hospital bed, singing softly to her comatose son, and I feel complicit in their injuries. Though I rail at the administration and express outrage at our aggressions, these are private rants, to like-minded people.

The returning soldiers are filling the beds of VA hospitals around the country. Seeing images of them in newspapers and magazines I am reminded of my early days in the hospital—how alien and terrible that time was and how raw the pain can feel when wounds are fresh.

A report in the *New England Journal of Medicine* in December of 2004, on the "lethality" of war wounds among U.S. soldiers, states that 10 percent of those soldiers wounded in Iraq have died, whereas in Vietnam 24 percent died, and in World War II 30 percent. The higher proportion of survivors is due, the report says, in large part to the presence of "Forward Surgical Teams" traveling with portable medical tents which can be positioned close to the battlefield. The tents, complete with operating tables, beds, sterile equipment, and more, can be set up in sixty minutes. Further, quicker evacuation procedures can now bring wounded soldiers from these units to U.S. hospitals on average in less than four days. During the Vietnam War, it usually took forty-five days.

The consequence of the larger number of survivors, of course, is that we have a growing veteran population with significant impairments. The report indicates a high incidence of blinding injuries, amputations of one or more limbs, and traumatic brain injuries. These men and women have wants and desires much the same as mine, when I was, like them, an emaciated hospitalized figure, frightened for my future.

No matter how one feels about the war in Iraq, the women and men who served honored their commitments and sacrificed in the name of our country. They are, for now, wounded warriors, as the Web site "The Wounded Warriors Project" calls them. After the war fades from view, though, and all the prostheses have been fitted and the VA support groups disbanded, they will become disabled citizens, subject to the definitions and constraints that come with that territory.

The medical advances have given them life and, for many of the disabled men and women, an unprecedented level of functioning and comfort. The teams of researchers and practitioners who have contributed to these interventions have done amazing work and are to be commended. Yet when these veterans go to get jobs, return to school, or live in the community, the work of the disability rights movement is what will sustain them.

Together, disabled people have fought for and won new freedoms and rights. The landmark legislation, the Americans with Disabilities Act, was passed in 1990, and a number of disabled Vietnam veterans were instrumental in its passage. In a hearing prior to the passage of the ADA, one veteran testified that he was wounded in Vietnam, returned home using a wheelchair, and found he could not get into his housing project or on the bus, was unable to get a job, and was now committed to the fight for the ADA.

In June of 2004, the National Organization on Disability (NOD) released a study indicating that only 35 percent of people with disabilities were employed full- or part-time, compared to 78 percent of those who do not have disabilities. Most of the unemployed want to work and consider themselves capable of working. Three times as many disabled people as nondisabled people live in poverty, with annual household incomes below fifteen thousand dollars. Recent Supreme Court rulings have eroded essential parts of the ADA, by, for instance, narrowing the definition of "disability" and exempting the states from prosecution under the act. The American Bar Association reports that of the 304 ADA employment-related cases decided by federal courts in 2003, nearly 98 percent were decided in favor of employers. More than two million disabled people are warehoused in institutions, often because of state policies that block funding for people to live in their own homes with needed supports and services. Polling places, courthouses, libraries, and public transportation systems are notoriously out of compliance with the ADA.

For disabled veterans and other disabled women and men, it takes legal measures to guarantee the right to get on a bus, go to college, get a job, and live on one's own. While the transformations over the last thirty-some years have afforded many disabled Americans opportunities and pleasures that would astound earlier generations, there are persistent obstacles—systemic and pervasive—that structure inequality. These veterans will, I hope, benefit from the advances, but will not be exempt from the ongoing discrimination.

If freedom is what we are supposedly fighting for in Iraq, it would be an ironic injustice to subject disabled veterans to a loss of freedoms available to other citizens in the United States, including those available to their fellow vets. We can't offer these men and women a salve for the pain of their loss or an easy means to forget the horror and mayhem they witnessed in Iraq. Yet our country must not add insult to their injuries by willful disregard of their rights.

I have tacked up a newspaper photo of a U.S. Marine in dress uniform on the wall to the left of my computer screen. He has penetrating brown eyes and strong hands with long tapered fingers. He is sitting alone on the sidelines of one of the inaugural balls that heralded the start of George Bush's second term. Both of the Marine's legs have been amputated above the knee, and he is sitting in a wheelchair with his pants legs carefully folded back and tucked under him. He appears to have a hospital-issued ID tag on his wrist. The caption tells us that he was injured in Iraq and is shown attending the "Heroes Red, White and Blue Ball."

If I could, I would tell him that I hope he finds excitement and passion in his life, a way to make sense of what has happened to him, and a use to put this experience to. I hope that he will not stay on the sidelines of any activity that he would find pleasurable or meaningful.

Most of all, I want to say to him: "I hope you have the good fortune to join a battalion of workers and friends. A *citizen* corps. If they are anything like the unit that I was conscripted into, they will welcome you, challenge you, and dance with you. Together, we will press the claim for what you, and all of us, need and deserve from America. Our job over the next few years is to convince the public that the burden of proof can no longer rest on our shoulders. It is not our job alone to point out inequities, frame legislation, and defend our rights. It is the responsibility of the nation."

I have gained freedoms and rights in the thirty-some years that I have been disabled. It is exhilarating to see so many young disabled people coming up with a surer sense of their place in the universe than, I venture to say, any disabled people have ever felt in the past. It is encouraging to see a workplace, an education system, a cultural arena, a political system increasingly, though only very slowly, making space for them. In the last decade, the disability rights movement and the field of disability studies have grown and gained strength. These factors keep me moving forward and acting as if more progress is possible.

Yet this remains, largely, an intolerant society with respect to disability. The gains we've made are precarious, and are inequitably distributed. Their distribution, as with other social benefits, is shaped by class, race, and gender. The visible accouterments of an accommodating society—the ramps, the sign language interpreters at public events, the wheelchair racer in ads for the forward-thinking bank—encourage us to think the battle has been won.

I fear that in the present century, the disability-line could wreak more havoc. It could increasingly determine who, based on their outward appearance or functioning and, significantly, on their genetic makeup, gets to do what, and under what circumstances. Where and how we live, and whom we mate with, where we go to school, and how we are incorporated into the life of the community. While this sorting system has been in place for centuries, this new science, genetics, will lend an air of authority and seeming rationality to these decisions that will be very hard to fight.

We can't wait for this century to unfold to reveal the truths in this forecast. We will have to act quickly to mark the line—to state for the record who is and who is not part of the community, the public, and the citizenry. From there it will take affirmative actions of a new and as yet unwritten form to make inclusion, integration, and participation a given of the twenty-first century.

17 *Epilogue*

The last story. The setting is an amusement park, a carnival, or a street fair, I don't remember which. A late summer evening. The memory is so fuzzy, I can't say with certainty that this actually happened to me, maybe I dreamt it, maybe I only saw it in a Lily Tomlin skit.

In the midst of the merry-go-round, the arcade, and the fun house, a round-faced little girl of four or five emerged from the crowd. She let go of her mother's hand and ran straight over to me. Her big saucer eyes looked me up and down. She took in a big swallow of the night air, raised up on her toes to bring her face close to mine, and asked: "Are you a ride?"